This book was donated by:

MR. PATRICK TAYLOR

For the love of the United States Marine Corps and for his dedication to provide a better life for our nation's children.

Today, thanks to Mr. Taylor, millions of American children have the opportunity to attend college based on their ability to learn and not their ability to pay.

You can read his profile and success in conquering the civilian world in this book on page 206. You can also learn more about the Taylor Plan and Mr. Taylor by visiting http://www.taylorplan.com.

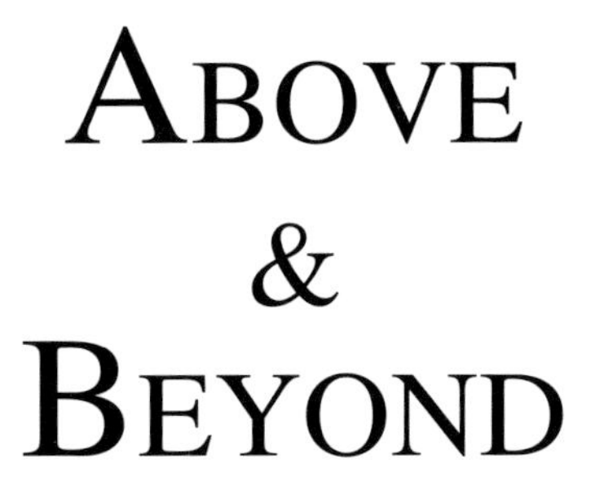

Above & Beyond

Former Marines Conquer the Civilian World

Rudy Socha & Carolyn Butler Darrow

Turner Publishing Company
Nashville, Tennessee • Paducah, Kentucky

Publishers of America's History
412 Broadway • P.O. Box 3101 • Paducah, KY 42002-3101
(270) 443-0121
www.turnerpublishing.com

Frene Melton, Designer

Second Edition.

ISBN: 1-59652-040-X

Library of Congress Control No.: 2003115111

Printed in the United States of America.

10 9 8 7 6 5 4 3 2 1

OTHER MARINE TITLES AVAILABLE FROM TURNER PUBLISHING COMPANY

Flame Dragons of the Korean War
1st Marine Division, Volume I
1st Marine Division, Volume II
2nd Marine Division, "The Heritage Years" Volume I
2nd Marine Division, Volume II
3rd Reconnaissance Battalion: Vietnam 1965-1969
3rd Marine Division: Two Score and Ten
3rd Marine Volume II
4th Marine Division
5th Marine Division
6th Marine Division
9th Marine Defense and AAA Battalion
Women Marines Association, Volume I
Women Marines Association, Volume II: Pictorial
Confess, Confess, Confess: The True Story of a Prisoner of War
MAG-24
Marine Corps Aviation, Volume I
Marine Corps Aviation, Volume II
Marine Corps Drill Instructors
Marine Corps Reserve Officers
Marine Corps Tankers
Marine Night Fighters
The Battle of Iwo Jima and the Men who Fought There
The Corsair Years
USMC/Vietnam Helicopter Association

Table of Contents

Profiled Non Profit Organizations

INTRODUCTION

The United States Marine Corps is the smallest unit of the four branches that make up the Armed Forces of the United States. In spite of its size and the relatively small number of people passing through its ranks, the Marine Corps produces a disproportionate share of this country's leaders. It is because Marines are different from the rest of the population. They have a different mindset and have been taught to handle problems in a different manner. They are taught to find a way to solve the problem, regardless of extenuating circumstances. They do not make excuses or try to determine why it can't be done.

This difference shows prior to the individual becoming a Marine. It takes an individual with a desire to be the best, and a desire to overcome all obstacles just to enlist in the Marines. No one who joins the Marines has illusions about what awaits them when they begin their training. They arrive for training with the "One of the Few" attitude and the Marine Corps training instills the self control, discipline, self assurance, and leadership skills that lead to high achievement later in life.

Other branches of the Armed Forces have elite units, the Marine Corps in its entirety is an elite unit. Everyone, regardless of military occupation in the Marine Corps is in top physical condition, a skilled marksman and prepared to fight. If you happen to visit a Marine base in the morning, you will see clerks, cooks, drivers, etc. running and doing PT (physical training).

If there is a former Marine in your business you will never find a more loyal, focused and driven boss, peer or subordinate. Never mistake his or her politeness and respect as weakness.

What we have done is profile some former Marines who took that winning attitude and applied it to the civilian sector. In this book you will meet a mix of former Marines who are very successful in the civilian fields they have chosen. For anyone who is currently in the Marines or is thinking about joining, this book will show you that the sky is the limit once you have served your time and mastered the discipline and leadership skills that the Marine Corps instills. It comes down to using the same focus and tenacity that got you through either boot camp or officer's basic training.

In this book you will read about some former Marines you already know and many you don't know. You will meet reservists, "one-termers" and out, "lifers," and a former Marine Commandant who is very successful in the private sector. You will find out a little bit about each person profiled, but as you read the stories collectively, you will see a camaraderie of many races, ages, and personalities that make up the Marines.

Another common denominator of the former Marines profiled is that each individual is giving something back through charities, foundations and various non-profit organizations.

One group of "de facto" Marines not included in this publication are the Navy Corpsmen. Many of these individuals, became Corpsmen, then were transferred and attached to Marine units. A long time friend, Ray Fredericy, joined the Navy but spent the last two years of his enlistment with a Marine Force Recon Unit. There are numerous Corpsmen who have won Medals of Honor, Navy Crosses, and Silver Stars, etc. for their bravery saving the lives of countless Marines. Not only did they provide life support, many times they stepped in and provided additional firepower to prevent the Marines from being over run. Thank you to those Navy brothers who served as "de facto" Marines.

If you are a former Marine or have an interest in the Marine Corps, we strongly encourage you to explore the Marine Corps non-profits profiled in this book. On their websites you will find links to many of the other Marine Corps non-profits related to individual units and methods for locating and reuniting with old contacts. Royalties from the sale of this book are being paid to the seven non-profits profiled.

There are many other former Marines who we wanted to profile, but for various reasons could not include them in this publication. If you know of someone you would like to see profiled when we update this book in 3 – 5 years, please send an email to *rudy@wildlifegifts.com*, or *carolyn@wildlifegifts.com*.

For us, this has been a great and very rewarding experience. We have made many new friends and have gotten to know many of those profiled personally. We would like to thank every participant along with many of the non-participants who assisted in providing referrals and support for the project. Along the way, we contacted over 400 former Marines and spent in excess of 2,500 hours working on this book. As many of the participants know, much of that time was evenings and weekends.

Rudy Socha & Carolyn Butler Darrow

Foreword

When, as a non-Marine, I was asked to write a foreword to a book about Marines, my instant reaction was "what a Marine-like thing to do." Yet again the Marines identify the task: "To ask how Marines do in civilian life; How Marine training and Marine Corps *Ethos* translate into the civilian theater?" And to do that they profile 88 Marines into civilian life and ask the son of a Marine to view the book through his eyes. In my experience nothing is more Marine-like than looking outside the predictable, safe and comfortable to achieve clarity and insight. After all, what are those, who are thinking about the broader impact of the U.S. Marine Corps going to learn or discover about Marines in a non-military setting by simply asking Marines?

The United States Marine Corps is a purpose-based phenomenon. The purpose is to train Americans to become the elite military protectors of the United States and its interests. To accomplish this, the Marine Corps has a set of standards for how it prepares, conducts and views itself. These standards have become so deeply ingrained into the mindset of the Marine Corps that they have become what many refer to as the Marine Corps *Ethos*. Finally, this Ethos has become so central to what it is to be a Marine that a credo has also been woven into the Marine Corps fabric: Semper Fidelis – always faithful. Here the Marine Corps has committed to a deep interest in Marines following their formal time in the Marine Corps, which makes this book about Marines so relevant. Further, Semper Fidelis as a concept accomplishes something further: it creates a sense of belongingness to a creed that is permanent both in its membership and its responsibilities. The result is that Marines continue to be Marines even after they leave the Marine Corps.

Communicating the Marine Corps Ethos is not an academic exercise. It is experiential and therefore deeply psychological which lends its explaining to specific anecdotes. Having lost my father, Al Lerner, a former Marine aviator, in 2002, I have found that many of his expressions, which seem to make more sense upon reflection, were pure Marine Corps vocabulary. Very often he would remind us that "Officers eat last." For example, some 30 years ago, flying to Florida from Cleveland on a family vacation, an airline attendant told my father that they needed two of our four seats toward the front of the plane but that there were seats available in the back. Instantaneously, he said, "Not a problem" and he and my mother were up and gone to the back leaving my sister and me where we were. "Officers eat last."

America senses the Corps as *Elite*. As infantrymen transported by sea there shouldn't necessarily be anything terribly elite about a Marine. Allan Millett, in his introduction to **Semper Fidelis,** explains that the Marine Corps, in many regards, began its tradition as an elite military in the 19th century, "when Marine officers stressed military appearance, strict obedience to orders, and disciplined behavior, in an effort to differentiate themselves and their men from the officers and sailors of the United States Navy." So often it has become the case that the admission process for many elite American institutions is considered more rigorous than the work to be done or the final duties to be performed. In the Marine Corps, it is well known that the elite nature of Marines results from what happens during training and subsequent performance.

Part of the experience of being the son of a Marine is coming down to the kitchen around 6:30 a.m. on school days as a kid (in the 1970s and long before the exercise craze) and seeing my father behind the dining room table on the floor doing push-ups. I knew not to say good morning because it wasn't respectful to distract him. Similarly, my sister and I used to steal glances at each other when my father would use pointing gestures as he pulled up to traffic intersections to identify whatever cars were heading in our general direction. He once caught himself doing it with us in the car, and told us that in flight school it was part of the training to use your hand as a redundancy for what you see. The point, of course, is that it is an elite person who is trainable both physically and emotionally continues the habits and patterns (that defined them as Marines) in their civilian life.

Of course, the anchor for the Marine Corps is the life and death nature of their underlying purpose. And for an American society with high expectations, anchors or anchored civilians will always be on the short list of elite people for which our society is searching. Just as a society searches, so do the individuals who comprise our society search for stabilizing habits that allow us to confidently maintain our direction. It comes as no surprise to anyone that people of college age can become overwhelmed by the choices American society offers. Institutions such as the Marine Corps, at first glance, seem a perfect fit for this predicament. Here, an interesting phenomenon of self-selection occurs in which the aura of the Marine Corps, its reputation, its ethos and its credo precede it to such an extent that in some way, the process of becoming a Marine begins unknowingly, especially for the sons and daughters of the Corps.

In this book you will find men and women who lead their businesses and families with the Ethos learned in the Marine Corps, just as my father led us.

Randy Lerner
Chairman MBNA Corporation
Owner, Chairman, Cleveland Browns NFL football team

Randy Lerner (left) with his father, Marine Aviator, Al Lerner (1933-2002).

Michael L. Allen

"My success in business is directly related to what I learned in the Marines while serving in Vietnam."

Born: 11 July 1945 in Ferndale, Michigan
Service: United States Marine Corps, 1965 – 1968, Enlisted, Infantry
Occupation: President, CEO, Owner, Crown Mortgage Company

At the age of 20, Mike heard the call to serve his country and enlisted in the Marine Corps.

Mike went in with the attitude that he was going to be the best Marine the Marine Corps had. He was the top recruit in his boot camp class (Dress Blues winner and PFC). His positive attitude and gung-ho spirit continued after boot camp. He was promoted to Lance Corporal and Corporal meritoriously within 12 months of enlisting.

"While serving in Vietnam in 1967, I extended my tour for six months to change from being the company radioman to a fire team. A few weeks later, I was promoted to Fire Team Leader. The day I became a rifle company fire team leader, all three of my fire team members asked to be assigned to other fire teams. I was shattered. I knew I would have the best fire team in the company. I couldn't believe they wouldn't want to be part of it.

"The company Gunny (Sergeant) heard what happened and talked to me. I've never forgotten his words, 'It's the best thing that could happen to you. You get to build your own team. Do it right and your fire team becomes the foundation of your future squad.' I must have done it right because a few months later I was an E-5 (Sergeant) Squad Leader and my fire team members became my fire team leaders."

After Mike was discharged in June of 1968 (received an early out to return to college), he returned to college and graduated with a BA in Business from Michigan State in 1971. In September of 1975 he started Crown Mortgage Company.

Crown Mortgage Company is one of the largest privately owned mortgage banking firms in the U.S. They have had as many as 14,000 people making their house payments to Crown ($1,100,000,000) and expect to surpass that number in 2004. Crown closed approximately $400 million dollars in new home loans in 2003.

"My success in business is directly related to what I learned in the Marines while serving in Vietnam. I used the same principle to build my company that I used to build my fire teams. I hired the best people and taught them how to do things the way I want them done. These people later taught their replacements how to do the job the way I taught them as they moved up to the next level in the company. The company grew as a structured cohesive team.

"Although I carry the titles President and CEO, my main job responsibility is leadership. I do the strategic planning and lead the company through new concepts. I also move from one area to the next working different positions to help managers systematize every function."

In 1991, Mike attended graduate school at the University of Chicago but dropped out after six months. The Dean at the University of Chicago asked why he dropped out. He told him "they were teaching me how to run a big company and I am an entrepreneur. I do not want to run a large company." The Dean recommended him for the Harvard Graduate School Program For Entrepreneurs; OPM (Owners, Presidents and Managers). He graduated from Harvard Graduate School of Business in March of 1995.

Mike's favorite charity is Opportunity International. Opportunity International uses entrepreneurial concepts to help the poorest of the poor help themselves. They make loans to the poorest of the poor (average $150) to start their own business. Then they train them, mentor them and build support networks. Loans and dignity – not handouts! Crown supports many charities. The preference is charities focused on food (Chicagoland Food Pantry), housing (Bridge Communities) and education (Scholarship Chicago).

Mike and his wife Laura currently reside in Hinsdale, Illinois. They have two children, Melissa and Michael, and a granddaughter, Katie.

SEMPER FIDELIS

Photo Credit (right photo) Worline Studio.

JAMES H. AMOS, JR.

"Never ask your troops to do something you wouldn't do."

BORN: 10 April 1946 in St. Louis, Missouri
SERVICE: United States Marine Corps, 1965 – 1973, Officer
OCCUPATION: Chairman Emeritus, Mail Boxes Etc., (The UPS Store); Founder and Partner of Eagle Advisory Partners

Jim Amos participated in the Marine Corps Platoon Leadership Corps program after high school. He attended college and spent his summers training to be an officer at Quantico Marine Corps Base, Virginia. Amos majored in political science, receiving his A.B. degree from the University of Missouri in 1968. In 1969, he found himself leading Marines into combat in Vietnam.

"What is paramount in my memory of Vietnam is a journey. The first part of that journey was the impact of arriving in Da Nang as a young green Second Lieutenant. I remember the first thing I saw was Marble Mountain dominating the terrain like a gray-white beehive rising abruptly out of the ground, except that the attending bees were helicopters appearing and disappearing like drones protecting some hidden queen within this hive of activity. I remember the heat that had a hidden presence that squeezed sweat out of every pore. I remember the dust, the heat and the noise all made breathing a chore and added to the feeling of disorientation and fear. I remember thinking, here I am ready to do what a lifetime has prepared me to do. I am confident, yet scared. I am supposed to be a man and a leader of men, yet sometimes feeling like a little boy who would like someone to tell me what the hell to do. I felt like a trained Marine and yet somehow still like a civilian. I remember thinking, here I am in Vietnam, I don't have a weapon and I'm still wearing green stateside utilities that stick out like a sore thumb against the camouflage utilities everyone else was wearing. I felt like I even looked screwed up.

"The second stage of this journey came after my first firefight in April 1969 along the Cam Lo River just outside Dong Ha, Vietnam. It seemed to me to be an amazing revelation that these guys were actually trying to kill me. Up until that very moment I understood the intellectual possibility of dying but not with the incredible force of the smell, chaos and intensity of actual combat. I will never forget that moment as long as I live. Along with all of the attendant emotions was also the new look of respect from the troops who recognized I had been 'blooded' and survived.

"Finally, in some odd migratory crucible, I remember finding myself standing at attention on a hot day in August of 1969 on a blistering black topped parade deck in Da Nang. Here as part of what was being called Vietnamization, the Ninth Marines who had been the first in Vietnam would be the first out of Vietnam. I remember squinting at the Paul Revere as Navy Frogmen swam around the ship that was to take us back to Okinawa to keep saboteurs from blowing it up. I remember listening to General Nickerson who said, 'The freedom we together have been fighting for we can continue to win … we will win.' I remember listening to the chairman of the Da Nang Citizens Council review the history of Vietnam and then saying, 'I want to thank you for your incomparable consequence to liberty and justice … never shall we forget …,' and then it was over. The Marines of Alpha, First Battalion, Ninth Marine Regiment, stood around looking at each other, unable to completely comprehend what was happening. Clean sheets, a bed, chocolate milk and salads. An incomprehensible journey from home to hell and home again.

"I am completely satisfied that without the incredible discipline, training and culture of the United States Marine Corps that journey would not have happened. I have had many blessings in life but some of my proudest moments have been in the uniform of The United States Marines."

A veteran of two combat tours in Vietnam, Amos received 12 decorations, including the Purple Heart and Vietnamese Cross of Gallantry. Amos made the very difficult decision to resign his Captain's commission in 1973 after eight years of service and dedication. "At that time, it was the most difficult decision of my life. I loved the Marines. It was part of my identity, and as I drove out that back gate at Quantico, I was wondering who I was and where I was going."

Immediately, Amos began work as an executive recruiter, and in a short time he and a colleague formed their own recruiting company. By 1984, he entered the franchising world, where he almost doubled Arby's franchises (13,000 units to 23,000 units) in three years. Over the next several years, Amos worked for a consulting firm and led a multi-brand frozen food company. His career with Mail Boxes Etc. began in 1996 and quickly flourished. Under his leadership, MBE forged a dynamic strategic plan that culminated in the acquisition of MBE by UPS in April 2001.

In 2003, Amos created Eagle Advisory Partners (EAP) assuming the role as Founder and CEO. EAP is an investing and consulting group that buys, invests and provides consulting services to high growth franchise concepts and those that have the potential to become growth companies through organic growth and or acquisition and conversion.

In addition to his executive responsibilities Amos is a successful published author. *The Memorial*, based on U.S. Marine involvement in Vietnam was published in 1990, and in 1998 his second work, *Focus or Failure: America at the Crossroads* became available. His third book, *The Millennial End Game*, is in progress.

Additionally, Amos gives his time and talent in many other ways. He serves on the boards of Mail Boxes Etc., The University of Missouri, The MBE We Deliver Dreams Foundation, San Diego Opera, Marine Corps Heritage Foundation, Marine Military Academy, Veteran's Administration Corporation, Ken Blanchard's Faithwalk Leadership Foundation, Alliance Franchise Finance and Meineke Mufflers. He is also the Immediate Past Chairman and Board Member of the International Franchise Association.

The MBE We Deliver Dreams Foundation was founded in 1998 by Amos. By delivering the dreams of individual children at risk, this non-profit organization strives to counteract the cycles of abuse, neglect, violence, poverty and illness that compromise a child's ability to grow and flourish physically, mentally and emotionally. His dream was to create a foundation that would help nurture and preserve our most precious resource – the children of the world. And dreams do come true!

The very busy Amos family resides in the Nashville, Tennessee area.

SEMPER FIDELIS

Photo Credit (right photo) Stahl Photographics.

JAMES A. BAKER, III

" James A. Baker, III, Marine And Secretary of State"

BORN: 28 April 1930 in Houston, Texas
SERVICE: United States Marine Corps 1952 – 1954, Naval Gunfire Officer
OCCUPATION: Senior Partner, Baker Botts; Partner, The Carlyle Group

After graduating from Princeton University in 1952, Mr. Baker served two years of active duty as a Lieutenant in the Marine Corps. His experience and reputation of being a former Marine has stayed with him since then.

"When I was Secretary of State, the Commandant of the Marine Corps at the time, Al Gray, asked if he could pay me a courtesy call. We had a nice visit in my office at the State Department. As he got up to leave, he said, 'Mr. Secretary, I have a present for you.' It was a box of business cards on a camouflage background that read as follows:

James A. Baker, III
U.S. Marine
And Secretary of State"

After his two years of active duty as a Lieutenant in the United States Marine Corps, Baker entered the University of Texas School of Law at Austin. He received his J.D. with honors in 1957, and practiced law with the Houston firm of Andrews and Kurth from 1957 to 1975.

Baker's record of public service began in 1975 as Under Secretary of Commerce to President Gerald Ford. Mr. Baker led presidential campaigns for Presidents Ford, Reagan and Bush over the course of five consecutive presidential elections from 1976 to 1992. Mr. Baker served as the 67th Secretary of the Treasury from 1985 to 1988 under President Ronald Reagan. As Treasury Secretary, he was also Chairman of the President's Economic Policy Council. From 1981 to 1985, he served as White House Chief of Staff to President Reagan.

James A. Baker, III has served in senior government positions under three United States Presidents. He served as the nation's 61st Secretary of State from January 1989 through August 1992 under President George H. Bush. During his tenure at the State Department, Mr. Baker traveled to 90 foreign countries as the United States confronted the unprecedented challenges and opportunities of the post Cold War era. In 1995, Mr. Baker published *The Politics of Diplomacy*, his reflections on those years of revolution, war and peace.

Baker's public service concluded with his service as White House Chief of Staff and Senior Counselor to President Bush from August 1992 to January 1993. In 2000, Mr. Baker led the legal team that argued the Florida election counts on behalf of President George W. Bush.

Baker received the Presidential Medal of Freedom in 1991 and has been the recipient of many other awards for distinguished public service, including: Princeton University's Woodrow Wilson Award, The American Institute for Public Service's Jefferson Award, Harvard University's John F. Kennedy School of Government Award, The Hans J. Morgenthau Award, The George F. Kennan Award, the Department of the Treasury's Alexander Hamilton Award, the Department of State's Distinguished Service Award, and numerous honorary academic degrees.

Baker is presently a senior partner in the law firm of Baker Botts and Senior Counselor to The Carlyle Group, a merchant banking firm in Washington, D.C. He is Honorary Chairman of the James A. Baker, III Institute for Public Policy at Rice University and serves on the board of the Howard Hughes Medical Institute. In 1997, Mr. Baker was appointed the Personal Envoy of United Nations Secretary-General Kofi Annan to mediate direct talks between the parties in the dispute over Western Sahara.

Baker and his wife, the former Susan Garrett, currently reside in Houston, and have eight children and 14 grandchildren.

SEMPER FIDELIS

Harvey Curtis Barnum, Jr.

(Medal of Honor Recipient)

"Through team work and taking care of your comrades, you can accomplish any task."

Born: 21 July 1940 in Waterbury, Connecticut
Service: United States Marine Corps 1958 – 1962 PLC Program; USMCR, 1962 – 1989 Commissioned Officer
Occupation: Deputy Assistant Secretary of the Navy

During the second week of his combat tour in Vietnam, H.C. "Barney" Barnum proved his courage and leadership skills in battle. On December 18, 1965, while most Americans were preparing for Christmas, First Lieutenant Barnum was assuming command of the rifle company he was attached to as an Artillery Forward Observer due to the deaths of the company's commander and radio man. He took command and proceeded to direct artillery fire, call in air support and direct counterattacks to overcome a force that was vastly superior in number. For these valiant efforts, First Lieutenant Barnum was the fourth United States Marine of the Vietnam War to be awarded the nation's highest honor, The Medal of Honor.

"I had been in Vietnam two weeks, been with my infantry company as its artillery forward observer for one week, was on my first operation and on the fourth day we were ambushed. That was the first time I was ever shot at. The company commander was killed. I took over and led the company against a force that was numerically superior, and as a team we were successful and defeated the enemy. That experience set the mold that has driven my life – through team work and taking care of your comrades, you can accomplish any task."

Barnum completed that tour of Vietnam and served another as an Artillery Battery Commander. He went on to serve a total of 27 and a half years in the Marine Corps before retiring as a Colonel. His tours included five tours as an artilleryman, Guard Officer at Marine Barracks Pearl Harbor and Operations Officer Hawaiian Armed Forces Police; Weapons Officer at the

Officer's Basic School; Commanding Officer of a Recruit Training battalion at Marine Corps Recruit Depot Parris Island; at Headquarters Marine Corps: aide to the Assistant Commandant as a Captain and Deputy Director of Public Affairs, Director of Special Projects and Military Secretary to the Commandant as a Colonel.

Barnum attended the Officers Basic School as a Lieutenant, U.S. Army Field Artillery School and Amphibious Warfare School as a Captain, U.S. Army Command and Staff College as a Major and the Naval War College as a Colonel. In 2002, Mr. Barnum was awarded an Honorary Doctorate of Law from his alma mater St. Anselm College in Manchester, New Hampshire.

While serving as Chief of Current Operations, U.S. Central Command, Colonel Barnum planned and executed operation BRIGHT STAR spread over four southwest Asian countries involving 26,000 personnel.

Barnum's personal medals and decorations include: Medal of Honor, Defense Superior Service Medal, Legion of Merit, Bronze Star with Combat "V" and Gold Star, Purple Heart, Meritorious Service Medal, Navy Commendation Medal, Navy Achievement Medal with Combat "V," Combat Action Ribbon, Presidential Unit Citation, Army Meritorious Unit Citation, Joint Meritorious Unit Award, Navy Unit Citation, two awards of the Meritorious Unit Citation, and the Vietnamese Cross of Gallantry (silver).

Colonel Barnum retired from the Marine Corps in 1989. He entered the civilian public service sector as the Principal Director for Drug Enforcement Policy in the Office of the Secretary of Defense. In that position he developed policy to enable the military to train and support drug enforcement agencies in the war on drugs. In 1998, Mr. Barnum took a position as Community and Corporate Affairs Advisor for Arltec, Inc. Arltec owned and operated five Sheraton Hotels in the Greater Washington, D.C. area. He worked extensively with chambers of commerce and local civic action associations on behalf of the firm.

As a Medal of Honor Recipient, he served four years as Vice President of the Congressional Medal of Honor Society and two years as its President. As one of the Society's senior officials he has traveled extensively speaking on the organization's behalf.

On July 23, 2001, Barnum was sworn in as Deputy Assistant Secretary of the Navy for Reserve Affairs. In this capacity he is responsible for all matters regarding the Navy and Marine Corps Reserve including manpower, policy, budgeting and mobilization. This entails oversight of more than 160,000 Naval Reserve and 100,000 Marine Corps Reserve personnel.

Barnum is married to Martha E. Hill of Parkersburg, West Virginia. The Barnums currently reside in Reston, Virginia.

SEMPER FIDELIS

James E. Bassett, III

"Entering the civilian sector, I soon discovered that the leadership I learned as a Marine was a life changing experience and was invaluable in providing me with the experience and competence in dealing with complex and difficult situations."

Born: 26 October 1921 in Lexington, Kentucky
Service: United States Marine Corps, 1943 – 1946, Officer, Rifle Platoon Leader, Company Commander
Occupation: Chairman, Emirates World Series Racing Championship

James "Ted" Bassett, III graduated from Kent School in Kent, Connecticut. Ted enlisted in the Marine Corps under the V-12 program and was sent to Yale to complete his degree. After graduating from Yale, he was sent to Parris Island for the "enlisted ranks" 16 weeks of boot camp. At the time, officer candidates had to complete boot camp and then qualify for Officer Candidate School, even if they were in a future officer's program such as V-12.

"Going through Parris Island gave me a great appreciation and understanding of the type of men I would be leading. We had the opportunity to know the men and they had the opportunity to know future officers on a personal level prior to rank and training separating us. I believe we had greater unit cohesion, confidence and respect for each other as a result of this method of officer training."

Upon receiving his commission, Ted served during World War II in the Pacific as an infantry officer in the 4th Marine Regiment, 6th Marine Division and was awarded the Purple Heart and the Presidential Unit Citation.

After his discharge from the Marines, Ted worked for nine years at Great Northern Paper. After GN Paper, Ted went to work for the Kentucky State Police and rose to become their Director and Deputy Commissioner for Public Safety for the State of Kentucky.

"Entering the civilian sector, I soon discovered that the leadership I learned as a Marine was a life changing experience and was invaluable in providing me with the experience and competence in dealing with complex and difficult situations. Many of the positions I undertook were with organizations that were in dire need of change, restructuring and organizational discipline. I would not have been able to implement the necessary changes and achieve the same level of accomplishment if at an early age I had not been given the training and responsibilities that the Marine Corps provided."

On January 1, 1968, Ted went to work for Keeneland, America's most famous thoroughbred institution. In 1970, Ted was elected President and in 1986, Chairman.

Keeneland is a combination thoroughbred race-course and sales company located six miles west of Lexington in the heart of Kentucky's famed blue grass region. Unique in organization, Keeneland is a non-dividend paying Corporation. Directors serve without monetary remuneration. Profits are returned in the form of higher purses to horsemen, capital improvements, and annual giving to charitable, educational, and research organizations.

Keeneland provides superior year-round training facilities and annually conducts race meetings of the highest caliber in April and October. Keeneland hosts the world's largest thoroughbred public auction. Average annual sales are $600-700 million dollars with $150-200 million in sales overseas to more than 28 different countries. Thoroughbred sales are held six times yearly with two-year-olds selling in April, yearlings selling in July, September and October, breeding stock in November, and horses of all ages in January. It is common at Keeneland events to see members of royalty, movie stars, and business tycoons from around the world. The grounds and buildings are listed on the National Historic Register and recognized worldwide for their intrinsic beauty and landscaping.

In 1998, Ted worked to form The Emirates World Series Racing Championship. In 1999, he assumed the Chairman's position for the organization. He retired from Keeneland in 2001 after 33 years.

The World Series Racing Championship was created to bring the Sport of Kings into the next century and in line with all other sporting activities by creating a world horse racing championship. In March 1999, the inaugural championship kicked off under the lights of Nad Al Sheba Racecourse with the world's richest race, the Dubai World Cup.

A major part of the philosophy of the World Series was to have a dedicated television program that would show each race in the Series and increase the global television audience and thus heighten the interest in the sport. The World Series field program is carried by ESPN on a live or delayed-programmed basis to more than 200 countries with a potential audience of a billion viewers.

Ted served as President of the Breeders' Cup from 1988 – 1996 and continues to serve as a member of its board of Directors. He is a member of the Jockey Club, past President of the Thoroughbred Racing Associations of North America and currently serves as a Trustee of Keeneland, National

Museum of Racing, University of Kentucky Equine Research Foundation, and Transylvania University.

He is an Honorary Member of the Victoria Racing Club of Australia, the Hong Kong Race Horse Owners Association, and the Association of Jockey Clubs of Latin America.

Ted has been the recipient of numerous awards including the U.S. Marine Corps Semper Fidelis Award, Eclipse Award of Merit, and Thoroughbred Club of America's Honored Guest.

Not only has Ted been involved in giving much of his time to many non-profit institutions, but he has been involved in distributing over $500,000 annually to more than 70 charities.

James E. Bassett, III and his wife, Lucy Gay Bassett were married on December 2, 1950 and currently reside in the Lexington, Kentucky area.

SEMPER FIDELIS

John Besh

"The Marines give you a sense of accomplishment and teach you how to push yourself to always go the extra mile."

Born: 14 May 1968 in Meridian, Mississippi
Service: United States Marine Corps 1986 – 1992, Reserves; activated for Desert Storm, Enlisted
Occupation: CEO, Executive Chef, Restaurant August; CEO, August Capital, LLC

Besh grew up hunting and fishing in Southern Louisiana constantly exposed to the essentials of Louisiana's rich culinary traditions. When he graduated from high school in 1986, John joined the USMC Reserves to test himself and be able to say he'd done it. After boot camp while working as a cook he was accepted at The Culinary Institute of America in Hyde Park, New York where he became a star student. His formal training was interrupted when he was activated to serve in Desert Storm less than a year before his scheduled graduation.

As a mortar man, infantry squad leader and forward observer Besh's Marine memories are many.

"Upon leaving to the Gulf, we trained and trained for desert combat in the swamps of Camp LeJuene, North Carolina and consequently shipped out with our mesh jungle boots and light utilities. None of us knew what to expect other than dry weather and plenty of heat. That wasn't the case … in fact it seemed to rain every day for the first weeks after our arrival, and it was cold rain too! I've never been so cold. We went immediately to the front and lived in holes we dug with our entrenchment tools. The tools were just as useful for killing rats that would raid your hole every night. Once the weather dried up the rats disappeared. And then came the bees. The Iraqis proved to be less of an adversary than the rats and the bees. Later, after the fighting, just prior to returning home, we were issued our desert boots and new desert utilities. None of it made sense to us grunts.

"Attached to the 1st Marine Expeditionary Force, our company spent most of our time moving from position to position along the Kuwaiti border in Operation Desert Storm. Just prior to the massive ground offensive we encountered an armored column of enemy bearing down on our position near the town of Khafji. I remember feeling a bit vulnerable with only 90 of us and very few heavy weapons to destroy tanks. Under different circumstances we wouldn't stand much of a chance. This lead to a couple of squads booby trapping their gear and belongings just in case we were overrun. Well, we were able to call in effective air support and with the help of a few TOWs we dispersed and destroyed most of the column. The next morning I remember laughing so hard at those fools for booby trapping their gear with high explosives, white phosphorus and incendiary grenades. They had a lot of explaining to do in order to receive new packs and gear from supply. Our commanding officer looked like he could have cried.

"After just liberating the Kuwaiti International Airport, our squad took 1,300 enemy prisoners of war and were left to our own devices as to how to keep them occupied while waiting on the Army to process them. So we struck up a game of football with an Iraqi gas mask. Lance Corporal Green instructed them how to perform the 'wave' and other such cheers. OK, maybe his pointing his weapon at them had something to do with their cooperation, but I saw no harm in it. The football game was good fun, and all was well, knowing we'd be going home alive soon."

Besh returned to the states, finished culinary school and embarked on a journey to further his education in the renowned kitchens of Maxim's, New York City; The Windsor Court's Grill Room, New Orleans; and Romantik Hotel Spielweg in the German Black Forest. A journal John kept while on active duty contained notions for dishes he eventually wanted to create, and became an important part of Besh's evolution as a chef.

Restaurant August is a fine dining restaurant located in New Orleans' Central Business District. Comprised of 120 seats in the main dining room, 100 seats in the private dining room, and up to 200 guests in the penthouse, they were ranked among the top five restaurants of 2002 by USA Today, and among the Top 50 restaurants of the world by Conde Nast Traveler. In 1999, *Food and Wine* honored Besh as one of the Top Ten New Chefs in America. There is a partnership with Harrah's Entertainment International, managing and developing fine dining concepts one of which is The Besh Steakhouse at Harrah's New Orleans. Besh has also partnered with the Marriott Corporation in developing and managing casual restaurant concepts, such as Besh on Fulton at the New Orleans Convention Center Marriott.

"The Marines gave me a sense of accomplishment and taught me how to push myself to always go the extra mile. Attention to detail, which had been instilled in me in the Marines, has helped me keep high standards in the food industry. Serving in combat and leading an infantry squad gave me a very different perspective on what constitutes a stressful situation. Now, as a chef, when things get very tense, I can look at some of my other leadership roles, and it really keeps things in perspective."

Besh is a proud member of the Crescent City Farmers' Market Association, Share Our Strength, St. Michael's Special School's Chef's Charity, ALD Foundation board member, as well as many other small charities that benefit his local area. The ALD Foundation is a charity that a dear friend of John's started in order to fund research for Adrinoluchiadistrophy, a disease that debilitates and kills thousands of young men every year. St. Michael's Special School, operated by nuns, gives physically and mentally disabled students self-esteem and love. Share Our Strength is a national charity founded by chefs to feed the poor and impoverished. The Crescent City Farmers' Market Association is a charity that promotes responsible farming, culinary education and the preservation of our culinary heritage by supporting family owned and operated farms.

Currently Besh is finishing his first book, *From Tomatoes to Truffles*, while operating his fine dining establishments in New Orleans, Louisiana. Besh conscientiously strives to balance his job with family, church, hunting, fishing and community service.

Besh's wife, Jenifer, was his pen-pal during Desert Storm. They eventually met then married and now have three young sons, Brendan, Jack and Luke. The Besh family resides in Slidell, Louisiana.

SEMPER FIDELIS

Photo Credit (right photo) Michel Varisco Photographs.

ANDREW J. BLUM

"A Marine Officer is responsible for everything his unit does, or fails to do."

BORN: 30 December 1964 in San Juan, Puerto Rico
SERVICE: United States Marine Corps 1982 – 1989, Officer
OCCUPATION: Founder and Managing Partner of the Trium Group

At the age of 17 and approaching his high school graduation, Andrew Blum decided that he wanted to be an officer in the Marine Corps. He told this to a recruiting officer during high school who in turn replied that "all Marine Corps officers are prior enlisted," so Andrew entered into his 85 day reserve program with the hopes that someday, he'd become a Lieutenant. Instead, he attended boot camp at Parris Island, in South Carolina.

"A story that stands out in my mind from boot camp at Parris Island was that on one particularly hot July day during drills (an activity that I had not yet mastered), I kept missing the same drills over and over. The drill instructor yelled at me, 'What the hell is wrong with you boy?' I looked straight ahead and said, 'This recruit is befuddled sir.' It was the wrong answer. The Drill Sergeant laughed for a few moments and said, 'Well then, all of you can spend the day in the pit, and be befuddled together.' With that, I and my entire displeased platoon spent the next two hours in the pit doing mountain climbers."

Following boot camp, Andrew was selected to be an Officer Candidate and attended Officer Candidate School (OCS) at Camp Upshur in Quantico, Virginia. After the first part of his OCS training was complete, he was given an education leave and went off to Reed College in Oregon for four years where, in 1986, he received a BA in Philosophy. After earning his degree, he completed Officer Candidate School and he went on to basic school. He then completed his communication officer course in Virginia, becoming a communications officer (25O2) assigned to the 3rd FSSG in Okinawa, Japan.

In his time overseas, Andrew became the commander of a radio platoon stationed in Korea where he participated in two multi-force exercises, "Valiant Blitz" and "Team Spirit," working closely with the ROK Marines. After completing his 13 months in South Korea and Japan, he was assigned to MCRD in San Diego where he was an Assistant Series Commander for the 3rd Battalion Kilo Company and served as the Aide de Camp to the base CG (Commanding General), General Frank Bredth.

In June of 1989, Andrew was honorably discharged from the Marine Corps and joined the software firm, Information and Communication Inc., where he became the Director of Sales and Marketing. Two years later he enrolled in Georgetown University, earning his MBA in 1993.

After graduating from Georgetown, Andrew worked as a business strategy and management consultant at Towers Perrin, serving clients around the world such as Pacific Bell and Cathay Pacific Airlines. Through this experience, Andrew observed that most business failures were, in fact, leadership failures and that very few firms were effectively addressing both strategy and leadership issues. Relying on his leadership training from the Marine Corps, Andrew resolved to address this issue and in 1999, founded the Trium Group (*www.triumgroup.com*), a consulting firm that helps businesses solve issues related to strategy, leadership and culture. Some of the clients that Trium serves are Nokia, Gap Inc., eBay, Home Depot, Barclays Global Investors, AXA Investment Managers, 24 Hour Fitness, Nextel, Vodafone and General Motors.

"Our approach combines best practices in strategy development and execution with state-of-the-art leadership development approaches. We help organizations develop a disciplined approach to aligning resources and activities in a way that creates benefits that are both self-reinforcing and a continual source of competitive advantage. Our expertise is in creating the conditions for leadership to emerge from all levels within an organization. We get people thinking and behaving like owners of their organizations. This sense of ownership translates into a renewed sense of passion, involvement, accountability and commitment. Once the organization has been introduced to this way of thinking, we focus on specific business strategies and goals to develop and implement lasting, innovative solutions."

Andrew credits the Marine Corps for giving him the leadership training and tools that have been fundamental in his work and his life. The skills that he gained during his service are the building blocks from which he has been able to develop leadership practices and tools in order to serve his clients and his firm.

Andrew is an avid triathlete and recently completed Ironman USA. He also takes part in the AIDS Ride, a charity bike ride from San Francisco to Los Angeles, and is the founder of Team Embrace, a team that raised over $70,000 for the San Francisco AIDS Foundation. Andrew is committed to serving the community and through the Trium Group has done Pro Bono work with a number of non-profit organizations including the YMCA, The Natural Step and Conservation International.

Andrew now resides in Mill Valley, California.

SEMPER FIDELIS

WALTER E. BOOMER

"A leader's position is with and in front of the people he is leading."

BORN: 22 September 1938 in Rich Square, North Carolina
SERVICE: United States Marine Corps, 1960 – 1994, Infantry Officer
OCCUPATION: Chairman, CEO, Rogers Corporation

Boomer spent the last two years of high school attending Randolph-Macon Military Academy in Northern Virginia. After graduating from the Academy in 1956, he entered Duke University under the NROTC program.

During Vietnam, Boomer served two tours and was awarded two Silver Stars, a Legion of Merit, and two Bronze Stars. After Vietnam, he rotated through the Corps and ranks. In February 1991, Lieutenant General Boomer served as Marine Commander for the retaking of Kuwait (Desert Storm).

"In 1991 during Desert Storm, the Marines of the 1st and 2nd Divisions had to cross a huge minefield and barrier as they launched the attack to liberate Kuwait from the Iraqi invaders. As Commanding General, 1st Marine Expeditionary Force, I was very concerned about the casualties we might take from Iraqi artillery and chemical weapons while crossing the minefield. When I learned that all of our training had paid off and that we had sliced through the minefields quickly, with essentially no casualties and we had not experienced chemical weapons, it was a great moment and I was immensely relieved. It was a signal to me that we would be victorious over the Iraqis even faster than we anticipated."

General Boomer's leadership during Desert Storm was chronicled by *Washington Post* reporter Molly Moore in her book, *A Woman at War*. Ms. Moore traveled with General Boomer and his staff during the retaking of Kuwait. She tells of Boomer moving into Kuwait in a small mobile command post, only 27 hours behind the attacking Marines, despite some concern that he might be too close to the front and risking capture.

While in the Marine Corps, General Boomer obtained a M.S. degree in Technology of Management from American University in Washington, D.C.

He also graduated with distinction from the Naval War College in Newport, Rhode Island.

In 1994, General Boomer retired from the Marine Corps as Assistant Commandant. He immediately went to work for McDermott International in New Orleans, Louisiana. After six months in New Orleans, he was transferred to Akron, Ohio to become the President of Babcock and Wilcox Power Generation Group.

On March 31, 1997, Walter Boomer became President and Chief Executive Officer of Rogers Corporation. On April 25, 2002, he was named Chairman of the Board and Chief Executive Officer.

Rogers Corporation develops and manufactures proprietary high tech materials for growing markets. Roger's products are found everywhere, from your car, to your cell phone, to the ATM used today, and the plane you will travel on tomorrow. There is a good chance that you will find Rogers materials in your personal digital assistant, your laptop or the server that runs your office network. By providing superior specialty material solutions to meet their customer demands, Rogers plays a key role in developing and supplying products now and for the future.

Although Rogers manufactures a broad range of specialty materials for a wide range of applications, their focus since 1996 has been on printed circuit materials and high performance foams for the wireless communications and network/computing segments of the electronics market. Recently, they have become increasingly engaged in the emerging and exciting new automotive electronics applications.

Rogers Corporation is a public company traded on the New York Stock Exchange under the symbol ROG. The company is very successful and has operations all over the world. Its latest expansion was into China with the addition of two manufacturing plants in the city of Suzhou.

Rogers Corporation participates in many charities at the local level. As a company they make their selections in support of their employee's active non-profit involvement. Walter is a member of the Board of Advisors to the President of the Naval War College; member of the Board of Trustees for the D-Day Museum and a founder of the Marine Corps National Museum.

Walter is married to the former Sandra Lokey of Alexandria, Virginia and has three children from a former marriage, Susan, Helen and Steven. Walt and Sandi currently reside in Pomfret, Connecticut.

SEMPER FIDELIS

Photo Credit (left photo) U.S. Army Photo.

Patrick Timothy Brent

"The Marine Corps does more than produce awesome warriors, they increase our nation's supply of much needed responsible citizens."

Born: 12 September 1942 in Chicago, Illinois
Service: United States Marine Corps, 1961 – 1967, Enlisted, Infantry
Occupation: Chairman, Baldwin Forrester & Company; CEO and Owner, Hawaii Polo Inn & Polo Tower

After graduating from high school, Brent went to Loyola University in his hometown of Chicago. During college, he joined the Marine Corps Platoon Leaders Course program and later made a transfer to the Marine Corps Reserves.

"My personal and business successes are chiefly due to the formative experiences derived from my time in the Corps. The Marine Corps does more than produce awesome warriors, they increase our nation's supply of much needed responsible citizens. My tenure in the Corps, albeit short, left me with many life long traits; one is still carrying my brief case in my left hand and keeping my right hand free. Physical Training (PT) has always been a ritualistic and daily event. My arrival is early every morning at work with a confidence most people who were not Marines will never experience."

After Loyola, Brent accepted a position with NCR as a programmer for accounting machines and computers. Later NCR had him working in sales on hotel and hospital systems. After three years he took a sales management position with University Company. While at University he was promoted to Regional Manager and relocated to Houston, Texas.

Five years later he moved to San Francisco, California. While in San Francisco, he founded Western Twenty-Nine, Inc., an IT firm. In four short years Western grew into a profitable operation with revenues exceeding $28 million. The company serviced customers in more than 30 states, Canada and Europe. Western migrated into data communications between airlines, and designed the first reservation and accounting system for travel agents. A few years later McDonnell-Douglas Corporation acquired the company.

Brent then became President of Charles Schwab's computer subsidiary, CRS. He undertook the job of reorganizing the company and increasing Corporate performance and efficiency. Once the reorganization was complete, Brent negotiated a sale of this Schwab firm to National Data Corporation.

Brent once again decided to start another business. He founded Hamilton Taft & Company. The company originated computer services for payroll tax reporting and processing trust funds exceeding four billion dollars annually throughout the United States. The company had more than 500 major Corporations as clients, and had assets worth approximately $80 million. In 1984, CIGNA acquired the firm.

He then left the high tech world of computer systems and founded the Laura Todd Cookie Company, which is fondly named after his grandmother. Laura Todd has one location in Chicago, six in California, and eleven in Europe. In 1987, he sold this venture to the San Francisco Sourdough Company.

From 1985 to 1999, Brent created Baldwin Forrester Company, an information system consultant firm, and Bradford Adams & Company, a digital publishing firm. He currently continues to serve as Chairman of Baldwin Forrester.

Along the way he also served in a consulting capacity for several firms including interim CEO of Windjammer Cruises in Hawaii. He successfully led the company through a dramatic "turnaround."

In 2002, he purchased 71% of the Hawaii Polo Tower (*www.hawaiipolo.com*) in Waikiki, Hawaii. This allows him the opportunity to have his many former and current Marine friends book their Hawaiian vacations through the hotel and stay close by.

In addition to work, he makes it a point to do his PT everyday, which includes an ocean swim. He plays polo, tennis, runs marathons (16) and triathlons, and holds a Commercial Pilot's License.

Brent is a trustee with the Marine Corps "Devil Pups," a summer camp for young people held on base at Camp Pendleton, California every year. He is a former trustee of the Marine Corps University Foundation and the Marine Corps Command and Staff College. He founded and sponsors the annual Irish Sprint in San Francisco, California.

He served eight years as Governor of the U.S. Polo Association.

"When my daughter Laura was twelve and we were touring the Pentagon, we made a bet. Laura was a fan of the Navy and we wagered $10 for every overweight Marine spotted against 25 cents for every plump Sailor. At the end of the day, Laura rescinded the gamble, she tugged at my jacket and said, 'No bet, Daddy.'

"I attended a 2000 Christmas party as the guest of Admiral Tom Fargo. He was showing clips of the upcoming movie *Pearl Harbor* in which he and his sailors had been involved. As I related Laura's Pentagon comments to the Admiral and his senior Pearl Harbor staff, the Admiral smiled and said, 'Careful Patrick, please remember the Marines Corps is only a department of the Navy.' I replied, 'You are right Tom ... it is the Men's Department' to a now silent and embarrassed room."

Brent and his daughter, Laura, currently live in Waikiki, Hawaii; San Francisco, California; and Lake Tahoe, Nevada.

SEMPER FIDELIS

Timothy Charles Brown

"I've been in both of America's premiere foreign policy Corps, the Marine Corps and the diplomatic Corps, but it was the Marine Corps that prepared me to succeed as a diplomat, not the other way around."

Born: 9 June 1938 in Anthony, Kansas
Service: United States Marine Corps, 1954 – 1964, Enlisted
Occupation: Chair of International Studies, Sierra Nevada College

Tim started his first enlistment at the age of 16. He states, "mother lied for me," and he made PFC during that first year. He was a Corporal at 17 and Sergeant at 18.

"As a 17-year-old first-enlistment Corporal, thanks to an administrative error and a buddy who deliberately made it for me, in 1956 I was an amazingly young Marine Security Guard assigned to the American Embassy in Managua, Nicaragua. Late one night while I was on duty at the then empty embassy's guard desk, Tom Whalen, the ambassador and himself a former World War I Marine private, suddenly arrived, returned my salute, handed me a stiff rum and coke, ordered me to drink it, and went upstairs.

"Just as I was beginning reluctantly to comply with his direct order, I almost dropped my drink when I heard him yelling at the top of his voice with his office door wide open. I quickly gathered he was talking with someone on the phone about a lively dust-up then underway between the armies of Honduras and Nicaragua that was apparently irritating his bosses in Washington. The conversation, or at least his side of it (during which Whelan in words his DI had probably taught him in his formative years) went like this: 'Damn it Louie, I don't give a (blank) if the (blanking) Hondurans did start the (blanking) war. You get your (blanking) troops off the border or we're going to shove a battalion of Marines right up your (blank).' Louie was better known to his compatriots as His Excellency President of the Republic and Commander in Chief of the Armed Forces Don Luis Somoza Debayle, so it seemed to me a rather informal way to be speaking to him. But then in private

Somoza addressed Whelan as Uncle Tom, so maybe that was just how it was done. In any case, being able to hear an ambassador as he delivered what is known in the trade as a forceful demarche was for me an early giant step up a career ladder that was to include 10-years as a Marine and then 27 as a diplomat. I never did, however, get a chance to quote my own DI to a head of state, or even an ambassador, except a few times under my breath. Perhaps that was just as well.

"Another memorable Marine incident occurred in 1962. A Marine Expeditionary Brigade was sent to Thailand to forestall possible Pathet Lao incursions into the northeastern region of that country. As the Fleet marine Force Pacific's only available Thai interpreter at Camp Smith, Hawaii, I joined the brigade as the personal interpreter of its commander, then Brigadier General and later Assistant Commandant Ormund E. Simpson. For a lowly NCO it was quite a high profile assignment, more political than military, and I was often asked to interpret for visiting VIPs as well, from King Phumiphon Adunyadet of Thailand to junketing congressmen. During one of these VIP visits, the American Ambassador to that country, Kenneth Todd Young, visited a nearby rice village with me as his interpreter. He was accompanied by the usual entourage of reporters, hangers on, headquarters pogs, and me. At one point he asked the villagers if they had any questions, and one of the village's elders asked the most obvious question of all: 'Why are the American Marines here?' The ambassador turned to me and issued an order: "Tell him why you're here." His order caught me off guard, especially since no one had even told ME why we were there. But I swallowed hard and winged it, on camera with microphones in my face. When I finished my spiel, Ambassador Young smiled and said: 'I hope you got it right, because what you said is going out over the Voice of America in about an hour as an official statement on American policy.' It was my first real foray into foreign policy making. But I must have gotten it right, since the Pathet Lao never did attack us."

As a Marine, Tim served in a number of overseas posts including extensive tours in areas of insurgent operations in Thailand, the Philippines and elsewhere. During these tours he served as an intelligence analyst and Thai and Spanish interpreter.

In 1964 he left the Marine Corps, finished his BA in Political Science and became a Foreign Service Officer in the diplomatic service in 1965. His diplomatic tours included service in Israel, Spain, Vietnam, Mexico, Paraguay, El Salvador, Netherlands, France, and Honduras. In Washington, D.C., Tim served as the Desk Officer for Paraguay/Uruguay, and then for the European Community. As the Deputy Coordinator for Cuban Affairs, Tim managed the economic embargo against Cuba and was involved in setting up Radio Marti, a U.S. radio station broadcasting into Cuba. His last overseas assignment was to Honduras where he was the Senior Liaison Officer to the Nicaraguan Contras managing budgets up to $125 million a year to provide food, housing and medical attention to more than 80,000 people daily.

After retiring from the diplomatic service in 1992, Tim returned to college. In 1998. he completed Ph.D. studies at New Mexico State University in four disciplines, international relations, economics, political psychology and history.

Tim is now a writer/lecturer/researcher/college professor. In his third career he is:

- A writer and researcher with three published books and a fourth in the works. He regularly lectures publicly and writes editorial and other articles on foreign policy issues and terrorism. His specialty is organized armed political violence and numbers among his primary sources several newfound friends who are former Communist revolutionaries and terrorists, Contra veterans, and intelligence operatives, and secret archival collections on their wars.
- A Research fellow, Hoover Institution on War, Revolution and Peace, Stanford University, he studies recent organized armed political violence, especially in Latin America. This has taken him into the homes and confidences of dozens of former Marxist revolutionaries. He then write articles and books based on this research.
- He is also Chair of the International Studies and professor at Sierra Nevada College, Lake Tahoe, a small four-year undergraduate liberal arts college with about 400 students. Sierra Nevada recently began trying to triple the size of its student body while simultaneously increasing the quality of its educational programs to levels comparable to the best colleges in the country. As part of this effort, Tim is building a new program of international studies to include an elite Diplomatic Academy and major programs related to national security and foreign policy.

Sierra Nevada College provides almost 40% of its students with scholarships, primarily needs-based. At the personal level, Tim works with several non-profit organizations of highlander peasant veterans and Miskito Indian veterans in Nicaragua.

Tim was married in 1958 while a Marine Guard in Managua, Nicaragua to Leda M. Zuniga of San Jose, Costa Rica, who is still his wife. They have four children (Barbara, Rebecca, Tamara, Timothy Patrick) and seven grandchildren.

SEMPER FIDELIS

Conrad R. Burns

"All the elements of success are included in all phases of Marine training."

Born: 25 January 1935 in Gallatin, Missouri
Service: United States Marine Corps, 1955 – 1957 , Enlisted
Occupation: United States Senator from Montana

Conrad Burns was raised on a small farm in northwest Missouri. The academic realm was never one of his youthful passions, but he was active in the Future Farmers of America and scholastic athletics, with a strong enthusiasm for football. After graduating from high school in 1952 he didn't want to feel left behind as his friends all went to college, so he sold his livestock to pay tuition and chose to work his way through the University of Missouri. In his first years of college he had trouble choosing a major and struggled to keep up his grades. As a result, he enlisted in the Marine Corps after his sophomore year, only calling his parents after he had passed his physical examination and his induction had taken place.

"If there's one thing I remember from boot camp it's the names of my Drill Instructors. They're a serious bunch, so serious that on my second day there, my nose was broken. I thought that we all looked a little funny after getting our military haircuts, and always having been able to find the humor in any situation, I laughed. Big mistake. Before I could catch myself I had my face jammed into a bulkhead. After I cleaned the blood and tears from my face I was ordered to sickbay. That was not for me. I just used my own thumbs to set my nose back in place and never went to the infirmary. I thought my nose would never stop hurting, but I realized that my introduction to the United States Marine Corps was now complete. Now I knew what to expect and I acted accordingly."

"After four weeks of combat training I was assigned to Camp Mathews, California as a small arms instructor, sniper trainer and team shooter. I was back among the ranks of the recruits again, only this time as an instructor. It was a great job as I got to pass along the message of tradition and the important role that every Marine plays."

"I requested and was granted a transfer to Fleet Marine Force Pacific, and my next assignment was overseas. There I joined F-2-12, 34th Marine Division on Okinawa. Actually, I was supposed to go to the 9th Marines but there was already another Burns aboard ship and they accidentally switched our assignments, he the rifleman and I the soldier trained in artillery! When I reported to my post the commanding officer asked if I was able to drive a truck. I told him that the Marines didn't have a piece of equipment that I couldn't operate (that was the farm boy coming out of me). As confident and excited as I was, I flunked my written test for the driver's license. I was ordered to take it again and told that if I failed again I would find myself working alongside the ground-pounders. That was all the incentive I needed. I passed."

"There's no doubt that the lessons I learned in the Marines have had more to do with my life than anything else. All the elements of success were included in my training and I gained great pride in myself, in the uniform and in being called a Marine. From day one the Marine Corps message was clear. It made no difference what rank, officer or enlisted, one was taught to assume a role of leadership when called upon. It's really amazing how much different the meaning of 'teamwork' becomes when your life depends on it."

"There was one more lesson gained from serving: learning about our America. There is great pride that comes from knowing and understanding the long line of men and women who have served this country. They come from every corner of our nation. They are wealthy and poor; they come from our cities and our farms, joining together to serve when their country needs them. And even though some have found their resting place in foreign soil, all of them remain in the grateful hearts of every freedom loving American."

Following his military service Burns worked for Trans World Airlines and Ozark Airlines until 1962 when he became a field representative for Polled Hereford World magazine in Billings, Montana. Named the first manager of the Northern International Livestock Expo in 1968, Burns began his career in radio and television broadcasting, reporting on agricultural market news and establishing his reputation as the voice of Montana agriculture.

In 1975, Burns founded Northern Ag Network, which grew to serve 31 radio and television stations across Montana and Wyoming by the time he sold it in 1986.

Burns began his career in politics when he was elected to the Yellowstone County Commission where he served for two years before deciding to run for the U.S. Senate.

Conrad Burns is only the second Republican Senator from Montana, defeating an incumbent opponent in 1988. Now in his third term, he is the longest serving Republican Senator in Montana history.

With a seat on the powerful Senate Appropriations Committee, Senator Burns has been able to bring more than $1 billion in federal funds to the state since taking office. He has been a champion of fiscally conservative government and a strong voice for lower taxes to create new businesses and jobs. He has expanded Montana's job base by establishing more balanced trade with Canada and has brought better education and health care to Montanans by encouraging hi-tech investments within the state. He has also pursued new markets for agricultural producers while securing millions of dollars in grants for research and marketing improvements.

Serving as Chairman of the Senate Interior Appropriations subcommittee for the 108th Congress, Senator Burns maintains jurisdiction over all of the country's federal lands and the National Park Service. His love of the outdoors brings him back to Montana several times each month and has made him a guardian of the state's vast natural resources. As a result of his work in the Senate, more than 70 rural Montana communities have adopted enforced potable water protection programs and funding has become available to safeguard acres of Montana through the Land and Water Conservation Fund.

On the national level, Senator Burns has criticized America's dependency upon foreign oil supplies, calling on Congress to ban imports from Iraq and increase domestic production and research in fuel cell technology. He has also cosponsored a Senate bill to voluntarily arm airline pilots to protect against future terrorist attacks.

In 1997, Senator Burns became Chairman of the Communications Subcommittee, one of the major regulatory posts in Congress. Since then he has been praised as "one of the fathers of the modern Internet," standing for deregulation, the roll-out of broadband in rural areas, and pushing for new Internet and mobile phone technologies. He authored section 706 of the 1996 Telecommunications Act and in 1999 unveiled the "Digital Dozen" proposal of telecom legislation. During the 107th Congress, Senator Burns pushed his "Tech 7" agenda, which aimed to bring greater security to the Internet. At the open of the 108th Congress, Senator Burns unveiled his "NexGenTen" Tech Agenda, ten top priority items to strengthen security and usher reform for 21st century communication.

Senator Burns' agricultural, military, communication and political interests have merged to serve our country well.

Conrad and Phyllis Burns have two children, Keely and Garrett and divide their time between Montana and Washington, D.C.

SEMPER FIDELIS

Drew Carey

"My Marine Corps 'buzz' haircut and black thick rimmed glasses became the successful TV image used in the Drew Carey show."

Born: 23 May 1958 in Cleveland, Ohio
Service: United States Marine Corps Reserves, 1980 – 1986, Enlisted
Occupation: Actor, Author, and Producer

At the age of eight, Drew's father died from a brain tumor. He was the youngest of three brothers and circumstances placed him at home quite often by himself while his mother and older brothers worked. After graduating from high school in 1976, Drew attended Kent State University. He dropped out after two years and then went traveling around the country. During these travels, he worked odd jobs to get by and fought bouts of depression.

"I was totally lost and had no direction or discipline. I joined the Marine Corps and found what I needed and had been looking for earlier in my life. Going through boot camp at Parris Island, South Carolina provided a real sense of accomplishment and instilled the discipline in me that had been lacking earlier in my life. Being in the Marine Corps Reserves provided therapy unlike anything a psychiatrist could offer. And 'summer camp' (two weeks active duty) always had a way of bringing reality back into my life."

Drew's friends always knew him to be funny, and one of them asked him to write some material for a show. Drew knew how to make people laugh, but he had no idea how to write comedy material for a show. He went to the library and not only learned, but became very good at it.

While serving in the Marine Reserves, Drew had a sense of confidence that allowed him to start doing stand up in the local comedy clubs. In 1986, he became the emcee at the Cleveland Comedy Club. This provided him with a real full time job in the entertainment industry.

In 1991, Drew had the opportunity to join Johnny Carson who has always been a big fan of Marines (Ed McMahon, Carson's sidekick, is a former Marine). This provided Drew with the exposure and opportunity he needed.

As with many new performers who have appeared on the tonight show, West Coast work and offers started arriving shortly thereafter.

One of the offers Drew received was from Disney. He co-starred in the series *The Good Life*. The series only lasted a half a season, but it provided the opportunity to meet and work with Bruce Helford. After the series folded, Bruce hired Drew as a staff writer for the *Gaby Hoffman Show*.

Drew and Bruce then moved through a series of HBO specials and television appearances before the two of them collaborated on writing and producing a show about an everyday white-collar worker from Cleveland, Ohio. This show has been lauded for being one of the most innovative comedy shows to reach television. They have accomplished multiple time-zone live episodes, website tie-ins, and audience participation games.

Another television innovation has been *Whose Line Is It Anyway?*, which is based on a British improv TV show. Carey is the producer and host of the show. The show debuted on ABC in August of 1998. The success of *Whose Line* led to the creation of the *Drew Carey's Improv All-Stars*, a live pay-per-view improv show telecast from the MGM Grand in Las Vegas. Featuring various members of the rotating *Whose Line* cast, the show was one of the most highly rated programs ever to air on pay-per-view. With the success of this show, he had achieved the rarity of having two highly rated prime time shows running simultaneously.

In 1997, Drew's first book *Dirty Jokes and Beer: Stories of the Unrefined* was published by Hyperion. It is a raw look at Drew's life and thoughts on many subjects including his friends, jobs, women, and places he has lived. The book spent three months on the New York Times Best Seller list.

Drew starred in his first full-length television movie in 2000. The movie was Disney's *Gepetto* and it provided the opportunity for this very versatile actor to sing and dance through this revised/musical version of a long time children's classic. *Gepetto* topped the ratings on the evening that it aired.

Drew has helped many people since achieving fame and success in the entertainment industry. He has made many USO appearances and troop visits.

Drew currently resides in Los Angeles, California and Cleveland, Ohio.

SEMPER FIDELIS

Photo Credit ABC Photo Archives.

George Ronald Christmas

"Marines fight outnumbered with uncommon valor and are the epitome of our motto, Semper Fidelis ... Always Faithful."

Born: 11 March 1940 in Philadelphia, Pennsylvania
Service: United States Marine Corps 1962 – 1996, Infantry Officer
Occupation: President, Marine Corps Heritage Foundation; Consultant

Ron Christmas attended the University of Pennsylvania and joined the local NROTC unit. He attended one summer session at T&T (Training and Test Regiment, precursor of Officer Candidate School). He graduated with a BA in History in May 1962. In June, he was commissioned a Second Lieutenant with a two-year obligation and attended TBS (The Basic School, mandatory training for all commissioned officers).

"My most memorable experience as a Marine was to command Hotel Company, 2nd Battalion, 5th Marine Regiment during the Battle of Hue City during TET 1968 in the Republic of Vietnam. These Marines fought outnumbered with uncommon valor and were the epitome of our motto, Semper Fidelis ... Always Faithful. They were truly faithful to their God, their families, their Country and Corps; but, especially, to their fellow Marines."

During the Battle for Hue City, TET 1968, Ron was seriously wounded and evacuated to the Philadelphia Naval Hospital. For his actions in Hue City, he was awarded the Navy Cross. During his career he also earned the Defense Distinguished Service Medal, Navy Distinguished Service Medal, Defense Superior Service Medal, Purple Heart, Meritorious Service Medal w/3 gold stars, Army Commendation Medal, and the Vietnamese Cross of Gallantry with palm.

Ron rose to the rank of Lieutenant General and held many command positions during his 34-year career with the Marine Corps. Prior to retirement he was assigned as the Deputy Chief of Staff of Manpower and Reserve Affairs, a position responsible for all aspects of human resource management. This job included the planning, budgeting, policy making and programs for an organization of 234,000 military and civilian men and women, with an operating budget of $5.8 billion.

Once a Marine, always a Marine. After retirement, Ron accepted a pro bono position as President of the Marine Corps Heritage Foundation. The Foundation was founded in 1979 and researches and chronicles the contribution of the Marine Corps to our great nation. They publish books about Marine Corps History, and support scholarly works with grants and fellowships. They provide direct monetary support to the History and Museums Division of the Marine Corps University in developing programs that celebrate and seek to preserve the culture of the Marine Corps. In 1999, following years of research and study, the Foundation's mission was expanded to include the planning and development of a new National Museum of the Marine Corps and Marine Corps Heritage Center. This Museum will forever document and depict the story of American history as seen through the eyes of Marines and will also help the American people to understand the steadfastness and strength of the elite, mystical institution known as the United States Marine Corps. The Marine Corps Heritage Center will be a multiple use complex of buildings and outdoor facilities devoted to the presentation of the Marine Corps history, professional military educational opportunities, and unique military events, and will be the showcase for our Marine Corps heritage and legacy to the Nation.

As President of the Marine Corps Heritage Foundation, it is his responsibility to bring this vision of a National Museum and a Marine Corps Heritage Center to reality. At the same time he continues to enhance the Foundation's support for programs that celebrate and preserve the glorious history of the Corps.

They have a small but very efficient staff that effectively operates the Foundation and Museum Gift Shop. With a permanent staff of only seven dedicated personnel, they have increased the assets of the Foundation from less than a million dollars to more than six million dollars. At the same time, the capital campaign to build the National Museum progresses with the ever-growing support of more than 47,000 charter sponsors.

In addition to serving as President of the Foundation, Ron began serving as a Senior Mentor for the Marine Air Ground Task Force (MAGTF) Staff Training Program (MSTP) and the Joint Forces Command. In this consultant role, he has helped train the Command Elements of the Marine Corps, three expeditionary forces, and Joint Task Force command elements serving throughout the world.

"The opportunity to teach and share one's career experiences with those professional soldiers, sailors, airmen, and Marines is personally rewarding. There is no greater feeling than to see them succeed."

He also performs consultant services for defense contractors and serves as a director on several boards including Stone Energy.

"Finally, I continue to be blessed with my wife, Sherry, of 38 years; and four great children, Tracy, Jim, Kevin, and Brian. All are married and successful in their careers – two are Marine officers, while two are educators and coaches. They, too, reach out daily to touch young people positively. They have also pleased us with 10 wonderful grandchildren. Life doesn't get much better than this."

SEMPER FIDELIS

Photo Credit (left photo) Defense Department Photo (Marine Corps).

CHARLES C. (CHRIS) COONEY

"The ethos of the Marine Corps was observed and instilled in me long before I knew what being a Marine really meant."

BORN: 12 October 1941 in Erie, Pennsylvania
SERVICE: United States Marine Corps, 1963 – 1967, Infantry Officer
OCCUPATION: Retired Vice President Sales (4/03), Co-Founder, Tellabs Operations, Inc., Equity Partner, MarketerNet and SimDesk Technologies

Chris' formative years began during World War II, with five of his father's brothers and two of his mom's brothers serving our country. As the oldest of what later turned out to be 40 grandchildren on the Cooney side, he had a steady stream of uncles returning from World War II. Many of these men, including three who were Marines, stayed at Chris' home for several months until they moved back into civilian life. As the oldest grandchild in the clan, his uncles (who seemed like royalty to him) accorded Chris a great deal of their attention. Hats, badges, medals, unit patches, play guns and stories galore were very important parts of his early childhood recollections. Not serving his country was never an issue that crossed his mind as a young adult, and the influence of his three Marine uncles left no doubt as to which branch of the military he would serve.

He entered the Corps through the PLC program and was commissioned a Second Lieutenant after graduation from Gannon College in June 1963. Upon completing basic school in the class of January 1964, he received orders to join the Fifth Marines at Camp Pendleton, California. He was accompanied to the West Coast by about 30 other Lieutenants from their Basic class. The FMF battalions returned from Okinawa and several of them were assigned to the 3rd Battalion 5th Marines; and he had a platoon in Lima Company. For the next year, it was PT and train and PT some more. Their officer staff and NCOs were seasoned Marines and while the war drums in Vietnam were still a very distant din, early in

1965 the Senior Staff became even more focused on company and battalion-sized operations.

"Since several of us were USMC 'R' on three-year hitches, in May of 1965 we were issued orders to Okinawa for reassignment. The battalion eventually followed us to Vietnam in September of 1965, and then became a part of the 7th Marines. Upon arriving in Okinawa, I was assigned to the 'Amphibious Warfare Raider Training School' started by the Corps to train a company from each battalion rotating through Okinawa to Vietnam. The idea was to train enough such companies to form a Raider Regiment for a possible excursion into North Vietnam, should the situation warrant. War being war, the call for warm bodies in the South was such that the school had to be abandoned. Battalions were now being called to Vietnam a week after arriving in Okinawa and that left little time to train for Carlson's wannabe's! During this transition, two sergeants and I went to Vietnam to visit Raider-trained companies in Danang and Chu Lai and saw first-hand night patrols and company-size recon and sweep activities. The Vietnam War became a reality, and soon I experienced the full measure of becoming a combat Marine.

"Upon returning to Okinawa, I was immediately reassigned to Vietnam and the Second Battalion 4th Marines, 'The Magnificent Bastards,' commanded by Lt. Col. Joe (Bull) Fisher in Chu Lai. Bull was a Marine's Marine and one of Chesty Puller's company commanders in Korea at the Chosin Reservoir. My assignment was that of Platoon Commander for Hotel Company. The next 11 months found the battalion heavily engaged in combat ranging from squad to multiple battalion operations. Operation Starlite in mid-August of 1965 was the most notable since it was one of the first major offensives that engaged regimental-sized enemy units. The battalion and Hotel Company performed admirably, spearheading the operation from choppers while other units landed on the beaches. Corporal Joe Paul was awarded the 'Medal of Honor' for his heroic feats and later a navy ship was named in his honor.

"In April of 1966 our battalion came under the command of Lt. Col. PX Kelley, later to become Commandant PX Kelley in the mid-1980s. He and his staff were consummate leaders and the battalion continued its proud heritage on their watch, moving from Chu Lai to the northern reaches of 'I' Corps. I returned home as the battalion moved toward Hue Phu Bai and continued heavy engagement with large enemy forces."

Chris spent his fourth year as a Marine in Quantico, Virginia, as a Company Commander for a main side services group; married his long-time sweetheart; and departed Quantico a year later with his bride and new son, Chris, for Jamestown, New York. "The Marine Corps left an indelible mark on my psyche and a deep abiding respect for my fellow Marines, past and present."

After working as a sales representative for Pfizer, he switched industries and joined a small telecom equipment supplier headquartered in Chicago. He found the change exhilarating and was asked to move to Chicago in mid-1973. There he met a cadre of overachievers who were destined to become the drivers of a new entrepreneurial venture named "Tellabs" in January 1975.

All of the founders, unlike the venture-backed seedlings of today, worked with no pay for the first year and nominal salaries well into the company's fourth year. Their President, Mike Birck, personified the leadership traits of the Corps and still does today, some 29 years later.

"Tellabs was successful beyond our fondest expectations and became a public company in mid-1980. In the next decade, Tellabs blossomed and technology breakthroughs, combined with intense focus on our customers, allowed us to expand beyond the North American markets to all regions of the world. In the boom of the '90s, Tellabs' revenues surged from $200M in 1992 to $3.3B in 2000. Unfortunately, the "dotcom bust" and the attendant telecom slump emerged in early 2001. The industry and Tellabs have experienced an extremely painful realignment that reduced revenues and personnel to numbers seen in 1997. Like the Marine Corps after World War II, "survival" has been the order of the day. And survive we will! Hoorah!"

Chris is also an equity partner in a number of small businesses including MarketerNet (*www.marketernet.com*) and SimDesk Technologies (*www.simdesk.com*). MarketerNet focuses on providing a pre-qualified list of prospects for companies. They focus primarily on the home lending, automotive, and wireless industries. SimDesk™, the premiere product at SimDesk Technologies, is a suite of web-enabled office productivity applications and was developed specifically to run on a variety of operating platforms including Windows, Macintosh, WebTV, Internet appliances, hand-held devices, and web-enabled cellular phones. The SimDesk™ suite has five major benefits that set it apart from other industry standard office productivity suites: cost, security, ease of use, transportability, and speed.

For a number of years prior to his retirement, Chris was actively involved with Junior Achievement. He would enlist Tellabs employees to teach classes for Junior Achievement. Chris is a member of the Scarlet and Gold committee for the Marine Corps Scholarship Foundation. For nine years he served as a Trustee for Gannon University in Erie, Pennsylvania, and he has served on various local boards over the years.

Chris currently resides in Downers Grove, Illinois. He is blessed to have two sons, Chris and Brendan, a daughter, Sara, and eight (soon to be nine) grandchildren.

SEMPER FIDELIS

J. Gary Cooper

"I instilled my Marine Corps values in my children and as a result they have become outstanding contributors to making this a better world."

Born: 2 October 1936
Service: United States Marine Corps, Active duty 1958 – 1970, 1988 – 1992, Reserves 1970 – 1988, Infantry Officer
Occupation: Chairman, CEO, Commonwealth National Bank

In 1958, Mr. Cooper earned his degree in finance from the University of Notre Dame and was commissioned a second lieutenant in the Marines through the NROTC program. He was sent to Officer's Candidate School in Quantico Virginia for training.

"On the evening of August 18, 1967, while in An Hoa, Vietnam, my Gunnery Sergeant came into my tent and told me that Private Walton wanted to see me. I asked him, 'do you know what Private Walton wants?' He replied, 'he stated that he wants to tell you something.' Young Private Walton was told to come in, he did, stood at attention and stated 'Sir, Private Walton reporting.'

"I asked him, 'Why do you want to see me?' he told me that he had a dream, and in this dream (maybe it was a premonition), he would die tomorrow. That as a result of this dream he felt that he should not go on patrol with the unit in the morning.

"I explained to Private Walton that he was the machine gunner in his squad and that Marines don't have the option of deciding when they want to go into battle based on dreams. I expected to see him in ranks at 0430 the next morning ready for patrol. I asked Private Walton if he understood me clearly and he stood at attention and said, 'yes sir' and did an about face and left my tent. The next morning when "Mike" Company, M/3/9, fell out, Private Walton was in ranks with his machine gun, with his squad.

"We left An Hoa that morning marching on a search and destroy mission. After an hour, we took a ten-minute break. We adjusted our gear and moved out again. As we crossed a rice paddy our company began to take fire. I deployed the Company and directed Private Walton's platoon to move toward the tree line while the other two platoons provided support fire. My command group was moving behind Private Walton's platoon. On the first burst of automatic weapons, Private Walton was hit in the head. As I moved forward, I saw Walton with a Corpsman at his side. Walton was dead. What a brave young man this was who knew what the day held, but also knew his responsibilities to his fellow Marines and his Country.

"Private Walton was one of the many unsung heroes among his fellow Marines. He is a real hero to us all."

During Vietnam, Captain Cooper became the first African American officer to lead an infantry company into combat in Marine Corps history. He earned the Distinguished Service Medal, Legion of Merit, two Purple Hearts and the Republic of Vietnam Gallantry Cross with Palm, Silver and Bronze Stars.

In 1970, after becoming a Marine Reservist, Mr. Cooper served as Director and Corporate Officer of his family's 70-year old insurance company and funeral home.

In 1973, Mr. Cooper served in the Alabama State Legislature. He was elected to his seat in a historic election during Alabama Governor George Wallace's administration. He served in the state legislature until 1978 when he was appointed Commissioner of the Alabama Department of Human Resources. In this state cabinet position, Mr. Cooper managed a staff of more than 4,000 and the largest agency budget in Alabama.

In 1976, joined by other distinguished local citizens, Mr. Cooper founded Alabama's first and only minority owned and operated national bank. Commonwealth National Bank is a full service commercial bank providing a wide array of deposit, loan products and services to the community. For more than 25 years, the bank has focused on providing quality services to the historically under-served inner-city communities in Mobile County.

From 1981 – 1989, Mr. Cooper was a Vice President of David Volkert and Associates, a regional engineering and architectural firm.

General Cooper was promoted to Major General in 1988, and returned to active duty as Director of Personnel, Headquarters, United States Marine Corps.

In 1989, President George H. Bush appointed, and the U.S. senate confirmed General Cooper as Assistant Secretary of the Air Force for Manpower, Reserve Affairs, Installations, and the Environment. He served throughout the Bush Administration.

He returned to David Volkert and Associates in 1992 as a Senior Vice President.

In 1994, President Clinton selected Mr. Cooper to serve as America's Ambassador to Jamaica. Upon senate confirmation, Ambassador Cooper presented his credentials to the Governor General of Jamaica on November 4, 1994. He served until December 1997 and returned to Mobile, Alabama.

In 1998, Ambassador Cooper returned to an active role at Commonwealth National Bank. Since then, assets have grown from $23 million to $46 million at the end of 2002. They have also set record operating results in 2001 and again in 2002. As Chairman and CEO of the Bank, his primary responsibility is to ensure that the wishes of the Board of Directors are executed and to gain value for the shareholders of the institution.

Mr. Cooper believes in and has practiced "giving back to the community" and has helped many community non-profit organizations.

"Through the grace of God, I have been able to develop a comfortable life. It is a joy to be able to enhance the quality of life for others. Two charities that are dear to my heart are the Heart of Mary Catholic School where I began my education and the 100 Black Men of Greater Mobile."

The 100 Black Men of Greater Mobile accepted the responsibility of administering the alternative high school in Mobile County with its Phoenix Program. Through this program troubled students who have been suspended are given a second chance to continue their education. Without the Phoenix Program, most of these students would drop out of school and face uncertain futures and crime. Students who complete this program are able to complete their education and are given a chance to live a productive life.

Mr. Cooper serves on the Boards of GenCorps, United States Steel Corporation, Providence Hospital, PNC Financial Services Group, Protective Life Corporation, The Marine Corps University, Mobile Industrial Development Authority, and the Mobile Community Foundation.

During the period he was still serving in the Marine Corps Reserve, he raised three children as a single parent. He is now married to Beverly Martin Cooper of Richmond, Virginia and they reside in the greater Mobile, Alabama area. His son Patrick is a graduate of Yale Law School, Joli is a graduate of Wharton School of Business and Shawn (also profiled) is a graduate of the JL Kellogg School of Business.

SEMPER FIDELIS

Shawn Cooper

"I found the key to my father's madness ... the United States Marine Corps."

Born: 27 February 1962 in Honolulu, Hawaii
Service: United States Marine Corps, Active duty 1985 – 1991, Reserves 1991 – 1994, Officer, Public Affairs
Occupation: Principal, Cooper, Nelson and Associates

In 1983, Shawn graduated from the University of Southern California and headed off to Paris, France. After a year in France, she returned to the states and followed in her father's footsteps by joining the Marines. In 1985, she went to Officer's Candidate School in Quantico, Virginia.

"My father, a single parent and hard charging Marine, raised my siblings and me. In our household we woke up to reveille, ate chow, ran with my dad for physical training, washed fingerprints from walls and prepared for inspections. I always thought dad was 'special' ... a little mental. Now fast forward ... I had survived my first two weeks of Officer Candidate School and was being acclimated to the culture (stress), the disciplined routine and unique terminology found in the Marine Corps. During my first weekend leave, I ran to a pay phone to call my father. I was so excited to tell him that I no longer viewed him as 'crazy' but yet found the key to his madness ... the United States Marine Corps."

In 1991, Shawn resigned her active duty commission in the Marine Corps and accepted a commission in the United States Foreign Service. She served as a diplomat at the U.S. Embassy in Mexico City, Mexico.

After a four-year tour in Mexico, she returned to the United States and earned her Masters in Business Administration in Finance and Marketing from Northwestern's JL Kellogg School of Management.

After completing her MBA, she went to work on Wall Street at JP Morgan as a sales trader. Returning to the South, she worked as the Vice President of Marketing for Jackson Securities in Atlanta. In 2002, she partnered with her sister, Joli Cooper Nelson and founded Cooper, Nelson and Associates (*www.coopernelsonassociates.com*).

Cooper, Nelson and Associates is a Tampa based market research and strategic management consulting firm dedicated to supporting the strategic, marketing and business development needs of their clients. This is a 100% female and minority owned business servicing a diverse group of public and private organizations nationwide.

Shawn handles market research business development for the company and is based in Atlanta due to the city's strategic location for Corporate clients and major airport accessibility. She believes in meeting face-to-face with their clients and performing an in-depth analysis of their market research needs. Her mission is to exceed her client's expectations by combining traditional research methodologies with value-added business insights.

Shawn believes in giving back to the community. She is a board member at the DeKalb Rape Crisis Center. Also, she also is actively involved in Cool Girls, a one-on-one mentoring organization that pairs disadvantaged, teenage inner-city children with successful and caring mentors.

Not placing boundaries on her community, Shawn recognized a void in Business Leadership material that focused on women and the issues they face in their quest to become outstanding managers and achieve professional success. To fill that void she has written a book titled *W.A.R.: Women Are Rising; from Combat Boots to Corporate Suits*. She has compiled insights from former women officers on how they incorporated their military training, the principles of military leadership, and the traits of leadership into their successful civilian career and management style.

Shawn currently resides in Atlanta, Georgia but frequently returns home to Alabama to spend time with her father, retired Marine Major General J. Gary Cooper.

SEMPER FIDELIS

Dennis Corso

"Discipline, physical and mental strengthening, stressful situations, and the quiet pride that comes from experiencing it all have contributed to the person I am."

Born: 17 November 1946 in Cleveland, Ohio
Service: United States Marine Corps, 1965 – 1967, Enlisted
Occupation: Founder, Owner, Dennis Corso Company, Inc.

Dennis graduated from Mayfield High School in 1964. In September of that year he enrolled at Cuyahoga Community College and stayed about long enough for a cup of coffee. After dropping out of college, he worked at a number of jobs, including construction and gas stations as a pump-jockey and so-so mechanic.

"In the evenings I went with my buddies to the bars, drank 3.2% beer, and mostly went home alone. In March of 1965, the Marines landed in Viet Nam and as we approached the age of 19, we started thinking about the draft. One evening in the fall after drinking too many of the above mentioned beers, we came up with a plan to beat the draft: 'We enlist!' The next question, of course, was what to enlist in. The Army was automatically out. We didn't like the Air Force uniforms, or the little white hats in the Navy. Needless to say, the Coast Guard was out: an 18 month waiting list and too many jokes: 'The ship sank and all hands waded ashore safely.' This only left one branch, and hey, the six of us were pretty tough guys. Besides, the Corps had so many cool slogans.

"A lot of things come to mind about boot camp. Card games on the train ride from Akron to South Carolina. Some guys playing 'tough guy' on the train (we think we're Marines now). In my case, a distant feeling of foreboding: NOW, what have I gotten myself into! A screaming DI getting on our bus as it arrived at the recruit depot and letting us know who was in charge.

"My favorite boot camp memory was the Chaplain's sermon. I went to church on Sundays, first out of habit, and second, to get out of the DI's sight for an hour. It seemed that every Sunday, the sermon ended the same way: 'My door is always open. HOWEVER, do not come and tell me that your DI is hitting you or picking on you. I know that isn't true (murmured chuckles). Remember: Thousands have come before you, and thousands will come after you.' My son has heard this any number of times when he complained about a teacher or a boss.

"Infantry training is now kind of a blur, as is the leave that followed. I reported to Camp Pendleton on Easter Sunday in 1966, the 23rd member of the newly forming Charlie Company, 1st Battalion, 26th Marines. We formed a battalion landing team (BLT-26) and in July sailed on the USS *Iwo Jima*, the first purpose built helicopter carrier. (Previous ships were converted World War II aircraft carriers.) We made a series of landings in country (Vietnam) and in October set up at Hill 55, 15 miles south of Da Nang. In May of 1967 we were attached to 9th Marines and went to Khe Sahn. I left in August with another vivid memory: All of our gear was turned in on the day of our flight out. The plane came in quickly, taking .50-caliber fire from the mountains. (The airfield was frequently under mortar attack when the planes came, but not this day.) As it touched down on the strip, the aircrew pushed skids of supplies off the tail as the plane taxied to the far end of the runway where we were waiting. As the plane came around for take-off, we ran up behind it and the aircrew pulled us aboard. When we were all on, the pilot went wide open on the throttles and we took off for Da Nang and processing for home."

After leave, Dennis spent three months at Quantico and then left the Marine Corps. He spent the next 16 years working for the railroad, as a brakeman, conductor, and yardmaster. Most of his railroad career was spent working on call, 24/7, including holidays. Missing a call for work took you off of the call list for 24 hours. Too many misses, and a suspension resulted. The railroad was quite strict in implementing its many safety and operating rules. He is quite sure that the discipline he learned as a Marine contributed to his success as a reliable and hard working railroad employee.

In 1985, Dennis caught the entrepreneurial bug and started his own business a few days before his son was born. He bought into a delivery business and opened a branch terminal in Akron. Partnership issues left him with the entire company.

In 1992, he purchased part of a product line manufacturing antique motorcycle parts. He started in his garage and today has a 7,500 square foot facility making more than 400 items for 1910 to 1984 Harley-Davidson and other American made motorcycles. He has the machining and manufacturing ability to reproduce almost any small motorcycle mechanical part. His business does very little advertising and has grown through word of mouth as a "can do" replacement motorcycle parts company. The easiest way for people to contact them is by email at dcorso@choiceonemail.com.

In 1996, becoming tired of operating two businesses, he sold the delivery business. "Five years of running two businesses and being a single parent was too much." In 1998 he bought his welder's business and now can also offer commercial welding and fabrication.

His son, Blaise, turned 18 in October 2003. He is in the National Honor Society at Walsh Jesuit High School. He's also very mechanically inclined, helping Dennis with their Hemi-powered 1932 Ford hot rod and will soon be sharing the driving chores of their injected front-engine nostalgia dragster which is currently running the quarter-mile in 8.20 seconds @ 160 mph. Blaise is now looking at colleges with an eye toward engineering.

Dennis, in 1990, joined Viet Nam Veterans of America in Geauga County. A very close friend (also a former Marine) had joined and really enjoyed it. Among other things, they collect toiletries for veterans in VA hospitals, provided benefit info to veterans, and speak about Vietnam in area high schools. He has also been actively involved in many of the various fund raising and capital campaigns associated with Walsh Jesuit. He personally gives financial support to many other local non-profits in the area.

"Everything that happens to us in life – good or bad – shapes us into the people we are. The United States Marine Corps made an impact on my life. Discipline, physical and mental strengthening, stressful situations, and the quiet pride that comes from experiencing it all have contributed to the person I am. It hasn't always been easy, but I wouldn't change very much."

Dennis, Pegi, and his son Blaise currently reside in Kent, Ohio.

SEMPER FIDELIS

WILLIAM V. COWAN

"You've got to be bad to be good."
(as stated on 60 Minutes when talking about his time as a clandestine operative in the Middle East.)

BORN: 17 August 1943 in Sacramento, California
SERVICE: Enlisted, USN, 1961 – 1962; Commissioned, USMC, 1966 – 1985
OCCUPATION: Chairman and CEO, the wvc3 group; Fox News Channel Contributor

Bill Cowan grew up in a military family, learning as a youngster that constantly moving was a way of life. He spent his high school years in Alaska. When the weather wasn't too brutal, he could generally be found in some remote section of the wilds, out by himself fishing, hunting, or practicing survival skills, all of which later served him well.

The day he graduated from high school, at age 17, Bill enlisted in the Navy. As he explains it, "the Marine recruiter was gone the day I went by the recruiting office, and the next thing I knew I was in the Navy!" His original orders out of boot camp were to go to sonar school and then into the submarine service. However, before he could execute them he was on his way to the Naval Academy Prep School at Bainbridge, MD. The following year, he was in the Academy as a Plebe.

Bill graduated from the Naval Academy in 1966 and accepted a commission as a second lieutenant in the Marine Corps. A year later, following Basic School and 12 weeks of Vietnamese language training, he was in Vietnam with the 3rd Battalion, 26th Marines. "I reported into the unit while they were in contact in the mountains near the Laotian border. My first issued utilities came from the willy-peter bag of a lieutenant killed the previous day. It was a sobering start."

With the 26th Marines, he was a platoon commander during the treacherous Fall of 1967 battles in and around the DMZ. "We had 55 Marines killed in one four-day on-and-off engagement with the North

Vietnamese." Later the battalion returned to Khe Sanh, just in time for the siege.

Bill subsequently served almost three years in Vietnam, all of it in combat assignments. The best part of it, he recalls, was the time in the Rung Sat Special Zone. "We had a small Marine Corps team and probably some of the best Vietnamese troops in the country. We worked closely with Navy riverine and Army helicopter units, and we were able to plan and conduct our own ops with virtually no guidance or interference from above. The result was success after success. Being a VC or NVA in the Rung Sat was not a good career choice. They just didn't live long."

In 1983, as terrorism blossomed in the Middle East, Bill was pulled away from a proposed plum assignment to the White House and sent instead to be the only Marine in the Pentagon's Intelligence Support Activity, a super secret, counter-terrorist organization under the auspices of the highest leadership of the Pentagon. "I was fortunate enough to serve with some of the Army's best – men who had served for years in Vietnam and elsewhere, mostly doing things that Marines of that era never got to do. It was an incredible experience, and the stories of many of the things we did in the unit will probably never be told."

In 1985, upon retirement, Bill joined the staff of U.S. Senator Warren B. Rudman, a former Army Ranger and Korean War vet. Bill served as a legislative assistant on defense and foreign operations matters, and as the Senator's principal staffer during the Iran/Contra Hearings. While there he was able to participate in what he considers to be his most significant contribution to his country – the drafting of the legislation creating the U.S. Special Operations Command in Florida and totally revamping the special operations community. "One of the results of that legislation was our ability to attack in Afghanistan, Iraq, and elsewhere around the world with special operations forces and capabilities we wouldn't have otherwise had. That legislation made the difference."

After leaving Rudman's staff, Bill entered the private sector as a budding business executive. But when Iraq invaded Kuwait in 1990, former CIA Director Bill Colby sought him out to put together an operation to rescue U.S. business executives trapped inside Kuwait City. "Considering the thousands of former CIA operatives Bill Colby had to draw from, it was the ultimate honor that he came to me to pull off such an operation. Of course, we did it. I'd learned well while working with the Army, and some of my former Army colleagues were the most important elements of our success."

Today, Bill is Chairman and Chief Executive of the wvc3 group, a small company working private sector and government homeland security issues. Bill founded the company with Alex Schultes, a close friend and former Marine with whom he had gone to Vietnamese language school in 1967 prior to both of them joining the 3rd Marine Division. Another founding member is Marine Vietnam veteran Carlton Sherwood, and James Webb, retired Marine and former Navy Secretary is a member of the company's Advisory Board.

Bill still maintains an active involvement in Middle East issues. Following the end of the Iraq War, the wvc3 group formed an international joint venture called ForcePro, Inc. In addition to the wvc3 group, the partnership includes distinguished Lebanese businessmen, politicians and retired military officers, as well as representatives of the 55 Sheikhs of the Al Anbar Region of Iraq. This relatively new joint venture is rapidly becoming known as "A Middle East Solution Provider."

Bill is also a member of the Fox News Channel team, where he provides analysis on a range of issues involving the military, counterterrorism, intelligence, and world affairs. During the Gulf War, he was recognized by a leading New York newspaper as the premier military analyst amongst all of the networks. As the paper noted, Bill was "the troops' biggest booster." Those who know Bill, know that he'd have had it no other way.

Bill has four grown children from a previous marriage – Linda, Mary, William, who is a member of the Army's 82nd Airborne Division, and John, who works with his father at wvc3.

Bill and his wife, Sue, have a young daughter Esther, with another child on the way. They currently reside in Northern Virginia.

SEMPER FIDELIS

John W. Davenport, Sr.

"The Marine Corps sets an example that inspires you to achieve much more than you ever thought you could."

Born: 1 October 1946 in Quincy, Massachusetts
Service: United States Marine Corps, 1964 – 1987; Enlisted 1964 – 1972, Officer 1973 – 1987, Adjutant
Occupation: Chairman and President of Management Services, Document Technologies, Inc.

Immediately upon graduating from high school, John visited his local recruiter and enlisted in the Marine Corps. He was placed in delayed entry to wait for a platoon opening. Later that summer he left for boot camp at Parris Island, South Carolina.

"A new general was taking over the base and was due to arrive at the headquarters for a briefing. I was assigned as the briefing officer and we had the staff assembled. The general arrived and everyone was called to attention. He commanded 'at ease,' and I introduced myself and attempted to begin my briefing. The general quickly interrupted me, saying, 'Major, you needn't introduce yourself, I know exactly who you are. Last night when I arrived on base and the staff car dropped me off at the BOQ, I was greeted by a 13 year-old boy who introduced himself as John Davenport, Jr. He politely, but firmly requested a few minutes of my time so he could fill me in on some of the things the teens on base needed me to pay attention to. I must say your son is very persuasive and I now know that one of my priorities must be to renovate the teen club. Now Major, you can continue with your briefing and I hope you are as well prepared and convincing as your son.' Today, John Davenport, Jr., also a former Marine, is the CEO of Document Technologies, Inc., a company he and I, and our team have built to more than $37 million in annual revenue in less than five years."

John, Sr. retired from the Marine Corps in January 1987 and immediately went to work in Atlanta, Georgia for a small copy service, providing outsourcing services to law firms. He advanced in the business while the company grew and he became the Regional Vice President of the company and was responsible for opening offices in Washington, D.C.; Philadelphia, Pennsylvania; Baltimore, Maryland; Richmond and Norfolk, Virginia. John returned to Atlanta in 1996 when the company was sold to a much larger entity. He stayed with the larger company as marketplace vice president for Georgia until forming DTI in October 1998.

Document Technologies, Inc. (DTI) is a national company with offices in 13 cities, providing document outsourcing services to Fortune 1000 companies, and some of the nation's most eminent law firms. They also manage business centers in some of the country's most prestigious hotels such as the Waldorf-Astoria, The Plaza and Palmer House Hilton. DTI earned recognition as Atlanta's fastest growing privately held company, and has grown from ten employees in one location to more than 750 employees in more than 50 locations in 13 cities. DTI brings the latest in technology to its customers and assists them in creating less paper environments. As a result of its reputation for providing superior service, DTI is well on its way to achieving its goal of having offices in 50 domestic cities and the top ten cities overseas.

John Davenport, Sr. is the Chairman and President of Management Services for DTI. Many of the 750 people employed by DTI are former Marines and veterans of other branches of the service. By employing the latest technology and fielding the most customer-focused team in the industry, DTI will generate more than $43 million in revenue for 2003.

The Marine Executive Association benefits from John's business acumen and experience. He serves as the vice-president, and on the board of directors of this non-profit organization whose goal is to assist Marines in transition from the military to the civilian job market and/or within the civilian job market.

John and his wife, Joanne, currently reside in Beaufort, South Carolina across the river from Parris Island. They are the parents of three children and have eight grandchildren.

SEMPER FIDELIS

Timothy T. Day

"The Marine Corps completed my transformation from youth to manhood, and in the process deeply instilled in me (perhaps burned into my core) values, principles, commitments, and attitudes."

Born: 9 May 1937 in Brooklyn, New York
Service: United States Marine Corps 1959 – 1962 active and 14 years Marine Corps Reserve, Officer
Occupation: Chairman and CEO, Bar-S Foods Co.

Tim joined the Marine Corps PLC program as a freshman at Wesleyan University, and received his commission upon graduation in 1959. He served his country for three years as an Artillery Officer achieving the rank of Captain. He then continued to serve many more years in the Marine Corps Reserve.

"I was attending winter mountain leadership training in Bridgeport, California and the final exercise was a 60 mile tactical march on skis through the Sierra Mountains. It was bitter cold and very hard work. At night, we would pack the snow down in a small area and drape a parachute over our skis to form a shelter. We were told our sleeping bags provided the most warmth if we slept naked. One night, I had to go to the bathroom. I held off as long as I could, but finally crawled out of my sleeping bag, lifted up a corner of the parachute and stepped outside only to sink up to my neck in powder snow! Some fellow Marines responded to my cry of surprise and pulled my frozen naked butt back into the shelter. I never did get warm again during that four-day journey."

Following his discharge in 1962, he earned an MBA from Harvard Business School, graduating in 1964. Over the next 17 years Tim held senior executive positions for Trans World Airlines and General Host Corporation, and served as President of Cudahy Company. The next challenge he met began in 1981.

"The Marine Corps gave me a great deal of responsibility at an early age, and had taught me leadership, command and control, organization skills, decisiveness, and made me action oriented. I learned the benefit of moving with speed and impact, and gained a "hands on" appreciation of working with a highly motivated and elite team. This, coupled with the specific business skills and work ethic honed at Harvard Business School, gave me confidence that I could excel in the business world and rapidly climb the ladder to the top of my profession."

Tim is the Principal founder of Bar-S Foods Co. and has been Chief Executive Officer, responsible for every aspect of this business, since it began operation in August 1981.

"Bar-S Foods Co. has risen from a little-known, heavily leveraged company into a recognized force in the processed meat industry. Over the past 21 years, we have focused on excelling in the basics and relentlessly pursuing continuous improvement in: fostering a culture of teamwork; building strong customer relationships; leading the industry in quality; providing superior service; and being a low cost operator. This solid foundation has enabled us to deliver real value to the marketplace. Bar-S is now the #2 sliced luncheon meat national brand, the #2 frank national brand, the #3 sliced bacon national brand, and the #4 dinner sausage national brand. Our vision to become the recognized Premier Company and Clear Value Leader in the processed meat industry is now within reach. Bar-S Foods Co. is among the ten largest privately held companies in Arizona and ranks in the top 40 meat companies in the United States. The company is headquartered in Phoenix, Arizona and has about 1,600 employees, in excess of $100 million in assets, and annual sales of approximately $400 million. More than 100 processed meat products are marketed in all 50 states as well as in many foreign countries. We operate four state-of-the-art facilities in Oklahoma that rank among the cleanest, most modern, and most efficient in the industry.

"While we contribute to many causes, our greatest support goes to the United Way because it covers so many different charities, and funds can be directed to communities that serve our people in Oklahoma, as well as other geographic locations. Further, we actively support the City of Hope because the organization has deep roots in the food industry, and they persuaded me to lead efforts to establish a major presence in Arizona. In addition, a great deal of support has been given to the Goldwater Institute, an Arizona "think tank," because it promotes philosophies we believe in —'limited government, economic freedom, and individual responsibility.' Finally, I am a contributor to the Marine Corps University Foundation and a founder of the Marine Corps Heritage Foundation."

Tim and his wife, Sandra, reside in Jackson, Wyoming where he spends his time when not busy at Bar-S Corporate Headquarters in Phoenix, Arizona. He is the proud father of four children: Eric Gleason, Leslie Pellillo, Timothy T. Day, Jr., and Bryan Day.

SEMPER FIDELIS

Marcel Desaulniers

"The extraordinary Marine Corps training I received imbued in me a sense of organization and loyalty that have contributed significantly to the discipline it has taken to be a successful chef and cookbook author."

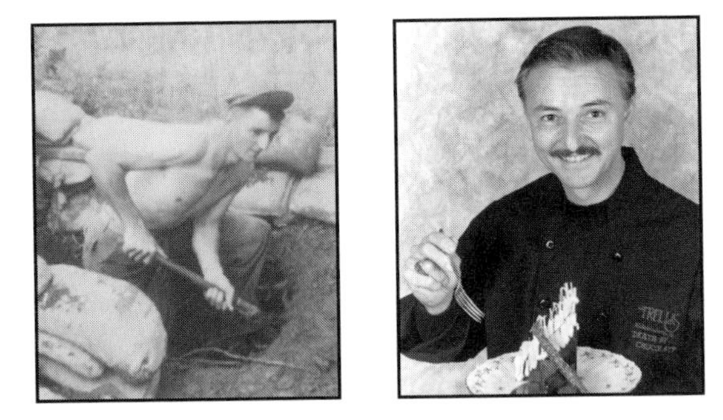

Born: 2 August 1945 in Woonsocket, Rhode Island
Service: United States Marine Corps, 1966 – 1968
Occupation: Executive Chef and Co-owner, The Trellis Restaurant

In 1965, Marcel Desaulniers graduated from the Culinary Institute of America and worked as a Rounds Cook at the Irving Trust Company, New York City, and then the Colony Club also in New York City. His culinary career was abruptly interrupted in February 1966 when he was drafted into the United States Marine Corps. Marcel's military occupation was a rifleman and his time was served in Vietnam.

"In boot camp at Parris Island raincoats were issued by height. When the supply sergeant asked me how tall I was I replied, 'Five foot 11 and 1/2 inches sir.' The sergeant replied, 'Look private (expletive added), you are either Five foot 11 inches or six foot.' I immediately and loudly replied, 'Six foot sir!'

"I have large feet for a man my size – thirteens! In Vietnam the boot supply was critical in that particular size. After several months in country, no size thirteen boots were available and I was tromping around in taped up boots. Finally I was taken out of the field for about three weeks until the supply department came up with more boots. During that time our company gunnery sergeant suggested that perhaps I should transfer to the mess kitchen for the remainder of my in country service. I refused, and told the gunny that I would go to the field in sneakers rather than give up my hard-earned role as a grunt. I did get boots and go back out to the field. Not long after that my platoon commander told me I had to chopper back to battalion headquarters to see the battalion commander. He had no idea what this was all about, but it must have to do with something stateside. I choppered to battalion headquarters in Phu Bai, worrying that a family member had died, and reported in.

Upon reporting to the battalion commander he ordered me to remove my boots. He then said, 'Marine, I just wanted to make sure your feet were that damned big. Now tell me,' he said, 'what the hell have you been telling your mother, because it seems that she has gotten the ear of both your congressman and senator, and they have raised hell with us.' I assured the colonel that I had never complained. I had simply mentioned that I was probably going to run out of boots before my tour of duty was over. 'Well,' he then said, 'Marine you're not in trouble, but our supply department is in a world of shit.' He then sent me back to enjoy the comfort of the boonies!"

When Marcel was discharged from the Marine Corps, he returned to New York City and spent two years at the Hotel Pierre as Saucier, and then moved on to The Colonial Williamsburg Foundation, Williamsburg, Virginia as Assistant Chef. From Assistant Chef he became Manager of Food Production and Quality Control. He spent the next six years as Executive Vice President and Co-owner of the Williamsburg Food Brokers, and then in 1980, he opened The Trellis Restaurant with partner John Curtis.

The Trellis Restaurant is on historic Duke of Gloucester Street in Colonial Williamsburg. Located in a busy tourist area, they serve more than 200,000 meals a year with a dollar volume of slightly less than five million. The Trellis enjoys a wonderful reputation and has garnered national recognition winning prestigious awards regularly.

In 1988, not only was Marcel inducted into the American Academy of Chefs, but his first cookbook, *The Trellis Cookbook*, was published, making that a very busy year for him. Since then Marcel has published several cookbooks including *Death By Chocolate* in 1993. This book won many awards and became the basis for Marcel's television cooking series on The Learning Channel. Marcel's most recent book, *Celebrate With Chocolate*, was published in October 2002 and was a winner of the Gourmand World Cookbook Awards, Best Chocolate Book for 2002. Foreign editions of his books have been published in France, Great Britain, Holland, Australia, Mexico, and Canada. Marcel is currently co-host of two PBS cooking series *The Grilling Maestros* and *Cook-Off America*.

Over the years, The Trellis has been very active in the community of Williamsburg. They frequently present special dinners that have raised many thousands of dollars for The College of William and Mary, The American Cancer Society, Child Development Resources, and many others.

The Desaulniers family resides in the Williamsburg, Virginia area.

SEMPER FIDELIS

JAMES D. DEVER

"The best way to get a job done is to build a team of experts."

BORN: 25 October 1955 in Oceanside, New York
SERVICE: United States Marine Corps, 25 years 1973 – 1998, Enlisted
OCCUPATION: President, 1 Force, Inc.

Jim Dever's military experience began at the age of 18 when he enlisted in the Marines. His 25-year military career was packed full of challenges, all of which he met proudly.

"One of my most memorable experiences was attending SERE instructor school (Survival Evasion Resistance Escape) conducted by the Special Forces Branch (Green Beret) at Fort Bragg, North Carolina. That was where I met the developer of the school, Colonel Nick Rowe. This man was a POW for five years in Vietnam before making his infamous successful escape. The stories he related surrounding his capture and how he survived his period of brutal captivity have continued to inspire me. He shared his experiences on his survival skills through torture and witnessing friends die. This man's shining example of strength aided me in instructing my Marines on how to endure hardships not only in their professional lives, but in their personal lives as well.

"In 1989, while attending the U.S. Army Special Forces Advanced Reconnaissance Target Analysis Exploitation Techniques Course at Fort Bragg, I received word that this great man was assassinated in the Philippines. I clearly recall the Special Forces community shutting down all training that day to honor this special man whose lessons have aided, and will continue to aid, countless fellow Marines."

Dever's military accomplishments are many. He began at the bottom as a Marine Recruit and rose to the highest rank possible as an enlisted man, Sergeant Major. He spent his Marine career in Infantry and Reconnaissance units and retired as the Battalion Sergeant Major for Landing Team 1/1 in 1998. Dever participated in retaking of Kuwait, evacuation of Phnom Penh, Cambodia, evacuation of Saigon, Vietnam, and his duties have taken him to Asia, Europe, Africa and Central America.

While he was a Gunnery Sergeant he was told to assist the director as a technical advisor on the filming of *Heartbreak Ridge*. The director was Clint Eastwood and the experience sparked a real interest in filmmaking. It was then that Dever knew he would go into technical consultation for filmmaking when his Marine commitments were fulfilled.

After his military retirement, Dever worked in TV doing special effects for films. This experience led him to start his own company, 1 Force, Inc. 1 Force was formed to meet the growing requirements of today's motion picture industry for technical advice covering an endless range of subjects. To answer this need, they have assembled a team of professional experts to service the film and television industry.

Dever and 1 Force have been involved in several motion pictures including *The Last Samurai*, *Windtalkers*, *Hostage*, *Dreamcatchers*, *We Were Soldiers*, *Death Before Dishonor*, and television programs including *Combat Missions*, *The Invisible Man*, and *ESPN Thrillmasters*.

As president of 1 Force, Jim researches all the films he is negotiating for or contracted to do. He works with the writers on the scripts and works very closely with the Director as well as the First Assistant Director. He also assists with props, art, costumes and weapons. By working with all the various departments Jim ensures that through research every detail for that time period is correct. In addition, he takes responsibility for battle choreography, weapons handling and safety, proper uniform attire. Depending on the project, he will train and coach the actors on military dialogue, customs, courtesies, protocol, as well as the dynamics of specific roles in Military hierarchy.

Jim Dever is married to the former Cathy Shepard and is the stepfather of two children. They make their home in southern California.

SEMPER FIDELIS

Jack G. Downing

"Be sure you're right, then go ahead." (David Crockett)

Born: 21 October 1940 in Honolulu, Hawaii
Service: United States Marine Corps 1958 – 1976, Reserve, 1963 – 1967, Active, Officer
Occupation: Consultant to U.S. Congress and the Intelligence Community

While an undergraduate at Harvard, Jack participated in the Marine Corps PLC program. Upon graduation in 1962, he was commissioned a Second Lieutenant. After earning a master's degree in 1963, he entered active duty, and completed Basic School.

While serving with the 3rd Battalion, 4th Marines at Kanoehe Bay, Hawaii, Jack was detached for a brief on-the-job training assignment with a U.S. Special Forces team in Vietnam in late 1964/early 1965. He soon returned to Vietnam when the Fourth Marines, along with other elements of the First Marine Brigade, were deployed there from Hawaii in April 1965.

"I have many vivid memories of my time in the Marine Corps. The most poignant of these is the loss of a very fine staff sergeant, fresh from service as a Drill Instructor at Parris Island, who was killed in action in Vietnam in late 1965. During a night action at close quarters with the Viet Cong, the sergeant was killed instantly by an incoming grenade as my platoon fought from an ambush position along the banks of a river near Hue. The Sergeant was lying on top of the grenade when it detonated, and there has never been any doubt in my mind that his death was an act of intentional sacrifice, which saved other Marines, including me, from serious wounds or death. However, due to the darkness and the confusion of battle, his act went unwitnessed and was subsequently recognized only by a Purple Heart. The selfless courage displayed by the Sergeant represents the Marine Corps at its best. No doubt, unrecognized valor was commonplace among Marine infantrymen in Vietnam."

After the Marine Corps, Jack began his long career with the Central Intelligence Agency in 1967. Fluent in Russian and Chinese, he served two tours in Moscow and Beijing and is the only Agency officer to have been station chief in both locations. Retiring from the Agency in 1995, Jack was asked by George Tenet, the Director of the CIA, to return in mid-1997 to rebuild the Agency's Directorate of Operations, then suffering from an ill-advised post Cold War draw-down. Jack served as the CIA's Deputy Director for Operations for the next two years, focusing his efforts on recruiting and training young officers, rebuilding the Agency's presence overseas, creating a cadre of reserve officers, and persuading Congress that the Agency, no longer able to "do more, with less," needed more funding.

Downing, a recipient of the CIA's highest award, retired from the agency again in 1999 and is now a consultant to Congress and the Intelligence Community. He is also a founding trustee of the CIA Officers Memorial Foundation, which provides assistance for the college education of children of CIA officers killed in the line of duty. This foundation was started in late 2002 following the death of a young CIA officer (and former Marine captain), Mike Spann, who was our nation's first casualty in the Afghan War.

Jack and his wife, Suzanne, have a son, John, and a daughter, Wendy, and two grandchildren. Jack resides in Arlington, Virginia and on occasional visits to the Vietnam Memorial, always pays his respects to the memory of the staff sergeant who sacrificed his life that night many years ago during the fire fight on the river bank near Hue.

SEMPER FIDELIS

Joseph N. DuCanto

"Doing your job as a Marine was more important than life itself."

Born: 18 March 1927 in Utica, New York
Service: United States Marine Corps, 1944 – 1946, Enlisted, Engineer and Light Machine Gun Crew Captain
Occupation: Senior Partner, Schiller, DuCanto and Fleck; Chairman, Securatex

Joseph "Joe" DuCanto enlisted in the Marine Corps in January 1944. He had been living with a foster family and had completed two years of high school. He was sent to Parris Island, South Carolina for training.

"Upon arriving at boot camp and going through the processing program, I together with my mates, was given the option to accept or reject the $10,000 G.I. life insurance policy which cost something like $3.60 a month deducted from our $50 per month pay checks. Since I was orphaned as an infant, spending time in an orphanage before becoming a foster child in the county welfare program, I declined to be covered. There was no one in particular who I wished to benefit one cent from my early demise. I was soon approached by Sgt. Peterson, senior drill instructor, seeking an explanation for this deviant behavior, since a $10,000 pay-out (equivalent to $100,000 today) was a hefty chunk of change not to go to somebody if I bought the farm. After listening to me for a very brief time, he asked me point-blank, 'Do you know what a point man is?' to which I replied, 'No, sir,' and he then proceeded to explain as follows: 'A point man is sent out 20 to 30 yards or more ahead of the platoon to seek out possible enemy contact and/or ambush. When the shooting starts, he is usually among the first to get it! Do you know, Boot, who we designate as point man?' Really a rhetorical question to which I quickly replied, 'No, sir,' with his rejoinder, 'The guy without G.I. insurance.' Suffice it to say that since nobody had ever explained it to me that way before, I very quickly signed the authorization card.

Mr. DuCanto served with the Pioneer-Engineers and the 3rd Marine Division during wartime and, following hostilities, with the 7th Marine First Marine Division, in North China. "Doing your job as a Marine was more important than life itself."

While trained to build things, most of their time was spent learning how to blow up and destroy hardened defense positions, which of course, came in handy at Iwo Jima. Although his primary MOS was "engineer," he was also the captain of a light machine gun crew.

He was discharged from the Corps late in 1946, short of 20 years of age, with two years of high school, no family and no prospects! After bumming around for a couple of years, Mr. DuCanto gained entry into Syracuse University under a special program for veterans and discovered he was college educable. He transferred to Antioch College, a highly prized and recognized school having a work-study program, and did exceedingly well, graduating in 1952 and receiving a National Honor Law scholarship to the University of Chicago School of Law. He graduated in 1955 and immediately commenced his career in Chicago where he has remained.

"I ultimately married a classmate of mine and had two children, Anthony, a former Marine, and James, now a physician. I was divorced 15 years ago and remarried nine years ago, adopting a son, William Heiman, who currently serves as a Corporal in Force Recon in the Marines."

Mr. DuCanto divides his time between two very successful and nationally recognized firms.

He is a practicing attorney in Chicago, Illinois and for nearly half a century, has specialized in representation of clients in divorce matters. The last 22 years he has been a partner in the law firm of Schiller, DuCanto and Fleck. This firm, consisting of 35 attorneys, is nationally known as the highest quality and largest divorce firm in the United States. The top echelon of our membership are acknowledged and named in *The Best Lawyers in America* and in similar publications. They have an enviable reputation for providing this much needed service to those from many walks of life, including titans of industry, professional athletes, movie stars, astronauts, the politically important, and assorted billionaires. Their reputation has been garnered by adherence to the highest professional ethics, quality, and for service with fidelity and loyalty to all who come to them for assistance. In 2003, Mr. DuCanto was rewarded by being named a "Laureate of the Illinois State Bar Association," an honor bestowed annually upon 12 lawyers (some posthumous) who exemplify the best of the legal profession and exhibit high standards and integrity. This award also serves as an example to all members of the practicing bar "to help all lawyers understand what a lawyer should be." The Illinois Bar currently consists of approximately 74,000 lawyers, so the receipt of such an accolade is an overwhelming professional honor.

Mr. DuCanto's second successful business and career is with Securatex, a private detective and private security agency.

"Securatex had its origin with my service in the Marines. I entered the Marines as an underage and undersized 5'3" wannabe, and never grew an inch more! Upon discharge I sought employment as a police officer, and was emphatically rejected because of my small size. In 1982, I, together with a former Chicago Police Detective, formed SECURATEX as a private detective and private security company. My motive in doing so revolved around one of my sons, Anthony, who had just completed six years of service as a United States Marine and had chosen to become a police officer with the Sheriff's Police of Cook County (Chicago Metropolitan area), working primarily as an undercover officer teamed with the DEA. It was my own thought that Anthony would eventually like to work with the company, and this expectation was realized a number of years ago when he left the Sheriff's Department and became an employee of Securatex."

From a very small beginning Securatex has grown to a company employing 600 to 800 people, operating in six midwestern states. The company provides hundreds of security officers to many national, big-board companies, hospitals, museums, educational institutions and offers substantial private investigative services covering theft, embezzlement, drug abuse, racial and sexual harassment, often involving covert, undercover operatives.

While there are 11,000 private security firms in the U.S., less than 50 of them, like Securatex, have gross incomes exceeding $10,000,000 a year. It has evolved into a woman-owned venture under the leadership of his wife, Patricia, who currently serves as President and Chief Executive Officer. It is unique as a successful, American-owned, family enterprise and takes great pride in its blue-ribbon clientele.

Mr. DuCanto has been an active supporter of many charities including the Marine Corps Scholarship Foundation, serving on their National Board. He looks upon this organization as a form of payback, his "force multiplier." Another non-profit with a tie to his military tour is The Salvation Army. During his service in China he became familiar with them. "They were there early and often in their attempt to relieve the massive suffering of hundreds of millions of poor Chinese during the days preceding the communist takeover."

Mr. DuCanto's favorite charity is Loyola University of Chicago. "This institution has become a favorite of mine because it early on offered me a platform for teaching at the law school. I have been a visiting professor and lecturer at the law school for more than 30 years, and have enjoyed the association and enhanced professional reputation which I have attained. I also feel gratitude for the fact that, after the Marine Corps, which I consider to be my first 'home,' I was cared for from birth to age four in a Catholic orphanage."

The other institutions receiving Mr. DuCanto's time and support are Antioch University and The University of Chicago. "These institutions offered much to me in my ultimate competence and the fulfillment of a life well lived. Life is a game of give and take; you take what you need when you need it and, when and if you can, you give some back."

Joseph DuCanto and his wife, Patricia, currently reside in the greater Chicago area.

SEMPER FIDELIS

ARCHIE W. DUNHAM

"Preparation helps you take care of your employees, meet the needs of your customers, and create wealth for your shareholders."

BORN: 20 December 1938 in Durant, Oklahoma
SERVICE: United States Marine Corps, 1960 – 1964, Officer
OCCUPATION: Chairman, ConocoPhillips

Geological engineering was Archie Dunham's chosen field of study for an undergraduate degree. He completed his course requirements and graduated from the University of Oklahoma in 1960. Archie then began his military service in the United States Marine Corps almost immediately. He directed a Marine Air Control Center in Hawaii.

"My four years of service in the United States Marine Corps were years of tremendous personal growth. I was privileged to lead at an early age and consequently learned much about leadership.

"I have never forgotten the five 'P's ... Prior Planning Prevents Poor Performance. Actually there were six, but I never repeat the sixth 'P' in public. Early in my career, I learned the importance of always being prepared. This single lesson helped me become an effective manager early in my career and a good leader later in life. Preparation helps you take care of your employees, meet the needs of your customers, and create wealth for your shareholders."

Having reached the rank of Captain, Archie was discharged from the Marine Corps in 1964, and returned to the University of Oklahoma earning a master's degree in business administration in 1966. Upon completion of graduate school, he began employment at Conoco Inc. as a Natural Gas Trainee. After many years of dedication and service, Archie became President and CEO in 1996 and was instrumental in Conoco's IPO separation from DuPont in 1998.

"ConocoPhillips is an integrated petroleum company with interests around the world. It is the third largest integrated energy company in the United

States, based on market capitalization, oil and natural gas reserves and production, and is the fifth largest refiner in the world."

Archie Dunham is currently Chairman of ConocoPhillips, which is headquartered in Houston, Texas. The company has a global presence, operating in 49 countries. At the end of 2002, there were approximately 57,000 employees and $77 billion in assets. ConocoPhillips is the fifth largest integrated international energy company in the world.

"ConocoPhillips plans to contribute some $35 million to charitable organizations globally in 2003. The primary areas of support are education and youth, health and safety, civic and the arts, and the environment. Organizations which ConocoPhillips support include the United Way, Boys and Girls Clubs, National Fish and Wildlife Foundation, Barbara Bush Foundation for Literacy, American Heart Association, Special Olympics, the University of Oklahoma, Oklahoma State University and the University of Texas."

In addition to his ConocoPhillips position, Archie Dunham serves on the boards of directors of Louisiana-Pacific Corporation; Phelps Dodge Corporation; and Union Pacific Corporation. Dunham is active in several professional business and advisory organizations. Nationally, he serves on the boards of directors of the American Petroleum Institute, the Energy Institute of the Americas, and the Horatio Alger Association of Distinguished Americans, as well as the National Board of the Smithsonian Institute. The George Bush Presidential Library Foundation, the Commission on National Energy Policy, and the National Infrastructure Advisory Council, a group providing advice to the President on the security of information systems for critical infrastructure supporting various sectors of the economy, including energy also benefit from Dunham's expertise. He proudly serves on the Marine Corps Heritage Foundation.

On the state level, Dunham is a member of the Texas Governor's Business Council and was inducted into the Oklahoma Hall of Fame in 1998.

In Houston, he serves the Greater Houston Partnership, The Houston Forum, Memorial Hermann Healthcare System, and the M.D. Anderson Cancer Center. Dunham is associated with the Houston Symphony, the Houston Grand Opera, and the United Way of the Texas Gulf Coast. He was named Houston's "Father of the Year" in 1998, and recognized as Houston's 2001 International Citizen of the Year.

Archie and his wife, Linda, actively attend the Second Baptist Church of Houston, the largest church in the United States. The Dunham's have three children and eight grandchildren.

SEMPER FIDELIS

Photo Credit (right photo) Gittings & Lorfing.

Ingrid Marie Duran

"Marine camaraderie is equivalent to a second family."

Born: 13 January 1966 in Los Angeles, California
Service: United States Marine Corps, 4 years, 1986 – 1990, Enlisted
Occupation: President and CEO, Congressional Hispanic Caucus Institute

Ingrid Duran's sense of community and her commitment to serving it began at the age of five. She attended rallies for farm worker rights and helped canvass neighborhoods to register new voters. By the time she was 20, she began serving our nation when she enlisted in the United States Marine Corps. At Twenty Nine Palms in California, Duran was an Honor Graduate from the Communications Center Operator School. Her military occupation was a Communications Center Operator.

"When I joined the Marine Corps in 1986, I was a misguided college student with no sense of direction. I had attended two and a half years of college and needless to say my GPA was very low. The Marine Corps taught me the importance of teamwork as we marched for hours on the parade deck at Parris Island while sand fleas ate us alive, until our Drill Instructors were satisfied that all 80 of us were moving as one and they only heard one boot hit the deck. The Marine Corps also taught me the importance of cross training when they assigned me to 45 days of mess duty while I waited for my Communications class to start. I had to learn the skills of food service while working in the chow hall. I also received cross training through numerous work parties that ranged from picking up garbage on the parade deck to taking apart an unused airstrip in the desert. I learned the art of time management in boot camp when all 80 of us had to be showered with only six shower stalls, dressed in five minutes and standing in line. I learned the importance of physical fitness while on a five mile forced march in Okinawa in 90 degree heat with an 80 pound Alice pack, a flack jacket, helmet and boots. I learned how to overcome my fear of heights while repelling down a 150 foot water tower with a Drill Instructor barking that if I didn't get down that wall, that wouldn't be my only fear."

"The Marine Corps instilled in me a solid work ethic and invaluable leadership skills that have given me a solid foundation that has carried me throughout my professional career. In addition, the camaraderie was equivalent to a second family. No matter where I may be when I meet another former Marine there is an instant connection and bond that is formed."

Upon Duran's military discharge, she again launched herself into public service. She worked for the Clerk of the U.S. House of Representatives in the Office of Systems Management and at the House Banking Committee under the chairmanship of U.S. Representative Henry B. Gonzalez (D-TX) in 1990 and 1993 respectively. She then worked as a legislative assistant in the office of U.S. Representative Gene Green (D-TX).

Next, Ingrid Duran became director of the Washington, D.C. office of the National Association of Latino Elected and Appointed Officials (NALEO). During her tenure with NALEO, Duran's leadership was instrumental in launching the Coalition for Hispanic Advancement, now called the National Hispanic Leadership Agenda, the largest and most influential coalition of Latino organizations in the country.

Duran's commitment to serving the Latino Community and our country has been a consistent theme throughout her professional career. Today, she is President and CEO of the Congressional Hispanic Caucus Institute (CHCI), a national non-profit and non-partisan educational organization dedicated to developing the next generation of Latino leaders.

"To fulfill its mission, CHCI offers nationally recognized educational and leadership development programs, services, and activities that promote the growth of its participants as effective professionals and strong leaders. As the premier national Hispanic educational organization, CHCI has created a pipeline for Latino youth from high school through college, graduate school, and on to the workforce. CHCI's educational programs, services, and activities have an extremely successful record of developing effective Hispanic leaders."

As President and CEO of CHCI, Duran continues to serve our nation by helping to empower Latino youth. She has consistently increased fundraising benchmarks, and in 2002, she and her small staff raised a record $3 million during the Institute's Hispanic Heritage Month events. Duran serves as a role model and mentor to all of CHCI's program participants and alumni. She works closely with CHCI's Board of Directors, comprised of Hispanic Members of the U.S. Congress, Corporate executives, and non-profit leaders, and Fortune 500 Corporations to ensure CHCI's growth and prosperity.

She currently serves as a Presidential appointee on the President's Advisory Council on HIV/AIDS and the Department of Veterans Affairs Advisory Committee on Minority Veterans. She also serves on the Executive Advisory Board of the Harvard Journal of Hispanic Policy, the Hispanic Association on Corporate Responsibility Board of Directors, the Shell Hispanic Advisory Council Board, Human Rights Campaign Board, and is a charter member of the Chase Home Finance National Housing Advisory Council.

Duran's professional affiliations include MANA, a National Latino Organization; Women in Military Service Memorial Organization; the Congressional Marine Corps Association; and the Congressional Hispanic Staff Association where she served as President. She successfully completed the National Hispano Leadership Institute Leadership Development program (the Harvard Executive Program and Center for Creative Leadership program). In addition, Duran continues her personal development through study in leadership and executive programs.

During her career, Duran has received numerous commendations from various organizations including the U.S. Department of Health and Human Services, the National Labor Relations Board, and Georgetown University's Greater Los Angeles High School Advancement Program.

A native of Los Angeles, California, Duran was raised in Wichita, Kansas. She earned her Bachelor of Science degree in Management from Park College in Arlington, Virginia and currently resides in the Washington, D.C. area.

SEMPER FIDELIS

Dale Adam Dye

"Semper Fidelis is not just a motto; applied to whatever you do, it can be a guideline for honor, dignity, courage, and success."

Born:	8 October 1944 in Cape Girardeau, Missouri
Service:	United States Marine Corps, 1964 – 1984, 13 years enlisted, 8 years commissioned
Occupation:	President/CEO, Warriors, Inc.

Dale Dye graduated as a cadet officer from Missouri Military Academy but since there was no money for college he enlisted in the United States Marine Corps in January 1964. He served in Vietnam in 1965 and 1967 through 1970 surviving 31 major combat operations. He emerged from Southeast Asia highly decorated, including a Bronze Star and three Purple Hearts for wounds suffered in combat. He spent 13 years as an enlisted Marine, rising to the rank of Master Sergeant before he was chosen to attend Officer Candidate School. Appointed a Warrant Officer in 1976, he later converted his commission and was a Captain when he was sent to Beirut with the Multinational Peacekeeping Force in 1982 – 1983.

Dye served in a variety of assignments around the world and along the way managed to graduate with a BA degree in English from the University of Maryland.

"Through a series of truly colorful leaders and mentors, the Corps shaped and molded me into what I am. In very effective fashion – in combat and out – Marines taught me to lead, to think independently of orders and to understand there are things much more important than myself. I learned Semper Fidelis is not just a motto; applied to whatever you do, it can be a guideline for honor, dignity, courage, and success. There's no MBA program in the world that offers anything close to that."

When he finally decided to retire from the Corps in 1984, he worked for a year at *Soldier of Fortune* magazine. He spent time in Central America, reporting on and training troops in guerrilla warfare techniques in El Salvador, Honduras and Costa Rica before leaving the magazine in 1985 and heading for Hollywood.

"Warriors, Inc. is a unique organization that provides technical advisory services to the entertainment industry worldwide. A full spectrum of services is provided including performer training, research, planning, staging and on-set advisory for directors and other key personnel. Warriors, Inc. creates themes including espionage/counter-espionage, terrorist/counter-terrorist operations, and military special operations involving all historical periods and all branches of foreign and domestic military services."

Dale Dye is an author, actor and film consultant. His accomplishments in these areas include many highly recognizable books and movies. Among his novels are *Platoon* and *Duty & Dishonor*. Dye has acted in or provided technical consultation for more than 35 feature films including *Platoon*, *Forrest Gump*, *Saving Private Ryan*, and *Under Siege*, just to mention a few. He has also contributed to several made for TV films broadcast on the major networks and HBO.

Dale Dye's favored charities include the Vietnam Veterans of America and the Veterans of Foreign Wars.

Dye travels widely and frequently as dictated by his career while maintaining his residence in California.

SEMPER FIDELIS

BERNARD T. EILERTS

"Surround yourself with competent, experienced staff, consider their recommendations and then make decisions."

BORN: 11 June 1932 in St. Louis, Missouri
SERVICE: United States Marine Corps, five years active duty beginning in 1955 and 15 years active reserve duty, Officer
OCCUPATION: Co-Chairman/Secretary of the Trust Fund and Chairman of the Employer Caucus, Western Conference of Teamsters Pension Trust Fund

Bernie Eilerts graduated from the University of Missouri, Columbia, Missouri in 1953 and continued his education at the University of Missouri Law School as the recipient of an NROTC Scholarship until 1955. That June he reported for active duty and was commissioned a 2nd Lieutenant, United States Marine Corps.

"When I was stationed at the Naval Weapons Station in Yorktown, Virginia, as the Assistant Security Officer, Marine Barracks, horses were used to patrol the perimeter fences in the more remote areas of swamp and tidewater sloughs. The Corps decided that more modern means and vehicles would be utilized, and the horses would be put out to pasture. Since this decision resulted in the end of an era of 'active duty' horses in the Marine Corps, it received a fair amount of publicity. Several television stations sent crews to record 'the retirement of the last of the Marine Corps horses.' I had the dubious honor of commanding the honor guard rendering the appropriate pomp and circumstance to the noble steeds. As the TV cameras were recording this historic moment and the horses passed in review, I ordered 'present arms' in my loudest command voice. This obviously captured the attention of one of the horses – he stopped, lifted his tail and dropped an impressive pile of manure. Amidst the cheering and applause from the spectators, particularly the troops that had ridden them, I could not help but believe that this was a statement from a tested veteran reflecting his opinion of forced retirement. All the local stations carried this segment on their evening news."

Bernie's military experience encompassed a variety of infantry and staff positions, including three years as the commanding officer of a Force Reconnaissance Company. After five years of active duty and 15 years of active reserve duty, he retired in 1975 as a Lt. Colonel.

An impressive civilian business career began for Bernie when he left USMC active duty in 1959. His legal background provided a substantial basis for many years of labor relations and negotiations. His business successes have continued through the years and he is now Co-Chairman of the Western Conference of Teamsters Pension Trust Fund and Chairman of the Employer Caucus.

The Western Conference of Teamsters Pension Trust Fund has approximately $23.5 billion in assets. It provides benefits to about 560,000 retired, active and vested employees in the 13 western states. The Trust Fund is ranked as the largest employer-union trust in the world and the 58th largest pension trust in the world.

"As Co-Chairman of the Trust and Chairman of the Employer Caucus, I oversee the day-to-day administration of the Fund through its three major administrative offices is Seattle, Northern California and Los Angeles. Also, I review the Trust's investment policies and the performance of investment managers, review and determine rights of individuals to benefits under the plan and modify or maintain benefits scheduled under the plan. There are 14 management and 14 union trustees on the board and a support staff of attorneys, actuaries, administrators, investment managers, data processing consultants, accountants and real estate advisors."

In addition to Bernie's current occupation, he has been a visiting professor at the University of Hawaii teaching advanced courses in Labor Relations and Contract Negotiations. He has also lent his expertise on city, state and national levels regarding labor management and dispute resolution. The Federal Mediation and Conciliation Service has benefited from Bernie's assistance in many educational programs.

Personally, the Eilerts do volunteer work as well as provide financial support to Community Outreach, a non-profit organization dedicated to helping needy families in Southern Arizona and making a positive difference in children's lives. Bernie also serves as a member of the Board of Trustees of the Marine Corps University Foundation, enhancing professional education and leadership development of Marine Corps officers and enlisted leaders.

The Eilerts are the parents of five and the grandparents of nine. They reside in the sunny, southwest city of Tucson, Arizona.

SEMPER FIDELIS

Donald V. Esmond

"The leadership qualities I learned in the Marine Corps give me a clear vision of what needs to be accomplished and how to succeed when others fail."

Born: 18 March 1944
Service: United States Marine Corps, 1966 – 1972, Helicopter Pilot
Occupation: Senior VP and General Manager, Toyota Division, Toyota Motor Sales USA

Don received a Navy ROTC scholarship to the Illinois Institute of Technology in Chicago, majoring in engineering before switching to business and economics. Out of the 30 Navy ROTC candidates, Don was the only one who chose a Marine Corps option. He was president of the university's Semper Fidelis Society, student body president, and president of his fraternity, Sigma Phi Epsilon.

Following graduation in 1966, he was commissioned a second lieutenant and married the former Cheryl Whigham, who he had met while in Chicago.

Upon completing Marine Corps Basic Officers training in Quantico, Virginia, he went to Navy flight school in Pensacola, Florida for training in T-34s and T-28s. Don earned his instrument rating and carrier-qualification aboard the USS *Lexington* before "the needs of the service" sent him to helicopter school. He received his wings in 1968 and transitioned to the CH-46 Sea Knight helicopter, known as the "workhorse" of the Marine Corps.

"My wife Cheryl went through her own Marine Corps initiation. I rented a basement apartment in Quantico without letting her see it first. That never happened again! I also spent all her dance money from the wedding reception on dress blues. I have been paying for that one ever since."

In January 1969, he was sent to Vietnam and was initially assigned to Marine Medium Helicopter (HMM) Squadron 346, the "Purple Foxes," at Marble Mountain outside Da Nang. He also served with the "Flying Tigers" of HMM 262 in Quang Tri and Phu Bai. "I served with Marines who had nicknames like Wags, Weird Harold, Chuckles and Easy Ed."

During his yearlong tour, Don flew more than 900 missions, including med evacs, recon inserts and extracts, troop lifts and resupply. Under the constant threat of hostile fire, he was shot down twice and wounded once. Don was awarded the Silver Star, Distinguished Flying Cross, 45 Air Medals, and the Purple Heart.

"The leadership qualities I learned in the Marine Corps give me a clear vision of what needs to be accomplished and how to succeed when others fail."

After his Vietnam tour, Don was promoted to captain and assigned to train new CH-46 pilots back in the states. He also served as officer-in-charge of Marine Air Traffic Control Unit 46 in New River, North Carolina.

When he was discharged from the Marine Corps in 1972, Don landed a job in Seattle with the Lincoln-Mercury Division of Ford Motor Co. After numerous field assignments with Lincoln-Mercury and Ford, he moved to Detroit in 1980 to work in Lincoln-Mercury's fleet department.

In 1982, he joined Toyota Motor Sales as national fleet manager. He was later involved in the startup of the Lexus Division where he served as vice president of field sales responsible for the luxury brand's four area sales offices, marketing, business management and market representation activities.

Following the Lexus assignment, he was named vice president of the Large Car Series Team for the Toyota Division. During this time, he successfully launched the fourth-generation Camry, which sold more than 1.6 million units during its model cycle.

In his current position as senior vice president and general manager of the Toyota Division, Don also serves as a member of the company's executive committee. He is responsible for all divisional operations, including sales, marketing, distribution, market representation, fleet, retail development and Corporate used vehicles. He has directed the successful launches of the Sienna minivan, the Camry Solara sport coupe, the Tundra full-size pickup truck, Highlander SUV and Prius electric-hybrid vehicle. Most recently, he was assigned the additional responsibility of overseeing Scion, Toyota's new brand vehicle aimed at younger buyers.

"I attribute a large portion of my current success to the Marine Corps, which taught me the importance of loyalty, respect, leading by example, competing with the best, dealing with adversity and accomplishing objectives through teamwork. I discovered very quickly that goals are achieved by a team effort and that your people always come first.

"The Marine Corps also taught me why diversity works because there were no color barriers in the Corps. Everyone was a Marine and you depended on each other to get the job done. You trusted each other with your lives."

That is why Don is proud of Toyota's diversity efforts, especially in hiring practices and appointing new dealers. Toyota employs more than 104,000 Americans with an annual payroll of $1.3 billion dollars. Toyota and its dealers have invested more than $15 billion dollars in the U.S.

Don is an active member of St. Luke's Orthodox Church in Garden Grove, California, is a past member of the Church Council and president of the Men's Club. He also is a founding member of the Irvine High School Pigskin Alumni, raising money for less fortunate students in the football program. And, he is a member of First Families and Families Forward, dedicated to providing food, shelter and counseling to needy families.

In 1999, he was presented the prestigious Semper Fidelis Award by the Marine Corps Scholarship Foundation. He was later named a director of the foundation, which raises money and awards college scholarships to the deserving sons and daughters of Marine Corps personnel.

Don and Cheryl live in Corona Del Mar, California. They have three sons, all residing in California. Mike is an electrical design engineer for Mindspeed and lives with his wife, Tiffany, in Irvine; Dan, a managing consultant with IBM Business Consultants in Los Angeles, is married to Nikki and they have a young son, Jake; and Chris works for Intel Corps. in San Jose as a business micro processor group account manager.

SEMPER FIDELIS

MICHAEL A. FEDORKO

"Whenever things get tough always remember that there have been many before you who have succeeded and that if you work hard you too will succeed."

BORN: 21 November 1944 in Lakeland, Florida
SERVICE: United States Marine Corps, 1966 – 1972, Enlisted, Weapons Platoon Machine Gunner
OCCUPATION: Vice-Chairman, New Jersey Casino Control Commission

Michael Fedorko enlisted in the Marines in 1965. When he talked to the recruiter, he told him he would go if he could go on the "buddy plan" with his friend, Tony DiCesare. The "buddy plan" enabled friends to be together throughout boot camp and ITR at Camp Lejeune. They arrived at Parris Island on January 14, 1966 and began processing. When they went for haircuts it was the last time they saw each other for 12 weeks. "Tony was assigned to the platoon upstairs from mine, and neither one of us had the nerve to tell the Drill Instructors that the Marines were not holding up to their part of the 'buddy plan' contract."

"After getting our haircuts, an old Sergeant Major came in and 'talked' to us. He told us that the next several months would be very difficult but not impossible. He said, 'Whenever things get tough always remember that there have been many before you who have succeeded and that if you work hard you too will succeed.'

"During boot camp at Parris Island, we were running the obstacle course. It was made from telephone poles. This particular part of the course was where you climb up onto the top of the poles, which were laid end to end. You then were expected to walk down the length of the pole and jump off. It had rained the night before and the poles were slick. About half way down the length of the pole I slipped, went up in the air, and came down on top of the pole with the widest part of my back. The pole snapped in half! Our company commander was present and was astonished to see what had happened. As a result, I was excused from PT for the rest of the day – I think they were afraid I might have broken my back."

On an unhappy note, Mike's friend, Tony, who he had known since they were 13 years old, was killed at Phu Bai during the TET offensive. Mike had seen him at Dong Ha. Mike was waiting to be flown by chopper to Khe Sanh when he noticed a group of Marines leaving a helicopter and walking toward him. The third Marine in line was Tony. They embraced and talked for a minute. Mike walked Tony to the next helicopter, they hugged again and parted. That was the last time they saw each other. Tony was hit by a 120 mm rocket in July 1967.

Upon discharge from active duty, Fedorko joined the New Jersey State Police. His initial assignment was as a general duty road Trooper. Later he was assigned to the Executive Protection Bureau, protecting the Governor, the Attorney General and other state officials, often traveling worldwide with them. Then Fedorko became Commandant of the New Jersey State Police Academy where raw recruits were trained and taught the meaning of their motto, "Duty, Honor and Fidelity."

During his 31 years with the New Jersey State Police, Fedorko earned a B.S. in Criminal Justice from the College of New Jersey, and a Masters in Governmental Administration from the Fels School of Government, University of Pennsylvania. He also attended the Program for Senior Executives in State and Local Government at the JFK School of Government, Harvard University. He retired from the New Jersey State Police as Acting Superintendent.

In November 1999, Fedorko was appointed to the New Jersey Casino Control Commission. This Commission is a panel charged with regulating New Jersey's casino industry. There are five members appointed by the Governor and confirmed by the New Jersey State Senate. They serve staggered five-year terms and regulate an industry grossing $4.5 billion. The Commission employs 350 people, has a budget of $24 million and is totally funded by the casinos operating in Atlantic City. Fedorko is currently Vice-Chairman of the Commission and also oversees the Compliance Division.

Outside of work, Fedorko donates his time generously. He is a Director for the Marine Corps Law Enforcement Foundation comprised of former law enforcement personnel and senior executives from the private sector. This group raises money for the children of Marines and law enforcement officers killed in the line of duty. Each of these children receives a $10,000 bond toward their education.

Fedorko is also a Director with the McGuire Air Force Base Memorial Foundation. He supports the Salvation Army, the Boys and Girls Club of Atlantic City, and the Children's Hospital of Philadelphia.

Mike and his wife Lisa live in Trenton, New Jersey with their three children, Michelle, Michael, Jr. and Carlton, a future Marine.

SEMPER FIDELIS

Adam Brooks Firestone

"With perseverance, chaos can be reduced to order."

Born: 12 January 1962 in Carmel, California
Service: United States Navy, Ensign 1984 United States Marine Corps, 1984 – 1991, Officer
Occupation: President, Firestone Vineyard; Founder, Firestone Walker Brewing Company

Adam Firestone was young and restless, finishing Middlebury College early and starting Pepperdine Law School.

"I felt a longing for some sort of purpose or to make some sort of a contribution. I started first in the Navy in the summer of 1984 and enrolled in its Officer Indoctrination School and was commissioned as Ensign and JAG officer. But it felt incomplete. The school was not challenging and restlessness continued. That fall I resigned my commission in lieu of OCS in Quantico. The drill instructors found me to be a good sport. Anyone with a Navy connection was fair game, resigning a perfectly good commission made me all the more their sport. It was a tough game; over the next two and a half months I dropped from 207 lbs. to 171 lbs. in the Virginia heat, but found it a life changing experience like so many others had before me."

A variety of assignments in legal matters and ground units kept Adam fully occupied for the next few years. He left active duty as a Captain in 1990, a few weeks before Iraq invaded Kuwait. By October, he was back on active duty, and shortly thereafter was deployed to the Gulf as Camp Commandant for one of the task forces with the 1st Marine Division.

"Shortly after arriving at the border, nightly incursions by Iraqi armor were keeping the net alive with chatter. Our position made one such sighting with a young Marine identifying two tanks dead ahead and moving slowly toward us. The missing engine and track noise was ignored in the excitement of the moment. The starlight scopes and first generation NVGs all confirmed the targets. Heads were lowered, coordinates plotted and weapons trained.

Finally, the images came up on TOW launcher thermal sight and revealed two nearly euthanized camels plodding across the desert. Only the sound of laughter cut the desert night air. Other nights weren't as funny."

"The salient lesson taught to me by the USMC is that with perseverance chaos can be reduced to order. Structure, organization and planning may accelerate that process, but never surrendering to the chaos is the precursor."

After his discharge from the Marines, Adam practiced law in Santa Barbara, California. In 1994, when his father, Brooks, was elected to the California State legislature, Adam took over the reins of the Firestone Vineyard.

The Firestone Vineyard (*www.firestonewine.com*) was established by Adam's father and grandfather in 1972. As the first estate vineyard in California's Santa Ynez Valley, it is now a family tradition. Adam, a third generation vintner, continues a family commitment to estate winegrowing. He has implemented new vineyard management, and winemaking and sales programs. His brother, Andrew, handles sales and scored a marketing home run while appearing on the television reality show *The Bachelor*. Andrew and Firestone Wines became instant celebrities.

Adam in conjunction with his brother-in-law, David Walker, founded Firestone Walker Brewing Company in 1996. It has moved from the 153rd largest brewery to 28th largest in 2003 and is still growing.

The Firestones are active in many local charities. Adam belongs to various trade and business organizations, and is the Director of Farm Credit West.

Adam and his wife, Kate, have four children: Nick, Madeline, Matthew, and Peter. The family resides in Santa Barbara County, California.

SEMPER FIDELIS

Photo Credit (right photo) Kirk Irwin, I&I Images.

James L. Fisher

"The Marine Corps provides drive and discipline useful throughout your life."

Born: 2 June 1931 in Decatur, Illinois
Service: United States Marine Corps, 1951 – 1954 enlisted, G-2, Intelligence
Occupation: Owner, James L. Fisher, Ltd.; Consultant and Author

James Fisher flunked out of Millikin University in 1950. Confused, patriotic, and in search of redemption, he enlisted in the United States Marine Corps.

"His name was Cooper Philips Speaks; an average looking guy who had been a college English teacher before being drafted into the Marine Corps. It was the Korean War, and I had enlisted after flunking out of college. We 'seasoned' Marines were anxious to see what a draftee looked like. After several 'tests' he turned out to be a nice guy, and we began to include him in our occasional forays into Jacksonville where we drank beer, got tattoos, and looked for girls.

"One night in our favorite haunt, mild-mannered Cooper mentioned to our attractive waitress that he read palms. By the end of the evening, Cooper had read the palms of every waitress in the place and had his pick of the lot. The rest of us lusting Marines were dumbfounded … and I was inspired.

"The next day I went to the base library and checked out all the books on palmistry, as well as other pseudo-sciences (phrenology, psycho-graphology, astrology, et al). I spent weeknights in Barracks 327, Camp Lejeune, reading and talking with Cooper; in short order I became a palmist extraordinaire. From that time on, virtually all of my pronouncements became authoritative and captivating.

"After being discharged in 1954, I was readmitted to college and finally finished a Ph.D. in psychology. Since that time, I have written several books, directed many doctoral students, and taught countless psychology courses; and to this day, I begin my general psychology course by flashing a lined palm on the screen before several hundred eager students. It never fails."

In 1956, Jim graduated with honors from Illinois State University. In the following years, he taught high school, was a school psychologist and a tennis professional. Jim returned to school at Northwestern University and earned a Ph.D. in psychology in 1963. A few short years later in 1969, James Fisher, who had earlier flunked out of college, became President of Towson University.

With a powerful enthusiasm for education, Dr. Fisher has taught at Northwestern, Illinois State, Johns Hopkins, Harvard, and the University of Georgia and has consulted at more than 300 colleges and universities.

While president at Towson, his government relations activities were sufficient to overturn gubernatorial vetoes. Newspapers styled him a "master educational politician" ... under his leadership, enrollment doubled, quality went up and costs went down, and leaders in both political parties encouraged him to run for Governor. While he was President of the Council for Advancement & Support of Education (CASE), they created and orchestrated the "America's Energy is Mindpower" campaign, "Higher Education Week," and "The Professor of the Year" awards. For several years, he did a popular daily radio commentary on WBAL in Baltimore.

Dr. Fisher is now President Emeritus of CASE, the largest organization of colleges and universities in the world, and President Emeritus of Towson University. He is presently Professor of Leadership Studies at The Union Institute and University and a consultant to boards and presidents. He coined the term "institutional review" and has conducted hundreds for private and public institutions. He also conducts board orientations and consults on presidential searches, evaluations and contracts.

Dr. Fisher has been a trustee at 11 private colleges and universities, and two preparatory schools. He presently serves as a trustee of the Marine Military Academy, Millikin University, and Florida Institute of Technology, and is on the advisory boards of Franklin University and South Baltimore Learning Center. He has received awards for teaching, writing, citizenship and leadership, and has been awarded 11 honorary degrees. At Illinois State, the faculty named The Outstanding Thesis Award, "The James L. Fisher Thesis Award." The faculty at Towson University recommended that the new psychology building be named after Dr. Fisher, and the CASE Distinguished Service to Education Award bears his name.

In addition to teaching and consulting, Dr. Fisher is a celebrated author. He is the most published writer on leadership and organization in higher education today. He has authored or edited ten books and has written scores of professional articles. *The Board and the President*, *The Power of the Presidency*, *Presidential Leadership: Making a Difference*, and *Positive Power* are must read books for college presidents and trustees.

Dr. Fisher is married to Kimberly, and he has four children and nine grandchildren. They lived in the Baltimore area for many years and now make their home in Vero Beach, Florida.

SEMPER FIDELIS

Charles W. Gittins

"I always put myself in the shoes of the guy who is making a tough decision and think about what he had to think about before he made such a decision."

Born: 26 October 1956 in Wilkes Barre, Pennsylvania
Service: United States Marine Corps, 1979 – 1992 active duty, currently a Lieutenant Colonel in the reserves
Occupation: President, Law Offices of Charles W. Gittins, P.C.

Charles Gittins graduated from the United States Naval Academy with Merit in 1979, and immediately was commissioned in the Marine Corps. He served one tour as a Radar Intercept Officer and was selected to attend law school under the Funded Law Education Program. Charles attended law school at Catholic University of America and then served six years as a Marine Corps Judge Advocate in Okinawa, Washington D.C., and Operation DesertShield/ Desert Storm.

"As a judge advocate, the most difficult thing I did was investigate an accident involving an A-6 aircrew that mistakenly bombed a Marine Corps artillery column in Kuwait just prior to the start of the Gulf War. I learned that no matter how good you are at your job as a Marine and aviator, the 'fog of war' can lead to tragic mistakes with terrible consequences. It led me to always put myself in the shoes of the guy who is making a tough decision and think about what he had to think about before he made such a decision."

Upon completion of his active duty, Charles joined the law firm of Williams & Connolly, the firm that represented Oliver North in the Iran Contra investigation. After three and a half years, he decided to open his own practice, Law Offices of Charles W. Gittins, P.C.

"My law practice is premised on providing representation of military personnel and other employees in administrative, criminal and military justice matters. My firm is the 'go to' firm for military members and federal employees, such as FBI agents involved in high profile accidents and incidents. I have represented the Commanding Officer of the Navy's Blue Angels in the 'Tailhook' investigation, and FBI agents who were targets of the Ruby Ridge grand jury investigation into the standoff with Randy Weaver.

"The Sergeant Major of the Army in the highly publicized investigation and court-martial for sexual harassment, the commander of the USS *Greeneville* after the collision at sea with the M/V *Ehime Maru* killing nine Japanese students and staff, and the pilot who was involved in the 'friendly fire' accident where four Canadians were killed in 2002 in Afghanistan during Operation Enduring Freedom have all been my clients."

Charles' law firm is committed to providing the best possible legal representation to military personnel at a reasonable cost.

The Center for Military Readiness is Charles' choice of principal charity. This charitable organization lobbies in Congress for military personnel on a wide variety of issues relevant to military personnel. The Center works hard to help ensure military personnel are provided the means and the leadership to fight and win wars.

Charles Gittins is married to Christine and they make their home in Virginia.

SEMPER FIDELIS

Eric J. Gleacher

"My 3 1/2 years in the Marine Corps convinced me that I might accomplish just about anything I put my mind and character to."

Born: 27 April 1940 in New York, New York
Service: United States Marine Corps, 1963 – 1966, Infantry Officer
Occupation: Chairman, Founder, Gleacher Partners, LLC

After completing his B.A. at Northwestern University in 1962, Eric enlisted in the Marine Corps. He went to Officer Candidate School in Quantico, Virginia, was commissioned an Infantry Officer with the rank of Second Lieutenant.

"Upon being given my own platoon of men to lead, we were sent to Jungle Warfare School in Coco Solo, Panama. The thing that I remember most about being there was the blackness of the jungle under the canopy of vegetation. I also remember the amount of insects a jungle supports within each square foot and what they like to eat (Marines).

"During our time in the field, I shared a pup tent with my Platoon Sergeant, James Dixon. We stayed up far too late many a night as he shared his Korean War stories with me. I had a first hand account of Marine Corps history. He told me about many of the hardships and the terrible cold that the Marines dealt with aside from fighting the enemy. I am forever grateful to Sergeant Dixon for sharing with me what was a defining time in his life. We all learn from those who take the time to share their experiences with others.

"My 3 1/2 years in the Marine Corps convinced me that I might accomplish just about anything I put my mind and character to."

After being discharged from the Marines in 1966, Eric obtained his M.B.A. from the University of Chicago Business School in 1967. In 1973 Eric became a partner at Lehman Brothers and founded their Mergers and Acquisitions department in 1978. In 1983, he left Lehman and went to work at Morgan Stanley and ran their Global Mergers and Acquisitions Department.

In 1990, Eric and several Morgan Stanley professionals left and formed Gleacher & Company. The firm's focus was to provide strategic advice to major Corporations and make private equity and venture capital investments in an entrepreneurial environment.

In October 1995, National Westminster Bank, a major U.K. bank, acquired Gleacher & Company as part of a strategy to establish a major presence in the U.S. investment banking market. In April 1999, the employees of Gleacher & Company purchased certain assets of the firm in order to regain the entrepreneurial environment upon which the firm had been founded. Gleacher Partners (as the firm is now called) has 85 employees and has completed more than 200 billion dollars worth of Mergers and Acquisitions transactions.

Eric currently serves as a trustee of the University of Chicago and New York University. His goal as a trustee is to work towards making these two institutions the best in the world. He has also been a strong supporter of many Marine Corps related non-profits including the Marine Corps Law Enforcement Foundation.

Eric and his wife, Annie, have six children and currently reside in New York State.

SEMPER FIDELIS

Frederick H. Graefe

"Whatever success we have on this earth is due in a large measure to being first and foremost a Marine."

Born: 16 April 1944 in Des Moines, Iowa
Service: United States Marine Corps 1967 – 1970, Infantry Officer
Occupation: Hunton & Williams, Partner

Fred Graefe attended Loyola University and completed the PLC program, graduating with an A.B. in 1966. Active duty in the Marines was his next challenge.

"My Marine experience has had, and continues to have, a most profound impact on my life. The crucible of Vietnam – the many friendships created by our shared Marine experiences are invaluable and permanent: Jim Jones, Pete Pace, Mal Mixon, Jimmy Stone, and Jim Webb – these are giants in the Marine pantheon. We all admit whatever success we have on this mortal soil is due, in large measure, to being first and foremost a Marine."

"My Vietnam experience was not unlike most Marines: searing, frightening, enlightening, unforgettable memories, especially of Marines who paid the ultimate price, relief and, thanks to God, that I came back alive and whole."

As an Infantry Officer, Fred served in Vietnam in 1967 – 1968. When he completed his military obligation, he was discharged as a Captain in 1970 and headed back to school. Georgetown University provided an M.A. in 1971. Next he enrolled in Georgetown's Law School and received his J.D. in 1973. With an impressive education under his belt, Fred was admitted to the Iowa Bar in 1973, the District of Columbia Bar in 1974 and the Supreme Court of the United States in 1976.

Fred's first legal employment was clerking for the Honorable Howard F. Corcoran, United States District Judge for the District of Columbia. From 1975 – 2001, he was associated with prestigious Washington, D.C. law firms. The last 13 years of which were as a partner at Baker & Hostetler.

Currently, Fred is a partner of Hunton & Williams. This practice is a major, 100-year-old international law firm with its headquarters in Richmond, Virginia. Practicing as a lobbyist, Fred has specialized in health care, trade and tax for the last 25 years. In addition, he serves as Washington counsel to trade associations and coalitions. Fred frequently meets with senior policymakers in the White House, Congress, the U.S. Department of the Treasury, the Office of Management and Budget, the Department of Health and Human Services including Medicare/Medicaid, and the National Institute of Health. His clients include Invacare, whose Chairman and CEO is Mal Mixon, also a former Marine; Trans World Assurance Co. and American Fidelity Life Insurance Co, both founded by former Marine aviator Charles Woodbury; the Cleveland Clinic; Amgen, the nation's leading biotechnology company; Cardionet, the pioneer in wireless telephone cardiac monitoring; and the Federation of American Hospitals, the trade association of investor-owned hospitals.

Fred's time and talent are put to good use outside his work arena as well. Involvement in the restoration and renovation of the Home of the Commandants, Quarters 6 at the Marine Barracks, Washington, D.C. has been a most rewarding experience for Fred. "The Home is the soul of our Marine Corps and is a legacy for all Marines everywhere, of whatever stripe or rank."

Fred Graefe resides in Bethesda, Maryland and is married and the father of four daughters.

SEMPER FIDELIS

Photo Credit Dupont Photographers.

Earl C. Hargrove, Jr.

"There is nothing that prepared me more for life than the training, discipline, responsibility, and values I learned in the Corps."

Born: 5 October 1928 in Richmond, Virginia
Service: United States Marine Corps, 1946 – 1948, 1951 – 1954, Enlisted, Infantry
Occupation: Chairman & President, Hargrove, Inc.

In 1946, after graduating from high school, Earl joined the Marine Corps and spent his 18th birthday (October 5, 1946) at Parris Island Marine Corps Boot Camp.

"Just outside the gates of Parris Island was a small town by the name of Yemassee. Our Drill Instructors had told us that we were now all hometown boys from Yemassee. One night I was on guard duty in the rain on the midnight to 4:00 a.m. shift. I wrote my mother and told her I had "made the biggest mistake of my life." As mothers do, she agreed and told me to tell the D.I. that I catch colds easily when I stand outside in the rain. When I relayed my mother's concern to the D.I., he listened quietly. After a moment he said in a loud voice, "You a——e. S—birds from Yemassee don't get colds!" Until the day she died, my mother couldn't figure out what Yemassee had to do with catching colds."

Earl joined the Marine Corps after World War II was over and the military was making adjustments as they always do after every war. He served his two years and was honorably discharged. He returned to the civilian world and worked with his father to establish and build Hargrove, Inc. Then in 1951, after the United States decided to enter the Korean "conflict," Earl reenlisted.

After being released from the Marines the second time in 1954, Mr. Hargrove returned to the family business. Soon thereafter in 1955, he married his wife, Gloria.

Early on Hargrove, Inc. developed an outstanding reputation in the specialty decorating and parade float business. The company expanded as a premier special events company in the 1950s, established a trade show division in 1961 and a custom exhibit division in 1977.

The company began its association with Presidential Inaugurals in 1949 and has been a principal contractor to every inaugural since that time, serving as the official general contractor to the Presidential Inaugural Committee in all recent inaugurals. Hargrove has decorated the National Christmas Tree and Pageant of Peace since its inception in 1954 and serviced the Miss America Pageant from 1954 – 2000. The company services major Corporate and association clients nationally and internationally from its 60-acre, 350,000-square-foot facility and campus just outside Washington, D.C.

Hargrove has serviced other major national celebrations and events, including the Homecoming celebration for Operation Desert Storm troops; dedications of the Franklin D. Roosevelt Memorial, the Korean War Veterans Memorial, The National Holocaust Museum, and the Women in Military Service Memorial; the National Bicentennial Parade, the Bicentennial of the U.S. Constitution, the Sugar Bowl Parade; Democratic and Republican National Conventions; Super Bowl Halftime; the Modern Day Marine show; and Marine South. The company also serviced international events, including: International Monetary Fund and World Bank conferences worldwide; Economic Summits of Industrialized Nations in Williamsburg, Virginia, and Houston, Texas; International Goodwill Games, Olympic Games (Atlanta), 50th Anniversary NATO Summit; TRANSPO 1972; the Universal Postal Union Conference; World's Fairs in New Orleans and Seville, Spain; and the World Figure Skating Championships.

Earl Hargrove remains the entrepreneurial force behind Hargrove, Inc., which employs more than 200 full-time workers, a number that swells to more than 500 during peak events. The facility includes a 35,000 square foot fabrication shop, 5,000 square foot paint shop, 4,400 square foot art shop, 3,600 square foot computer graphics shop, 25 all weather loading docks, 145,000 square foot warehouse, and complete design studio.

Earl Hargrove is an active charter member of HEROES, Inc. of Metropolitan Washington, D.C., an organization that assists widows and children of police officers and firefighters who lost their lives in the line of duty. He has served on the Board of Directors for the USO and Goodwill Industries, in addition to the Marine Corps Scholarship Foundation. Hargrove, Inc. also actively supports the National Children's Medical Center in Washington, D.C. and the Susan G. Komen Breast Cancer Foundation.

Earl and his wife, Gloria, reside on a 125-acre farm in Southern Maryland that they bought in 1958. They have five children, Chris, Cathy, Carla, Cindy, and Carey and five grandchildren.

SEMPER FIDELIS

Jack Hawkins, Jr.

"Leadership is the management of hope."

Born: 30 March 1945 in Mobile, Alabama
Service: United States Marine Corps, 1967 – 1970; USMC Reserve 1970 – 1976, Officer
Occupation: Chancellor, The Troy State University System

Although Dr. Jack Hawkins, Jr. has made a career in higher education, he knew he wanted to be a Marine even before he decided to attend college. As a senior at Murphy High School in Mobile, Alabama, in 1962, service in the Marines was his first career choice, and he visited the local recruiting station ready to enlist. After some tests, however, the recruiting officer encouraged Hawkins to attend college. He chose the University of Montevallo, a public liberal arts school near Birmingham, Alabama, and spent his summers in Platoon Leaders Class, a special Marine officer-training program for college students.

Upon graduation from college in 1967, Hawkins was commissioned a Second Lieutenant. Following further training at The Basic School and at Camp Lejeune, Hawkins was assigned to Vietnam where he served as leader of a combat engineering platoon. During the majority of his time "in country," Hawkins' platoon was attached to the Korean Marine Corps. His platoon's responsibilities included daily mine sweeps along Route One, patrols, removing booby traps and construction projects in support of the Korean infantry battalion. He saw considerable combat, engaging regularly in firefights with VC/NVA in I Corps, south of Danang. For his service, he received the Purple Heart, the Bronze Star and a special citation from the Korean Marine Corps.

During his Vietnam service, Jack Hawkins began forming the philosophies that have served him throughout his professional life of service in Alabama higher education. Directing men in combat made him see the leader's role in a new light.

"When you are in a combat situation with brave men, you know that they must have plenty of hope in their hearts to face the inevitable terror that war breeds. Leadership, when stripped to the barest essentials, is managing that hope. It's similar in civilian life, because the people you lead have hopes and dreams that must be considered; it's just that the stakes are nowhere near as high as on a battlefield.

"The bottom line of my military experience is this: Service as a United States Marine has had a profound influence on me and my life. No other experience has shaped my values, beliefs, determination, and 'duty above self' philosophy as did the USMC."

After leaving active duty in 1970, Jack Hawkins began in earnest his career in higher education, earning a master's degree from the University of Montevallo in 1971. From 1971 – 1979, Hawkins served in positions of increasing responsibility, rising to assistant dean/associate professor with the University of Alabama Birmingham's School of Health-Related Professions. Hawkins earned his Ph.D. from the University of Alabama in 1976.

In 1979, Dr. Hawkins took on the challenge of the presidency of the Alabama Institute for Deaf and Blind in Talladega. When he arrived at the school, major Alabama newspapers were castigating AIDB for its deplorable conditions. In 1988, the New York Times called the school a model institution of its kind. He improved programs and services and restored fiscal solvency to the institution. Moreover, he was forever changed by daily contact with and service to these students with so many hurdles to overcome.

But serving as a university president had been Dr. Jack Hawkins' goal since leaving the Marine Corps, and that opportunity presented itself in 1989, when he was chosen as Chancellor of the Troy State University System. As Chancellor, Dr. Hawkins leads a multi-campus system that serves more than 22,000 students. He is accountable to a Board of Trustees and is responsible for more than 1,200 full-time faculty and staff with an annual operating budget of $135,000,000.

Interestingly, the attraction to lead TSU was borne of Hawkins' interest in the military. In addition to traditional campuses in Alabama, Troy State University offers educational programs on more than 50 military bases in 14 states and six foreign countries. TSU is also a primary provider of Internet programs for the E-Army U, which extends educational access to soldiers around the globe. The prestigious list of TSU graduates includes four NASA astronauts and more than 60 active or retired general and flag-rank officers.

The international nature of Troy State University led to an interesting personal footnote for Dr. Hawkins. In 2002, he returned to Vietnam for the first time since his Marine Corps service, as TSU is exploring the possibility of a cooperative program with the University of Dalat as well as graduate programs to be offered in Hanoi and Ho Chi Minh City.

"In more than 13 years of serving as the Chancellor of Troy State University, I have found that the same principles of leadership so vital to the mission of the Marines, such as teamwork, loyalty, recognition, and integrity, are equally valuable in a university setting," Dr. Hawkins said. "A university has one key mission – educate her students – but many different moving parts. To get the job done it's important for the leader to set the example.

"The first thing you learn in dealing with Marines is that it is 90 percent what you do and 10 percent what you say. Students are no different. So it follows that the cornerstone concept is 'the walk is more important than the talk.' The words 'follow me' are critical, whether going on an early morning run or approaching a tree line filled with NVA/VC!"

Dr. Hawkins added that the lessons of the Corps remain with him in practically every phase of his life. For example, he still believes in a regular physical training program of running and exercise to keep fit. And, every weekday morning finds him up at dawn to read several newspapers, a habit instilled by the Marine officer's need to be mentally sharp and fully briefed in order to get the most out of the workday.

In addition to his service to Troy State University, Dr. Hawkins serves on the Executive Council of the Commission on Colleges, Southern Association of Colleges and Schools; the board of directors of the Better Business Bureau of Central Alabama, Troy Bank and Trust Company, and Edge Regional Medical Center. He is chairman of the Governor's Committee on Employment of the Disabled, and he is the past chairman, Council of University Presidents in Alabama. He is also the President of the Atlantic Sun Athletic Conference. He is a member of the Troy Rotary Club and the First Baptist Church of Troy. He has served as a trustee of Talladega College, the Helen Keller Eye Research Foundation and is Trustee Emeritus of the American Foundation for the Blind.

He has been honored as the alumnus of the year for the University of Montevallo and in 1999 was presented the Golden Eagle of the Year Award, Alabama Senior Citizens Hall of Fame. He is a member of seven national professional/honor societies, including the Honor Society of Phi Kappa Phi.

Dr. Jack Hawkins and his wife, the former Janice Grindley, are the parents of three children; Jay, a small business owner, Katie, an officer in the U.S. Air Force, and Kelly, a 2002 TSU graduate who plans to attend law school.

SEMPER FIDELIS

Ralph W. Heim

"The teamwork and discipline that was so skillfully instilled in us early on paid off then and has continued ever since."

Born: 22 May 1946 in Orlando, Florida
Service: United States Marine Corps Reserves, 1966 – 1972, Enlisted
Occupation: President and Chief Operating Officer, Trailer Bridge, Inc.

Ralph attended college for a short while following high school but then began working full time as a freight handler for now defunct REA Express. This proved to be a great introduction to the freight transportation business and a future career path. The next event to further shape him was his enlistment in the Marine Corps in 1966.

"One of the things Marine Corps Recruit Training taught me was the importance of consistent effort. At graduation my platoon was the Honor Platoon of our Series, but it wasn't because we finished first in all the competitions held during training. In fact, we may have finished first in only one or two of the events, but more importantly we were contenders in nearly all of them. The teamwork and discipline that was so skillfully instilled in us early on paid off then and has continued ever since.

"An unforgettable experience was the time our recruit platoon participated in a parade with full Colors, and the Depot Band played the Marine Corps Hymn as we marched along. For perhaps the first time in my life I felt I was really about something much larger and was where I belonged."

Upon returning from active duty in the Marines, Ralph went back to college, married his childhood sweetheart and graduated shortly thereafter from Jacksonville University with a degree in Business Administration. After graduation he was recruited by SeaLand Service Inc. as a management trainee in the newly emerging field of containerized freight transportation. Containerization was doing then for ocean freight transportation what the jet airplane had done for air transportation. It turned out to be an exciting career choice for Ralph and has included a variety of responsibilities in a number of domestic and international locations. The fact that Malcom P. McLean, who created this industry back in the 1960s, was the same person he would end up working with in the 1990s during the start-up of Trailer Bridge was a special twist and experience that Ralph treasures.

Today, Ralph is President and COO of Trailer Bridge, Inc. (NASDAQ: TRBR) an integrated trucking and marine freight transportation company. The company was founded in 1991 by legendary transportation pioneer, Malcom P. McLean, who is globally recognized as the Father of Containerized Shipping. Trailer Bridge provides truckload service between all points in the continental United States and the island of Puerto Rico utilizing their own trucks, drivers, vessels, 53 high cube containers and exclusive marine facilities. They are one of four companies that connect the island of nearly four million U.S. citizens with the U.S. mainland.

According to Ralph, "Trailer Bridge has been associated with growth and innovation since opening their doors for business, from the introduction of 48 foot long highway equipment, transition into even larger 53 foot equipment, and 'stretching' the initial two vessels to increase capacity by over 50%. A public stock offering, building five new vessels designed exclusively for 53 foot high cube equipment, developing and patenting specialized Vehicle Transport Modules (VTM), achieving ISO 9002 registration and the unveiling of Internet Shipment Tracking have made the last decade an exciting time for customers, shareholders and employees. In spite of a hyper-competitive business environment, Trailer Bridge has built and maintained an impressive following of blue chip customers and loyal employees."

Trailer Bridge reaches out to the community in a number of ways but is especially proud of their involvement with Habijax, the local chapter of Habitat for Humanity. This organization provides affordable housing for low-income families and the company has sponsored and built two of these homes in the last several years. Trailer Bridge is also a participant in a current USMC recruiting campaign, applying USMC graphics to select companies' highway freight trailers, transforming them into rolling billboards for the Corps.

Ralph is active in outreach and non-profit organizations through his church, his company and the community. He has served the last three years as Director of Outreach and Missions for the Episcopal Church of the Redeemer in Jacksonville, in a diverse program that is supportive of approximately 15 local and non-local faith based ministries. He also currently serves on the Advisory Board of St. Mary's Episcopal Church and Outreach Ministry, an inner city mission in Jacksonville that reaches out to the mentally and physically ill, a large addict community and kids at risk. Ralph serves on the Board of the Jacksonville Marine Transportation Exchange, whose primary concern is harbor safety and was a Vice-Chairman of the 2000 Greater Jacksonville Kingfish Tournament.

Ralph and his wife, Marilyn, have two grown children and have been blessed recently with a beautiful granddaughter. The Heim family resides in Jacksonville, Florida.

SEMPER FIDELIS

John E. Hoban

"The Marine Corps motto 'Semper Fidelis' remains the core of my value system and guides my relations and decision-making both in my personal life as well as in business. It is not always easy to remain true to the motto, but in times of doubt and confusion, the phrase 'Semper Fi' is like light that illuminates the high road."

Born: 13 October 1955 in Miami, Florida
Service: United States Marine Corps, two years reserves, 1975 – 1977; five years active, 1977 – 1982, Officer
Occupation: President, Living Values Institute; Vice President, Health Ware Concepts

John (Jack) Hoban attended Villanova University, Villanova, Pennsylvania and earned a B.A. in political science. Through PLC he became a combat engineer officer in the Corps.

"I had many life-defining moments in the Marine Corps. They ranged from the tragic to the humorous. As a Series Commander at MCRD San Diego I once had a recruit request emergency leave because his pet killer whale had died. I am still trying to decide what category that incident belonged in!

"But, some were truly tragic; I was the COC watch officer on an exercise in Korea when a whole helicopter full of United States and Korean Marines flew into a mountain during a snowstorm. I had to wake the General to tell him, and then help initiate the recovery operation.

"I was never in heavy combat, but like most Marines, I faced my share of hardship and separation from home and family. I think my greatest learning experience, however, came in an unexpected way. I was having dinner at the Globe & Laurel in Triangle, Virginia. Most Marines who have been to Quantico have dined at this landmark restaurant that is almost a Marine Museum (if you haven't been there, you need to go!). I was fortunate enough to witness a heart to heart talk between an old Iwo Jima veteran and a Marine who had been on Tarawa. After decades of holding in their private memories, unable to explain themselves to anyone who hadn't been there, they opened up to each other and discussed their true experiences, feelings, and fears. It was just one of those amazing moments. I was mesmerized as I listened to their stories of courage in the face of unimaginable horror, their modesty regarding their clearly heroic actions, and, most of all, by the love they felt for their fellow Marines. I also learned things of inestimable value about what hot combat is really like and what it takes to survive and accomplish the mission when you are nearly overwhelmed by the shock of real war. I feel the tears coming every time I think about that night and those two Marines."

Jack left active duty in 1982 as a Captain, finished his MBA at National University in San Diego, California, and then headed back to his home state of New Jersey.

Jack's company, Living Values Institute (*www.livingvalues.com*), is officially his "other job" as he is also a Vice President of a software company. With Living Values, Jack enjoys the privilege of working with professionals from the military, the law enforcement establishment, and other related groups (such as martial arts schools) to provide training in the areas of moral/physical values and warriorship.

The Living Values training methodology draws heavily from Jack's nearly 30 years of martial arts training, and especially from the Life Value Theory of Dr. Robert L. Humphrey. Living Values worked with Dr. Humphrey to publish his book, *Values for A New Millennium* which chronicles his life works on the subject of universal human values and cross-cultural conflict resolution.

"Humphrey was a U.S. Marine rifle platoon leader on Iwo Jima. Near the war's end, a gunshot wound ended his hopes for a professional boxing career. For 12 years he passed through eight colleges and universities looking for answers to that eternal question: 'Why?' Why that terrible Depression that devastated his peaceful little hometown? Why that insanity on Iwo Jima that killed most of his Marine friends?

"Bob Humphrey took a Harvard Law degree and settled into teaching economics at MIT. Then came the Cold War with the predictions that the Communists would win. He went back overseas to see if his global experiences would guide him in solving America's self-defeating Ugly Americanism. He taught culture-transcendent, 'win the people' values in the most vital overseas areas – those surrounding the Communist Block. The approach did overcome the Ugly Americanism. It did win back the foreign peoples. And it kept the lid on sabotage and violence in his assigned areas. It opened up a new social-scientific pathway to human conflict resolution.

"Dr. Humphrey passed away during the summer of 1997. He is sorely missed. In my opinion, we need his insights now more than ever. You have probably guessed that Bob Humphrey was the Iwo Jima Marine mentioned in the Globe & Laurel story described earlier. The other man was retired Marine Major Rick Spooner."

Working with Living Values, Jack travels around the world giving seminars on martial arts and values. He has written three books on martial arts and philosophy, and also has a four part video series that supports his work. Jack's most rewarding work currently is as a Black Belt Emeritus and Subject Matter Expert (SME) for the Marine Corps Martial Arts Program (MCMAP). This fairly new program has already proven to be very effective in helping shape Marines as proficient close-quarter combatants who are also ethical warriors/defenders who understand the proper use of their skills. As an SME, Jack provides oversight on the physical and moral aspects of the Program. He is honored to address the instructor classes on the subject of warrior values and ethics.

Jack's charitable interests lie in helping victims of injustice around the world. With this in mind, he contributes to Catholic Charities and Amnesty International.

In addition to his hectic work schedule, Jack coaches Little League baseball and Pop Warner football. He, his wife and two sons live on the Jersey Shore.

SEMPER FIDELIS

Baldemar Huerta "Freddy Fender"

"Life is just a matter of what kind of day you're having."

Born: 4 June 1937 in San Benito, Texas
Service: United States Marine Corps, 1954 – 1957, Enlisted
Occupation: President/International Entertainer, Freddy Fender Music

Baldemar Huerta was born in the Rio Grande Valley town of San Benito, Texas in a poor Hispanic neighborhood. His parents were migrant workers and the family constantly moved during the picking season.

"I was not a particularly motivated student when in school due to the fact that my family kept migrating seasonally. Since I was never able to catch up with my classmates, I had this bright idea of joining the Marines to be a 'John Wayne' ('Sands of Iwo Jima'). I eventually had my mother lie about my age and enlisted in the Corps when I was 16 years old. While in the Marines, I had the memorable experience of meeting General Thomas during an inspection of the troops. He talked to me, but to this day, I can't recall what we talked about.

"I remember singing and playing my guitar for my Drill Instructors while in Boot Camp. They would awaken me during the middle of the night and take me to the Platoon Headquarters to serenade everyone. I know that I was already picking and singing before I got to the Marine Corps, but I honestly don't know how they found out. This was a major part of my life as a Marine for later on, when I was stationed in Japan and Okinawa, I was a tanker, but unofficially, I was allowed by the Battalion Commander to join Special Services. (Hey, little did I know that I would be the future Freddy Fender, the Singing Marine, and proud of it.)"

Freddy's entertainment success and popularity has spanned more than four decades. Rhythm and blues, country, pop, rock and Tejana have all played an enormous part in the development of Freddy's long musical career. In

1975 with "Before the Next Teardrop Falls," he made musical history as the first artist to reach number one on Billboard's pop and country charts with his first single release. He was named "Best Male Artist of 1975" by Billboard.

Over the years Freddy Fender has received more awards and honors than it is possible to mention. During his long career he overcame the influences of alcohol and drugs and has now been sober for almost 20 years. Fender states, "Sobriety has brought me dignity." Through it all his love of music and entertainment grew steadily.

Freddy Fender Music (*www.freddyfender.com*) is managed by his wife, Evangeline Huerta (Vangie). She has been his agent and manager with great success for nearly 20 years. Freddy entertains around the world, and has played for at least three presidents; Jimmy Carter at The White House, George Bush, Sr. at an Inaugural Ball, and Bill Clinton at an Inaugural Ball.

Fender has won three Grammys, has a Star on the Hollywood Walk of Fame (1999), a European Walk of Fame Star in Rotterdam, Holland (1993), and a Country Music Award. In 2002 Freddy was the recipient of an ALMA (Spanish for spirit or soul) Pioneer Award.

The Freddy Fender Scholarship Fund, organized in 1994, provides Scholarships for deserving Rio Grande Valley graduating high school seniors that are "average B/C students." Since Freddy was not a bright student, he understands how difficult it can be for the average student to find funds for college. An annual concert, usually held in the fall, provides the revenue for the scholarships.

In 1999, The Freddy Fender Golf Tournament was added to the fundraising activities so the number of scholarships could be increased. This is held annually in late spring with all proceeds going to the scholarship fund.

Freddy also does benefit performances for "Charlie's," an alcohol abuse center.

In recent years Freddy was diagnosed with Hepatitis C and regular kidney dialysis became necessary making performances more and more difficult. In spite of his worsening condition, Freddy continued to perform. His medical team began the search for a suitable kidney donor. His three older children were tested, but were not compatible matches. Freddy's youngest daughter, Marla, (21 at the time) was not asked or tested because of her age and because she and her husband had a one year old to care for. When Marla found out what was going on she wanted to help her dad so she volunteered to be tested – a perfect match! The kidney transplant took place in January 2002. Freddy and Marla both recovered remarkably well. Freddy has now returned to the stage performing with increased vigor and enthusiasm.

Freddy Fender is an international entertainment success. The legendary performer is noted for all his contributions to rhythm and blues, country, pop, rock, and Tejano music worldwide.

Freddy and Vangie make their home in Corpus Christi, Texas.

SEMPER FIDELIS

Jerry D. Humble

"Tough transformational training and team work creates the Marine Family with a heritage to uphold."

Born: 4 November 1947 in Jamestown, Kentucky
Service: United States Marine Corps, 1969 – 2003, Major General
Occupation: State of Tennessee, State Cabinet Member/Director of the Office of Homeland Security

Jerry Humble graduated from Western Kentucky University in 1969, and was commissioned as a Lieutenant shortly thereafter. At Quantico, he played football before serving as an Infantry and Reconnaissance Platoon Commander and deploying to Vietnam.

Humble was promoted to Captain in 1974, was the Security Officer at Marine Barracks, Norfolk, Virginia, then attended Amphibious Warfare School, served as Platoon Commander at Officer Candidate School, followed by a tour with the British Royal Marine Commandos.

"When presenting the Royal Marine Company that I commanded as a young Captain to His Royal Highness, Prince Phillip, he asked me where my billet was. I replied, 'Here Sir, as the United States Marine to The Royal Marine Exchange Officer Program in 42 Commando.' He Looked amused. He smiled, asked again but added, 'I mean where do you live?'"

Humble established the 2nd Marine Division Arctic Warfare Training Program and was a battalion Operations Officer as a Major. Later, he commanded a Recruiting Station in St. Louis, Missouri and then graduated from the USMC Command and Staff College with distinction, prompting his promotion to Lieutenant Colonel.

As a Lieutenant Colonel, Humble served with the 2nd Marine Division where he commanded two battalions, co-authored the MEU (SOC) Training Program and developed the Rapid Response Planning Process. After attending War College, he served with the State Department's Bureau of International Narcotics Matters. During Operation Desert Shield/

Storm he was the G-3, 1st Marine Division, and in 1991 was promoted to Colonel.

While a Colonel, Humble commanded a special operations capable, Marine Expeditionary Unit in the Asia/Pacific theatre. Following that he was Director of the Marine Air Ground Task Force, Quantico, Virginia where he was selected for Brigadier General.

General Humble took a command at Parris Island and then of 3rd Marine Division where he was promoted to Major General. He became Commander, USMC Forces Korea and Assistant Chief of Staff, C/JS, United Nations Command, Combined Forces Command, and United States Forces Korea. His last assignment was as Commanding General, Marine Corps Recruiting Command.

General Humble's personal decorations include the Defense Distinguished Service Medal, Navy Distinguished Service Medal, the Legion of Merit with two Gold Stars and Combat "V," the Meritorious Service Medal with one Gold Star, the Joint Service Commendation Medal with Oak Leaf Cluster, the Navy and Marine Corps Commendation Medal with one Gold Star, and the Navy Achievement Medal and Combat Action Ribbon.

Upon retirement from the United States Marine Corps in January 2003, General Humble applied his leadership and management skills as a business and defense industry consultant. His long, impressive military career gave him many attributes for use in his civilian career.

General Humble accepted a Cabinet appointment from the Governor of Tennessee as the Director of the State's Office of Homeland Security. The goal of this office is to build a successful "team of teams" among federal, state and local agencies to support our national strategy against the threat of terrorism. There are three regional field-coordinating offices.

The Humbles, Jerry and Margaret, reside in Nashville, Tennessee. They are the parents of one son, Scott, and one daughter, Lee.

SEMPER FIDELIS

James A. Johnson

"In the Marine Corps, always remember you are unique, just like every other Marine."

Born: 15 August 1933 in McCrory, Arkansas
Service: United States Marine Corps, Active 1951 – 1954 and 1967 – 1973, Reserve 1957 – 1960 and 1973 – 1977, Enlisted, Officer
Occupation: Consultant, Non-profit Institutional Advancement and Development

James "Jim" Johnson was born on a small, hot and dusty cotton farm in northeastern Arkansas, and attended McCrory schools where he was an All District Football player. Working in a funeral home while in high school, Jim received an apprentice embalmer's license. Then immediately following graduation at age 17, Jim enlisted in the Marines.

When basic recruit training concluded in mid-July, Jim was sent to Camp Pendleton, California for assignment to a future replacement draft to Korea. Discovery that he wasn't yet 18 resulted in re-assignment to miscellaneous duty at Camp Del Mar. He served four temporary assignments before the realization of the "powers that be" that he had turned 18 and was eligible for a replacement draft. His assignment – 3rd Battalion, Fifth Marines, Korea.

While assigned to the Battalion Observation Post, Sergeants Nye and Johnson developed a dangerous, but very simple and uncomplicated observation procedure for use Forward of the MLR. This allowed the two sergeants to position themselves singularly in a highly concealed forward area, and observe the Chinese trench lines and specific enemy activities during the daylight hours.

"When occupying these carefully prepared and very forward positions, with the intent of totally blending into the topographical surrounding area, one spent nearly 24 hours concealed with absolutely no movement, and very little opportunity to escape to the MLR if discovered. These forward 'lay-out' positions were carefully selected using the latest topographical maps, current aerial photos, photos and sketches from the battalion OP, MLR and from combat outposts situated in front of the MLR. Being in the layout position was extremely dangerous, and support fire coordination was critical for the support and ultimate survival of the 'layout' positions if the observer was discovered.

"After some time on the Main Line of Resistance (MLR), I was running supply trains, attempting to lay communications wire to combat outposts and other forward positions and treating some wounded Marines. As the cold rains commenced, I spearheaded the collection of USMC camouflage ponchos from those units not on the MLR, arranged the movement of medical material forward, and assisted the evacuation of the dead and wounded. My youthful experience in the funeral home became a stark reality.

"In late July we were given 72 hours to salvage or destroy all of our trench line and bunker fortifications. Working around the clock in true Marine fashion, we salvaged every piece of fortification material, every nail, every spike, every piece of 782 gear, all rations and communication wire. The heat during this three day salvage detail was 100 degrees plus, and "G" Company Marines found or constructed temporary shade, slept mid-day and worked throughout the slightly cooler nights."

After his return from Korea and discharge in 1954, Jim attended the University of the Ozarks earning a Bachelor of Science in biology, chemistry and physics. He continued his education attending graduate school at Texas Tech University and the University of Arkansas on fellowships from the National Science Foundation.

After a short, successful career teaching and coaching, the Marine Corps Reserves commissioned Johnson directly to the grade of Captain through the Officer Specialist Program. He later augmented to the regular Marine Corps.

In addition to the normal junior officer assignments, Johnson attended the Army Defense Inventory Management School, the Instructor's Training School, the Unit Supply Officer's Course, the Army Graves Registration Course and the Marine Advisor's and Vietnamese Language Course. On his Vietnam tour, he was Advisor to the 4th and 5th Infantry Battalions, Supply Advisor and Logistics Advisor to the Vietnamese Marine Corps.

Upon his return from Vietnam, Johnson was assigned as Head, Casualty Section, Personnel Department, Headquarters Marine Corps. While in that position he was the Marine Corps member of the White House/Department of Defense Missing and Captured Task Force, and was involved in the development and implementation of the 1973 return of prisoners during "Operation Homecoming." Johnson reached the rank of Major before his USMC discharge.

Since the mid-1970's, Johnson has been a foundation executive, vice-president of a major consulting firm, a campaign director and a consultant to non-profit institutions in the United States and abroad. His foreign clients include the London School of Economics, United Kingdom; the Kimbe Bay Research Station, New Guinea; and St. Paul's Outreach, Mexico. Jim's U.S.

client list includes the U.S. Naval Academy, Texas A&M International University, the Muscular Dystrophy Association, The College of the Ozarks, The National D-Day Foundation, the PGA and the American Heart Association.

As a consultant to a variety of non-profits, Johnson has directed and trained governing boards, executives and volunteers so campaigns remain on schedule and reach their intended campaign goal. Since the mid-1970's his non-profit clients have raised slightly over $400,000,000.

Jim has a special interest in World War II and Korean War history with a collection of 8,500 items. Another special interest is aviation. He is a licensed commercial pilot with instrument rating and holds three national powered flight records.

Jim and his wife, Linda, have five children. The Johnson's are active members of St. John's Episcopal Church and reside in Bedford, Virginia.

SEMPER FIDELIS

DENNIS M. JONES

"I believe that utilizing the many lessons learned in the four short years I served in the Marine Corps benefited my family, my colleagues, my shareholders, and of course myself, every single day of my business career."

BORN: 12 September 1938 in Terre Haute, Indiana
SERVICE: United States Marine Corps, 1957 – 1961, Enlisted, Jet Mechanic
OCCUPATION: Consultant, King Pharmaceuticals

"I was very fortunate as a child, my father taught me the value of money and exposed me to the polished world of sales by bringing me with him to trade shows and sales meetings. My father believed that each of his five children should contribute financially to running the household. In high school, I was paid 25 cents an hour and earning $15 dollars a week. My room and board charge at home was $12 a week and I had to buy my own school lunches. This left me with about 75 cents in disposable income each week. At a young age I learned what profit margin was."

Upon graduating from a small town high school in Marshall, Illinois, Dennis realized that college was not an option, so he went to work for Ford Motor Company. After a year of working in a factory environment he enlisted in the Marines.

"While at Boot Camp, our Senior Drill Instructor was Sergeant A.J. Fisk, who was from St. Louis. Following boot camp I dreamed of going to St. Louis someday (only two hours from home) and finding Sgt. Fisk. I wanted to beat the hell out of him for the strict discipline he imposed on us. By 1968, however, (seven years after being discharged) I moved to St. Louis. By then I had already come to appreciate the many valuable lessons that I had learned in boot camp and at Advanced Infantry Training at Camp Pendleton, California. The most valuable of which was to be able to discipline myself, in my business training, studies, and long work hours. This I found, gave me a great edge over my peers against whom I was competing for promotions and additional compensation.

"The Marine Corps was what I needed at the time. The Marines provided a real world post high school education that forced me to grow up and mature. A year after enlisting, I was mature enough to assume the most important responsibility of my life. I married my high school sweetheart, Judy Pearce.

"I believe that utilizing the many lessons learned in the four short years I served in the Marine Corps benefited my family, my colleagues, my shareholders, and of course myself, every single day of my business career."

After being discharged from the Marine Corps in 1961, Dennis wanted to go into pharmaceutical sales but was not considered without a college degree. Instead, he took a sales job with Rockford Life Insurance and quickly became the youngest regional manager in the company's history.

In 1964, Jim O'Neal, the owner of a small upstart pharmaceutical company, Sig: Laboratories, gave Dennis the sales opportunity that he wanted. After a couple of years O'Neal sold Sig: Laboratories to a division of Revlon.

Dennis and Jim O'Neal then formed OJF Pharmaceutical Sales Company. In 1978, they sold their company to Chromaloy American.

Dennis formed his own company, Jones Medical, in 1981, and later changed it to Jones Pharma. The concept of the company was to purchase products and companies, eliminate duplicate overhead, and make profitable acquisitions. The acquisition focus was on successful products that large companies didn't have time to promote. Jones Pharma would then aggressively sell these products. This strategy became known as the "Emerging Specialty Pharmaceutical Sector" and Dennis is credited with creating it.

As with any entrepreneur growing his business, Dennis worked seven days a week 12 hours a day. His company eventually had 600 employees and five manufacturing plants. This was the result of 19 well planned, strategic acquisitions. During the start up and growth phases, the most important and reliable employee Dennis had was his wife, Judy.

In August of 2000, Dennis amazed Wall Street by selling his company for 20 times annual sales. King Pharmaceuticals acquired Jones Pharma for $3.4 billion. An early stockholder who purchased $10,000 in Jones Pharma could now cash out at $45 million. Dennis had provided stock options and bonuses to his employees as the company grew. This sale made a lot of people very wealthy.

Dennis officially retired on September 1, 2000 and now serves as a consultant to the company. He is also Vice-Chairman of Junior Achievement of Mississippi Valley, an active Trustee of the St. Louis College of Pharmacy, Trustee of Boy Scouts of America – St. Louis Council, and Trustee of the Evans Scholarship Foundation. Dennis is a past National Board Member for the Marine Corps Scholarship Foundation.

After a lifetime of hard work, Dennis and his wife, Judy, are enjoying the fruits of their labor. They have built a 32,000 square foot French Chateau in Ladue, Missouri, and have traveled the world to acquire its furnishings. They also enjoy two motor yachts, the 151' D'NATALIN and the 156' D'NATALIN II, as they take time to cruise the Mediterranean and Caribbean Seas.

Dennis and Judy have two married children, Denise and Matt, and three grandchildren with whom they spend as much time as possible.

SEMPER FIDELIS

JAMES K. KALLSTROM

"The discipline, values, leadership and ethos of the Marine Corps was and is the major basis for any success I had in life."

BORN: 6 May 1943 in Worcester, Massachusetts
SERVICE: United States Marine Corps, 1966 – 1969, Artillery Officer
OCCUPATION: Senior Policy Advisor to the Governor of New York for Counter-Terrorism Planning and Operations; Senior Executive Vice President, MBNA

James "Jim" Kallstrom graduated from the University of Massachusetts at Amherst with a Bachelor's Degree in Business Management. After graduation, he enlisted in the Marine Corps and went to Quantico, Virginia for Officer Candidate School.

In March 1967, Jim was sent to Vietnam and served a 13 month tour as an Artillery Officer/Forward Observer. He was with 1st Battalion/3rd Marine Regiment until being rotated out in May 1968.

"It was difficult to return to the United States in the Spring of 1968 from South Vietnam and see the tremendous change that had taken place in the country. The confusion of America's goals, as directed by politicians in Washington, with the heroic and dedicated patriotism of its Marines, was very disappointing."

After leaving the Marine Corps in 1969, he was accepted to the FBI Academy in Quantico, Virginia. He entered on duty with the FBI as a Special Agent in February 1970 and following a period of training, was assigned to the Baltimore, Maryland FBI Office. In 1971, he was transferred to the FBI's New York Office.

"I returned once again to Quantico for training. Since it had been only four years since going through OCS, I was very aware of what the differences and similarities were between the two institutions. I found the training at OCS had been substantially more difficult physically and emotionally; while the FBI training was more difficult from a traditional classroom setting. Both the Marine Corps and FBI firearms training were exceptional."

From 1971 to 1993, Jim had numerous assignments of increasing responsibility in New York and Washington, D.C. In September 1993, he was promoted to Special Agent in Charge of the Special Operations Division in New York. In February 1995, he was designated the Assistant Director in Charge, New York Division, a position he held until his retirement on December 31, 1997.

"During the decade of the 1980s, I was involved, with many others, in the successful takedown of the Mafia (five families) in New York; that was very rewarding as it benefited society greatly. My saddest case was the investigation of the tragic crash of TWA Flight 800 and the loss of 230 people. My biggest disappointment was that the FBI could not convince the political crowd in Washington that we were in a war against Radical Islamic Fundamentalist Terrorists, who would not stop in their goal to kill us, our society, our economy and our freedom."

In January 1998, upon his retirement from the FBI, Jim joined MBNA America Bank in Wilmington, Delaware where he was the Director of Sales. MBNA Corporation is a bank holding company and the parent of MBNA America Bank, N.A., a national bank. MBNA America has two principal subsidiaries: MBNA Europe Bank Limited (which is run by Charles Krulak) and MBNA Canada Bank, both are fully chartered banks that issue credit cards in the United Kingdom, Ireland, Spain, and Canada.

After September 11, 2001, at the request of Governor Pataki, Jim took a leave of absence from MBNA America to become the Director of Public Security for the state of New York. In this capacity he was responsible for Counter-Terrorism Planning and Operations for the State of New York. He also was New York State's point of contact with Tom Ridge at The White House Office of Homeland Security. In June 2002, Mr. Kallstrom was elevated to the position of Senior Policy Advisor to the Governor of New York for Counter-Terrorism, and returned to MBNA splitting his time between both jobs. Mr. Kallstrom is currently a Senior Executive Vice President, a Management Committee Member, and the Director of Government Affairs with MBNA America.

Jim currently serves as the Chairman of the Marine Corps Law Enforcement Foundation. He and his fellow board members have taken a very active role to make this the premiere non-profit supporting military and law enforcement families. The Foundation is providing a $40,000 Scholarship Bond to each child of U.S. service members and allied service members who lost a parent in Afghanistan or Iraq.

Mr. Kallstrom has appeared numerous times on national television shows commenting on law enforcement and terrorism issues. He is the long time Host of *The FBI Files*, shown weekly on the Discovery Channel and recently was a task force member on the Council on Foreign

Relations Task Force report titled, *America Still Unprepared – America Still in Danger*.

In addition to his Bachelor's Degree in Business Management from the University of Massachusetts, Mr. Kallstrom holds a Master's Degree in Criminal Justice from Long Island University. He has also been awarded Honorary Doctorate Degrees from Becker College in Worcester, Massachusetts and Long Island University.

Jim and his wife, Susan, currently reside in the New York City area. They are the proud parents of two daughters, Erika and Kristel.

SEMPER FIDELIS

MICHAEL T. KELLY

"Do the right thing, even when it is not expedient or easy."

BORN:	9 April 1953 in Paulsboro, New Jersey
SERVICE:	United States Marine Corps, U.S. Naval Academy 1972 – 1976, Active Duty 1976 – 1981, Officer, Infantry and Intelligence (S-2)
OCCUPATION:	President and CEO, TMP/Highland Partners

Mike Kelly graduated from the U.S. Naval Academy in 1976, took the Marine Corps option and immediately began active duty in the Marine Corps.

"As a young second lieutenant in the 3rd Battalion, 5th Marines, I learned many of the valuable lessons that are taught to every Marine NCO and Officer:

- Leaders lead from the front – never ask your men to do anything that you wouldn't do yourself.
- People watch what you do, not what you say.
- You must accomplish the mission in spite of all obstacles.
- You can't accomplish the mission without the support of the troops – take good care of the people who work for you.
- Do the right thing, even when it is not expedient or easy.
- You must be able to adapt – few experiences unfold the way you planned them.
- You can delegate authority but not responsibility – you are ultimately responsible for the results.
- Expect the best from people and you won't be disappointed.
- All Marines are green – there are no white, black, or yellow Marines."

Kelly was a Captain when he was discharged from the Marine Corps in 1981. He went to Pepperdine University and earned a Masters in Human Resources. After graduating he applied his education, experience, and people skills to the civilian world. His career began with senior-level human resource positions at General Foods in Dover, Delaware and Pepsi in Houston,

Texas. Following that he was employed by Recognition Equipment and was a vice-president at St. Jude Medical in Minneapolis. Next a major executive search firm, Korn/Ferry International had Kelly leading the global healthcare sector of their business. Currently, Kelly is President and Chief Executive Officer of TMP/Highland Partners.

Hudson Highland Group, Inc., one of the world's largest specialized staffing and executive search firms, delivers a full spectrum of recruitment, staffing and human resource consulting services worldwide. With approximately 4,000 employees in 27 countries, Hudson Highland Group defines a new breed of staffing and search enterprise. Hudson Highland Group consists of TMP/Hudson Global Resources, TMP/Hudson Human Resource Consulting and TMP/Highland Partners, and serves more than 10,000 staffing clients and more than 1,000 executive search clients.

As President and CEO of TMP/Highland Partners, Kelly is responsible for driving revenues by developing sales across all sectors and industries worldwide. Kelly also serves as a member of the company's Executive Search Board of Directors.

Because TMP/Highland Partners is organized along both industry and geographic lines, it offers clients exclusive access to an international talent base across all major industries at the very highest levels of management. TMP/Highland Partners includes specialty teams focused on Consumer Products & Services, Financial Services, Healthcare, Industrial, Technology, E-commerce/Internet, Energy & Natural Resources, Board of Directors, Human Resources, Legal, Professional Services and Supply Chain Management.

Specializing in recruiting at the CEO, COO, CIO, CFO and Board of Director level, as well as senior level operations and staff positions, Kelly helps clients find leadership for their organizations. And he helps the leaders themselves find a place where they can shape tomorrow's technology and trends.

The Kellys personally support the St. Croix Catholic School and the St. Paul Children's Hospital, both in Minnesota.

Mike Kelly and his wife, Barbara, have three sons and reside in Minnesota.

SEMPER FIDELIS

William Morgan Keys

"Take the message to Garcia."

Born: 29 March 1937 in Fredericktown, Pennsylvania
Service: United States Marine Corps, 1960 – 1994, Infantry Officer
Occupation: President/CEO, Colt's Manufacturing Co., New Colt Holding Co., Colt Defense LLC

Bill Keys grew up in the coal-mining town of Fredericktown, Pennsylvania. After graduating from high school, he entered the U.S. Naval Academy and selected the Marine Corps as his service. After graduating in 1960, he entered the Basic School at Quantico, Virginia.

As an Infantry officer, General Keys served at every level of operational command, platoon through regiment. As Commanding General, 2nd Marine Division during Desert Storm combat operations in the Middle East, he led the Division in its successful assault across the Kuwait border, breaching Iraqi barriers and minefield land, into Kuwait City. He additionally served two tours in Vietnam, and held numerous principal staff assignments both in the Marine Corps and on the Joint Staff. His personal decorations and medals include the Navy Cross, Silver Star Medal, and other high-ranking military awards.

"In the retaking of Kuwait during Desert Storm, we had to move the heaviest armored division in Marine Corps history through a minefield and anti-tank barriers. Breaching these defenses upon entry into Kuwait would route 16,000 Marines and 4,700 Army Tiger Brigade forces through what would essentially become a funnel. We chose a point approximately 80 miles inland from the Persian Gulf. We were east of where the 1st Marine Division would enter and west of the Arab Forces intended point of entry.

"For a week prior to the invasion, our engineers were out every night crawling and probing with their fiberglass sticks locating mines and working to create the funnel for us to enter. The planes worked the area in an attempt to remove the ground forces and armor protecting this part of the

Iraqi defensive perimeter. The lanes being cleared were not very wide, so any problems crossing could cause a bottleneck and high casualty situation for us. Once the invasion started, I was very concerned about vehicles hitting undetected, unexploded mines and incoming mortar rounds and artillery from remaining Iraqi forces in the area stalling our troops moving through the breach area. The unknown wildcards at the time were chemical and biological weapons. During the initial phase, congestion of the breaching operation is when we would be most susceptible to this type of attack. Once the invasion started and we had successfully breached their lines and safely passed through the initial minefields, I knew that overall we were going to be okay."

Lieutenant General Keys retired from the U.S. Marine Corps on September 1, 1994. His last active duty assignment was as the Commander, U.S. Marine Corps Forces, Atlantic.

In 1995, Bill Keys accepted a board position with Colt's Manufacturing Company, Inc. in Hartford, Connecticut. In 1999, when Colt's Manufacturing was in extreme financial duress, he assumed responsibility as President and CEO of Colt's Manufacturing and its parent company, New Colt Holding Corps.

Colt is one of the most recognized and prominent names in the firearms industry. The company has been in business for more than 160 years and there are millions of arms bearing the Colt name attesting to the company's keen knowledge of shooters' needs coupled with the ability to deliver a quality product.

More than 400 distinct models of handguns and long arms of muzzle and breech loading designs together with thousands of variations and subtypes are included in this phenomenal accomplishment.

Colt has many notations in our nation's military history as a result of their contributions to the development of modern firearms technology. These include:

- Percussion black powder classics such as the Walker and Dragoon models, 1860 Army and 1861 Navy.
- The most famous revolver ever, the 1873 Single Action Army (or Peacemaker) that signaled Colt's move into the metallic-cartridge era.
- The Model 1911 Automatic Pistol that still defines the standard for modern day .45 semiautomatic pistols and was the sidearm for the U.S. military for more than 100 years.
- The Python often referred to as the Rolls Royce of double action revolvers.
- M16 rifle that has set the standard for modern small arms for the world's armed forces.
- M4 carbine is the enhanced/upgraded variant weapon system that is now replacing the M16 as the most combat proven assault weapon for the US and allied military organizations.

Suffice it to say that no other name has contributed more to the legendary history of American firearms than Colt. That's what makes Colt the most revered and collectible name in the history of firearms. They will certainly hold a place in the future of firearms with their continued ingenuity.

Colt has always been an innovator, a pioneer – implementing mass production techniques, designing for part interchangeability, always striving to improve production methods. Today, Colt maintains its position as one of the world's leading gun manufacturers by blending state-of-the-art technologies and modernized manufacturing methods.

In November 2002, Colt Defense LLC was formed and Colt's defense business and law enforcement sales transferred to Colt Defense. Bill also assumed the duties of President and CEO of Colt Defense.

Having twice served in Vietnam, Bill was personally aware of the importance of the issues surrounding the Colt M16 weapons system to the safety and survival of our troops in that theatre. The M16, purchased over the objections of the Army, is the most widely used weapon in U.S. history. Over the course of time this weapon has been kindly embraced, like many of its predecessors, by those soldiers who depend on it day-to-day.

During the early 1980s Colt developed a new weapon system, the M4 carbine. While maintaining a legacy to the M16, and capitalizing on all its combat experience, the M4 operating characteristics were quite different, and is, in fact, a completely new weapon system. Typed as classified in August 1994 and with shipments to U.S. Armed forces beginning shortly thereafter, the M4 was originally designed as a rear echelon weapon. The compact size and lighter package that delivered nearly identical effective range, found a receptive audience with the elite troops of our nation. Bill, being keenly aware that Colt was successful as a company when it focused itself on the military, used the M4 platform as the product of the future. Under his leadership, Colt was able to rededicate itself, focusing on high quality weapons for the military. By achieving ISO registration in record time and continuing on this path, the company has achieved the desired results. The M4 carbine is now the weapon of choice for all service branches, and will serve as the primary weapon of choice for the next decade for both the U.S. and many of the elite forces of our allies. These systemic changes assure all Colt customers, most importantly military and law enforcement, of the reliability of a firearm when needed, and of the knowledge that quality is paramount to all decisions made at the Company. Colt tradition dictates that the technology be the best available and quality is never compromised.

"In the Marines and now in the Corporate world as a civilian, I have tried to impart to those who have worked for me one simple bit of guidance, and one that I have done my best to abide by, that being to 'Take the message to Garcia.' This little booklet and the message it contains are the real essence and foundation of good leadership (in my opinion). To do what has to be done to get the job done, or get the mission accomplished, and do it with as little fanfare as possible. It's all about accepting responsibility and accountability for one's actions, while never losing sight of the final objective."

Bill and Colt are actively involved in supporting the Marine Corps Law Enforcement Foundation as well as the many law enforcement agencies in their local area. He and his wife also support the Women's Cancer Care Foundation.

Bill currently resides in Hume, Virginia with his wife, Gail, their family and new Pit Bull puppy, Captain Jenks.

SEMPER FIDELIS

Donald R. Knauss

"Always take care of your people first."

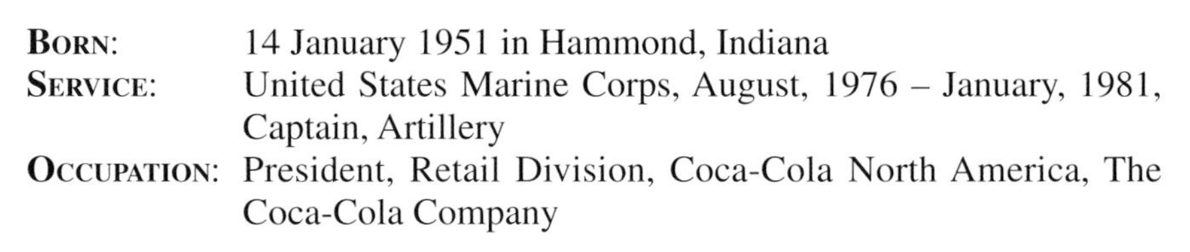

Born: 14 January 1951 in Hammond, Indiana
Service: United States Marine Corps, August, 1976 – January, 1981, Captain, Artillery
Occupation: President, Retail Division, Coca-Cola North America, The Coca-Cola Company

After high school Don attended Indiana University and earned a B.A. in history. After earning his degree, Don enlisted in the Marines and went to Quantico, Virginia for Officer Candidate School.

"One indelible learning from the Marine Corps came my very first day in the Fleet Marine Force (FMF). I had just arrived at Kaneohe Marine Corps air station in January 1978. I was quickly flown over to the Big Island of Hawaii to join my unit: Charlie Battery, 1st Battalion, 12th Marines. My unit had been on live fire exercises for several weeks. I joined them as they were breaking for noon chow. Given that the unit had been in the field for several days, without hot food, the Battery C.O. had the Base Camp bring out hot chow. I was standing and talking with the Battery C.O. and Gunney. The line was forming for food, so since the introductions were over I began to move to get into the line early in the process. As I walked to the line I felt a big hand grab my shoulder – it was the Battery Gunney. He said, "Sir, in the field the men eat first. If there is any left after they finish, you can have some." I got the message – your people always come first. It's a rule I have held by for the last 25 years."

In 1981, after leaving the United States Marine Corps, Don began his civilian career with Procter & Gamble in Marketing. After four years at P&G, he moved on to PepsiCo where he spent almost nine years at Frito-Lay, in Canada and the USA.

In 1994, Don moved to The Minute Maid Company as head of Marketing. And in 1998 moved to South Africa as President of Coca-Cola Southern

Africa. In 2000, he returned from Coca-Cola Southern Africa as President and CEO of The Minute Maid Company. In January 2003 Coca-Cola combined The Minute Maid Company with all Coca-Cola brands in North America and he took on his current assignment as President of the combined retail group.

Don is currently President of the Retail Division of Coca-Cola North America. This division sells all Coca-Cola brands/products, including Minute Maid, to all retail customers: supermarkets, convenience stores, club stores, mass merchandisers, etc. Total sales for the Retail Division is more than $5 billion with approximately 5,500 associates. The majority of these associates manage and run their 24 manufacturing facilities across the United States and Canada.

Coca-Cola supports many local community events and charities. The Corporation has also established The Coca-Cola Foundation. The Foundation's mission is to improve the quality of life in the community and enhance individual opportunity through education. They support educational programs primarily within three main areas: higher education, classroom teaching and learning, and international education. Their programs support scholarships for aspiring students; encourage and motivate young people to stay in school; and foster cultural understanding. Over the last ten years, the Foundation has contributed more than $124 million in support of education.

Don is on the Board of Trustees for the USMC University Foundation Board, the Board of Trustees for Camp Coca-Cola, and he and his wife are co-chairs of the Capital Campaign of Strake-Jesuit College Preparatory School of Houston, Texas.

Don and his wife, Ellie, and their four children, Jack, Mickey, Alec and Kara, live in Houston, Texas, with Don spending significant time in Atlanta.

SEMPER FIDELIS

Charles C. Krulak

"It's all about anticipation, agility and thinking things through, so as not to be surprised if at all possible."

Born: 4 March 1942
Service: United States Marine Corps, 1964 – 1999, Officer
Occupation: Chief Executive Officer, MBNA Europe Bank

Charles C. Krulak was the 31st Commandant of the Marine Corps and retired in 1999. Very few people have ever achieved this level of success, and are as modest about it.

"It still stands out in my mind that I was once told, 'The road to hell is paved with the bleached bones of Second Lieutenants who failed to put out their local security.' That simple concept has been important to me over a lifetime of service in the Corps and in business. It is all about anticipation, agility, and thinking things through, so as not to be surprised if at all possible."

Many social issues were examined with regard to the military during Krulak's command. He went head to head with the Clinton Administration regarding gender integrated vs. gender segregated basic training. Through his efforts the Marines maintained gender segregated basic training, exclusion of women from direct combat including armor, artillery, and direct fire support units. He was instrumental in upholding the UCMJ Article on Adultery maintaining the seriousness of the offense. "We raised the bar on who could become a Marine … mental and physical standards as well as standards regarding drug testing, tattoos, and gang membership, etc. All other services were lowering their standards as we increased ours. We still met and exceeded our recruiting goals. Finally, we installed the 'Crucible' as the final test in boot camp. The tough 54-hour 'gut check' ensures that we graduate a battle tested Marine."

Upon retiring from the Marine Corps in September of 1999, Krulak immediately went to work for MBNA. "As CEO of MBNA Europe Bank Limited, I have the honor of working with more than 4,000 great people spread across multiple countries. MBNA is the largest independent credit card company in the world. Its entire ethos is based on the simple precept that each person at MBNA should 'think of him/herself as the customer.' MBNA is world re-known for its customer focus. It is a Fortune 500 Company and one of the 'top 10 places to Work' in America. MBNA Europe is only nine years old and has already captured 15% of the United Kingdom market and recently expanded into Spain and Ireland. It is the fastest growing credit card company in Europe, managing over $12 billion in loans.

"Our company supports 12 charities in the United Kingdom and numerous charities in the United States. We have an education foundation that gives grants to individual teachers to provide extra learning experiences for their students. MBNA gives millions of dollars a year to charities and to education."

The Krulaks reside in England and have two adult children. One is a flight surgeon with the rank of Lieutenant Commander in the Navy and the other is earning a Ph.D. in religious studies at the University of Pennsylvania.

SEMPER FIDELIS

Sherman R. Lewis, Jr.

"After boarding the ship and spending my first day around Marines, I immediately knew I was to become a Marine and not a Sailor."

Born: 11 December 1936 in Ottawa, Illinois
Service: United States Marine Corps, June 1958 to June 1961, Officer
Occupation: Vice Chairman and Director, Lehman Brothers Inc.

Sherman Lewis received his undergraduate degree from Northwestern University in 1958 and immediately began three years of active duty in the United States Marine Corps serving as a communications officer.

"During college I was in the Naval ROTC program. As a 3rd class midshipman, I served my duty cruise aboard the USS *Wisconsin*. After boarding the ship and spending my first day around Marines, I immediately knew I was to become a Marine and not a Sailor.

"One of my early memories as a Marine involved knocking over a table of food. I reflexively snapped to attention when, by surprise, I saw my former basic school Drill Instructor – Sergeant Crosby – being interviewed during the Huntley-Brinkley national news program as he 'stormed the beach' during the ammunition-less landing in Lebanon in 1959. The last time I had seen him was when he personally and profanely 'braced' me against the bulkhead in the barracks at Quantico."

Following his discharge from the Marine Corps in 1961, Mr. Lewis returned to the Chicago area and began employment with American National Bank & Trust. During this employment he attended evening classes and received his M.B.A. from the University of Chicago Graduate School of Business in 1964. The next year he was transferred to New York City where he still works and resides.

Sherman Lewis has held many key executive positions with premier financial institutions. He has been in this business for over 40 years and has been with Lehman Brothers or a predecessor firm for more than 30 years.

“Lehman Brothers is an innovator in global finance, serving the financial needs of corporations, governments and municipalities, institutional clients, and high net-worth individuals worldwide. Founded in 1850, Lehman Brothers maintains leadership positions in equity and fixed income sales, trading and research, investment banking, private equity, and private client services. The firm is headquartered in New York, London, and Tokyo, and operates a network of offices around the world.”

Since late 1990, Sherman Lewis has held the title of Vice Chairman with the responsibility for maintaining the firm’s most senior relationships with its corporate clients as well as government officials throughout the world.

Sherman Lewis and his wife, Dorothy, have been active and financially supportive of many educational, charitable, and health related institutions. While they contribute generously to many causes, their major commitments include Northwestern University, The University of Chicago Graduate School of Business, The Newark Museum, The New York Eye and Ear Infirmary, Southampton Hospital, and The New York City Mission Society. In addition to his above affiliations, Sherman Lewis is an active member of the Marine Corps Heritage Center Founders’ Group and the Council on Foreign Relations.

Mr. Lewis has risen steadily through the ranks of the financial world even though it is a very turbulent and competitive industry. In his chosen field, Sherman Lewis has reached the pinnacle of success.

Sherman and his wife, Dorothy, currently reside in New York City. They are the proud parents of four children, Thomas, Catherine, Elizabeth and Michael.

SEMPER FIDELIS

Charles Lynn Lowder

"From this day on, you are and always will be a United States Marine."

Born: 19 December 1945 in Decatur, Illinois
Service: United States Marine Corps 1967 – 1968 Enlisted, 1968 – 1983 Officer
Occupation: Corporate/Litigation Counsel, Piper Rudnick

Lynn served 16 years active duty in the Marine Corps. A collegiate football player for Northern Illinois University, Lynn, in 1967, left college his junior year and reported to Marine Corps Recruit Depot, San Diego as a Marine recruit. Graduating Honorman of Platoon 3016, he served one year as an enlisted Marine before being selected for the Enlisted Commissioning Program. After commissioning, he initially served as a team leader with 1st Force Reconnaissance Company in Vietnam where he received the Silver Star, Bronze Star with Combat V, and Purple Heart. Upon his return stateside, he played for the 1970 Quantico Marines football team.

Following an Okinawa tour as a rifle company commander, Lynn was selected for the Degree Completion Program. At the University of Illinois, he completed his undergraduate degree with honors. He later was selected for the Law Program and graduated from DePaul University College of Law in the top 15% of his class. His last active duty tour was in the JAG Corps at Quantico, Virginia.

"The Marine Corps was where I found myself and my first role model in the person of my Senior Drill Instructor, Gunnery Sergeant Bell. I will always remember the comments made by Lieutenant Colonel Terry at my boot camp graduation ceremony. He said, 'From this day on, you are and always will be a United States Marine.' I thought my chest would explode with pride. I still remember his comments vividly and they are a continuing source of motivation.

"Another Marine Corps memory is when two other Lieutenants and I decided to go to Saluda, Virginia and pay our respects to Marine Corps legend and hero Chesty Puller before going to Vietnam. Appearing on General Puller's doorstep, unannounced, we were warmly welcomed in by Mrs. Puller. As it turns out General Puller was recovering from a stroke, so we spoke with Mrs. Puller for more than an hour before she awakened the General. During this time, she allowed us to see his original medals (kept in a shoebox in the sewing room) and page through his copy of Caesar's Gallic Commentaries which he carried throughout his entire Marine Corps career. We later visited with the General and Mrs. Puller for more than two hours. They were charming, caring hosts. General Puller signed my boot camp yearbook and inscribed it as follows: 'Saluda, VA. 29 September 1968. To 2nd Lieutenant Charles L. Lowder, U.S. Marine Corps, a platoon leader and patriot, with best wishes. Be a leader and not a commander. L.B. Puller.' Later, he walked us out to my car and apologized that he was not going with us ... that he wanted to but had been told he was too old to serve again in combat. Imagine ... Retired General Puller apologizing to us. What honesty and humility from a Marine's Marine. I will forever remember that experience."

Upon being Honorably Discharged in 1983, Lynn returned to Illinois and entered civilian law practice. For the next 16 years, he defended numerous lawsuits filed against medical doctors, non-profit organizations and Corporations. He has authored numerous professional articles and has been a featured trial advocacy speaker at various legal seminars.

In 1998, Lynn entered the Corporate world and became Executive Vice President/General Counsel for Mail Boxes Etc., the largest non-food franchise chain in America. Subsequently, in 2000, he became COO of Colt's Manufacturing Company, Inc. (Colt Firearms) in Hartford, Connecticut. This was a significant and poignant assignment for Lynn, as he and his Vietnam recon team had used the Colt M-16 rifle in combat. Although still producing M-16 rifles for America's military services in 2000, to insure the highest quality standards and qualify for future U.S. Government contracts, Colt's needed to achieve ISO 9000:2001 qualification, a rigorous quality standard for manufacturers. With Lynn's leadership, Colt's achieved this all-important milestone within one year.

In 2002, Lynn went to work for Piper Rudnick, a nationally known business law firm with offices in 11 cities nationwide. The firm's core practice is focused on business and technology, real estate, litigation (securities, labor, commercial and products liability), government affairs and international commerce and litigation. He draws upon his significant Corporate experience to assist the firm and his clients as a Corporate litigation attorney.

Lynn is a prolific speaker on the topic of character and leadership. For the past several years, he is a scheduled speaker at Drill Instructors School in San Diego. He emphasizes to each new class of "soon-to-be" Drill Instructors the life changing role and example they can be to Marine Recruits ... the same role model that his Senior Drill Instructor, Gunnery Sergeant Bell was to him.

He is on the Board of the Marine Military Academy in Harlington, Texas. The MMA President (Major General Wayne Rollings, USMC Retired) and

Lynn were team leaders with 1st Force Recon Company, Vietnam (1968 – 1969). The school does an incredible job building character and leadership in young men. "With General Rollings at the helm, there is outstanding leadership provided to the MMA cadets … second to none."

Lynn's proudest accomplishment in life has been as a father to his three children, Kathy, Lisa and Danny. "They are now adults and very fine people."

SEMPER FIDELIS

Robert A. Lutz

"The Marine Corps provided me with the opportunity immediately after high school to fulfill my childhood dream, becoming a fighter-pilot."

Born: 12 February 1932 in Zurich, Switzerland
Service: United States Marine Corps, 1954 – 1959 Active duty, 1959–1965 Reservist, Jet-attack pilot
Occupation: Vice Chairman, Product Development – GM, and Chairman – GM North America

Robert "Bob" Lutz is the son of a Swiss banker. His father's professional assignments in the United States enabled Bob to obtain a dual U.S. – Swiss education. In 1943 he became a United States citizen. Upon graduating from a Swiss high school in 1954, he joined the United States Marine Corps.

Bob joined as an enlisted Marine and completed boot camp at Parris Island, South Carolina. "I went through Parris Island before the congressional investigations and human dignity had been discovered as essential in American life, it was an interesting time. I could tell many stories, but since obscene and profane language had, at that time, not yet been banished from the Corps, they are not fit to print."

Based on his early weeks' performance and I.Q. testing, he was selected for Officer's Candidate School and applied for his great love, fighter aviation.

"In April 1955, after a minor nose operation to improve breathing (believed in those days to be essential to flying high-performance jets, but proven to be useless other than ruining the appearance of my nose), I was ordered to Naval Air Station, Pensacola, Florida for pre-flight training. To those of us who had endured USMC boot camp, it was easy. I made class officer, then Battalion Commander, then Regimental Commander of my pre-flight class. A succession of assignments to "outlying fields" ensued, as flight training progressed from basic, to formation, to instruments, to carrier qualification, and finally to "advanced training" in the Corpsus Christi, Texas area. I was assigned to fighter training which was my boyhood dream, and trained at

NAS Chase Field, in Beeville, Texas. A mistake had been made in my orders: I missed a three-month stint in T-28s (a high-performance propeller-driven aircraft designed to facilitate transition to jets). By the time the oversight was discovered, I was already flying a then-current combat aircraft, the F9F-2 Panther. I graduated from flight school in August 1956, and was commissioned a second lieutenant. A proud moment!"

During Bob's enlistment he accumulated roughly 1,300 hours of flight time in Panthers (F9F-5), Cougars (F9F-8), Banshees (F2H-4), and Skyhawks (A4-A, A4-B). While stationed in Okinawa, he served as an Air Liaison Officer to the 3rd Marines and participated in training the ROK Marines in improving their air-ground coordination skills. Upon being released from active duty in 1959, he served in the reserves until GM transferred him to Europe in 1965.

"While stationed in Okinawa, Japan, and staying with the 'Grunts,' I was facing a combat readiness inspection. I had neglected to withdraw two magazines for my Colt .45 from the armory prior to their closing. I knew that not having magazines was not an option, so I went about 'making' two. I used shoe polish, markers, cardboard and tape.

"The Battalion was arrayed for inspection and as was so frequently the case on Okinawa, a torrential downpour occurred. The inspection that day was being conducted by the Commandant, General David M. Shoup. When his gray Chevrolet arrived, it parked adjacent to what he believed was a brown puddle, but which was, in fact, an over-full 3-foot drainage ditch. The Commandant, all 5'7" of him, mostly disappeared for a moment, then re-emerged as a sopping swamp creature. His composure was intact.

"Being a member of the Battalion Staff, I stood in front of the troops and to the right of the Battalion Commander. General Shoup led the inspection with the Battalion Commander (all well there), then the various staff members. When he got to me, he checked more closely, since I was an aviator. He felt my magazine pouch, then felt it again. He opened the flap and withdrew my two counterfeit and soggy cardboard magazines. He dropped them to the ground with some disgust and fixed his glaze, through muddy glasses, on my 1,000-mile stare. Trying to ease my burden, he suggested that maybe I didn't have the magazines because, as an aviator, my normal sidearm was a .38 S&W revolver. I replied 'No sir, I neglected to go to the Armory before it closed.' He made a comment to the effect that he appreciated my honesty. It was a humiliating moment. To this day I do not know what made him check those magazines so closely, if it was intuition on his part or if someone ratted on me."

After active duty, Bob received his bachelor's degree in production management from the University of California – Berkley in 1961, and earned distinction as a Phi Beta Kappa. He received his MBA from the same university with highest honors in 1962.

"While at UC Berkeley I found the adjustment to civilian life difficult, especially as the left-wing environment of Berkeley was antithetical to all I believed in and had been trained to defend. A few of us Marines on campus aided by a couple of Special Forces veterans, were in the process of forming a radical right-wing cell which was to devote itself to blowing up the headquarters of such communist-sympathizing organizations as Students for a Democratic Society (SDS) and Students for Democratic Action (SDA), all later proven to be Communist front organizations. Luckily, for them, we were all too busy with studies, reserve duty, family, part-time jobs and graduation to ever realize our fantasies."

In 1963, he began his automotive career with General Motors at their Overseas Operations office in NYC. In 1965, he was transferred to Europe and served in senior executive sales, marketing and operations positions in France and Germany. At the time General Motors' hottest selling European vehicle was the Opel.

In 1972, he took a position with BMW as Executive Vice President of Worldwide Sales and Marketing. In this position he was a member of the company's board of management.

In 1974, Bob left BMW and assumed the position of Chairman, Ford of Germany. In 1977, he became President of Ford of Europe, and Chairman and CEO, Ford of Europe in 1984. In this position he became an Executive Vice President and a Member of Ford's Board of Directors. In 1985, Bob returned to the United States as Executive Vice President of North American Truck Operations. This started Ford's era of improved quality and construction: "Built Ford Tough."

In 1986, Bob accepted an Executive Vice President's position with Chrysler and soon rose to become their President, COO, and finally Vice Chairman. He was responsible for all of Chrysler's car and truck operations worldwide. His years with Chrysler are chronicled in his 1998 book: *Guts: The Seven Laws of Business That Made Chrysler the Hottest Car Company.* He is widely credited with being the architect of Chrysler's turnaround and the introduction of exciting new car styles including the Viper, Prowler and PT Cruiser.

In 1998, Bob went to work for Exide Technologies, the world's largest battery manufacturer. He assumed the role of Chairman and CEO. He was instrumental in refocusing the company efforts in new product development, reducing debt and once again making Exide a premier automotive supplier.

On September 1, 2001, Bob returned to General Motors as Vice Chairman of Product Development. In November 2001, he was named Chairman of GM North America. He is focused on bringing some excitement and increased efficiency to the GM automotive fleet while continuing GM's domination in the light truck and SUV market.

Bob is generous with his business acumen and his time outside of work. He serves as Chairman of The New Common School Foundation and as a trustee of the Barbara Ann Karmanos Cancer Institute. He is also a member of the board of trustees for the U.S. Marine Corps University Foundation and vice chairman of the board of trustees at the Marine Military Academy in Harlingen, Texas.

Bob and his wife, Denise, both have multi-rated pilot's licenses. They both fly helicopters: she a Bell "Jet Ranger;" he an MD-500 and Aero L-39 ex-Soviet jet fighter/attack aircraft. He also has a collection of vintage cars and motorcycles that they both enjoy driving.

The L-39 "Albatross" is one of the first Soviet advanced trainers to enter the U.S. He paid $230,000, probably 5 cents on the dollar for what it cost the Soviets to manufacture. After a 30-year absence from military high-performance aircraft, Bob went through training with former Soviet Air Force Major Makarenko. Bob soloed in the "Albatross" on May 5, 1995, exactly 30 years after his last flight in a Marine A4. The plane is painted in the 1965 era USMC flight operations standards, including his old squadron markings.

Bob and Denise currently reside on their 140-acre ranch in Ann Arbor, Michigan. Denise's son, Elliott Cambell, is a graduate of the Marine Military Academy. Bob has four daughters from a previous marriage: Jacqueline, Carolyn (also a former Marine), Catherine, and Alexandra.

SEMPER FIDELIS

Carolyn Lutz-Mannelli

"Opportunities can be created!"

Born: 17 January 1960 in Oakland, California
Service: United States Marine Corps, active1983 – 1988; Reserves 1988 – 1993, Officer
Occupation: Managing Partner; Korfmann Burnett Lutz AG, Geneva, Switzerland

"I had originally become interested in the Marine Corps as 'something to do after college' due to my father's love of the Corps. This, my sisters and I gleaned from the many formative incidents he described from his time at Parris Island. Like Dad, I wanted to become a jet pilot. Alas, the USMC in the early eighties still had no female pilots or plans for any. But this didn't stop me.

"According to my father, the USMC is a great training ground for leadership and resulting business success. Although my father had no sons, he was not going to miss this chance to have one of his offspring benefit from the same 'school of hard knocks' that he credits with much of his own success. So off I went to OCS, TBS and Air Traffic Control school – the closest I could come to naval aviation.

"A few years later, on liberty while in Pohang, South Korea for Operation Team Spirit, I was in a downtown bar where most of the Marine Officers came at the end of our long days, still in our camouflage utilities. At the bar, I spotted a Marine Corps Major General, wearing the wings of a naval aviator. I decided I had nothing to lose by giving him my opinion on women's ability and motivation to fly for the USMC. He listened politely, and I figured that was the end of it. Imagine my surprise when, a few weeks after the end of the deployment, Major General Chuck Pitman requested me to come to 1st MAW HQ in Okinawa to serve as his new Aide de Camp & Protocol Officer. The year with the General was, for me, the best job any 1st Lt. could have. Following the General to almost every country in the Western Pacific was invaluable learning: lead by example, be flexible, keep your 'men' informed, be tough but fair, and surround yourself with good people. Most important, opportunities can be created! And, the happy ending: The General was promoted to Lt. Gen., Deputy Chief of Staff for Aviation at HQMC. And during that time, women Marines were finally allowed to become naval aviators."

Carolyn was urged by the General and his Colonels to pursue her dream of an MBA and a career in business. She left the USMC in the spring of 1988 in California and drove almost non-stop over three days to Philadelphia, and the following day started an intensive two year dual-degree MBA/MA program at the University of Pennsylvania's Wharton School. Never having touched a personal computer before, she was in for a huge challenge; most of her fellow students had worked in consulting or investment banking while she was literally running around in combat boots. She had quite a bit of catching up to do just to manage one master's, let alone two at the same time in a very competitive environment. Luckily, by this time Carolyn had learned to appreciate a good challenge.

After completing her graduate programs, Carolyn took a job in marketing with Procter & Gamble in Geneva. This led, after a few years, to Director of International for the prestigious Swiss skin-care brand La Prairie. From there, she joined Korn/Ferry to learn the executive search business. Carolyn left them four years later to open the Geneva office of Heidrick and Struggles, another premier global search firm. Finally, a year ago, Carolyn became a partner and owner in her current company. And received a call from her Dad, "Congratulations. Finally, you are working for the best boss: yourself!"

Korfmann Burnett Lutz AG is a global "boutique" executive search firm with offices in San Francisco, Chicago, Zurich and Geneva. The company values long-term relationships, and helps its clients with CEO, board, and executive appointments. The company has not only survived the current severe downturn in the consulting business, they have actually grown, added staff, and opened a new office during the past 18 months.

Carolyn's role for the past year has been to open a new office for the partnership group in Geneva. Pan-European business development has been a key priority, since in this economic environment there is more of an oversupply of good candidates than of great jobs to be filled. Equally important is to find the best candidates for your clients. "Luckily, executive search is a relationship business built on trust and performance. Once you have satisfied clients, they tend to stay with you. For this reason we have a relatively small number of clients, but for whom we work fairly extensively, over time and across geographies."

Carolyn is on a mission in Switzerland (still a very male-dominated environment): to help women aim high and advance professionally. She speaks at conferences, mentors and advises women of all ages.

Carolyn is married to an Italian particle physicist, Marcello Mannelli, and they have a son, Anthony, and a daughter, Isabella. The family makes their home in Geneva, Switzerland, sharing it with their two cats, Max and Moritz.

SEMPER FIDELIS

Robert J. Maguire

"You learn something everyday of your Corps life, developing strength of character, empathy, compassion, and leadership."

Born: 4 April 1937 in Brooklyn, New York
Service: United States Marine Corps, 1958–1962 active, 1963–1978 reserves, Infantry Officer
Occupation: Chairman, National Automobile Dealers Association, McLean, Virginia; CEO, Maguire Automotive Group, Bordentown, New Jersey

Bob Maguire grew up on Long Island, New York, and attended LaSalle Military Academy, a product of a Christian Brothers' education. In June 1954, he was admitted to the U.S. Naval Academy, Annapolis, Maryland, as a member of the Class of 1958. During his plebe year, he experienced an "academic deficiency" in marine engineering and his choice was to be set back to the Class of 1959 or be discharged. Not wanting to lose any time for continuing advancement and development, he left the Naval Academy and enrolled at Duquesne University in Pittsburgh, Pennsylvania. While at Duquesne, he took Army ROTC and was designated a distinguished military graduate. Having earned such a distinction allowed him to receive a regular commission as a 2nd Lieutenant in the Marine Corps.

From June 1958 through February 1959, he attended Basic School, Class 3-58 at Quantico, Virginia. Upon graduation, he had orders to attend flight school at Pensacola, Florida, but after the graduation ceremony, his orders were changed to the 1st Marine Brigade in Hawaii. As an All American Collegiate Rifleman at Duquesne, he demonstrated his marksmanship prowess, which FMFPAC Commander, Lt. General Vernon McGee, wanted in order to develop a Marine Corps rifle team that would successfully compete against the Army team at Scoffield Barracks, Hawaii.

"Keenly disappointed that I was not going to be a Marine Corps aviator, I arrived at Hickham AFB in August 1959, as people were partying in the streets of Waikiki and Honolulu, convinced that I had been sent to a South Sea Island paradise. The next day I learned Hawaii was admitted to statehood.

"Inasmuch as the Brigade was participating in amphibious exercises on the shores of Camp Pendleton, I was assigned to participate in the Pacific Division Rifle matches which were about to commence at the Puolola Rifle Range. With my arrival, the 1st Marine Brigade formed a second four-man team comprised of an officer member, two experienced enlisted members, and a new marksman. The odds on favorite to win this championship was a team from the 3rd Marine Division, Okinawa. On the day of the competition, trade winds made it possible for anyone to win. To the total surprise of the shooters' community, 1st Marine Brigade, Team #2, won the championship and I was a celebrity before the Brigade returned to Kaneohe MCAS."

Joining the Brigade now became the highlight of his career as he was assigned to be a platoon leader in Foxtrot Company, 2nd Battalion, 4th Marine Regiment, a grunt – the heart and soul of being a Marine.

Shortly afterwards, while reading the Navy Times, it was reported that his roommate from Basic School was killed, along with his instructor, in an aviation accident during training at Pensacola. He wondered for a long time afterward if being "infantry" was indeed a blessing.

Hawaii – Marine Grunt – Distinguished Rifleman. He learned something every day that remained a core of his life, developing strength of character, empathy, compassion, and leadership, while valuing the importance of training.

Within a year, he was transferred to MTU (Marksman Training Unit) at the Marine Corps Recruit Depot in San Diego. This assignment, as a permanent member of the Marine Corps Shooting Team, allowed him to compete on an international basis in preparation for the Pan-American and Olympic Games as well as the National Matches held each August at Camp Perry, Ohio. In June 1962, he transferred to the Ready Reserve and spent the next 16 years training for combat, which never occurred because President Lyndon Johnson expanded the draft in lieu of calling the 4th Marine Division to active duty.

Meanwhile, his additional duties as a member of the Marine Corps Reserve Shooting Team lead him to continue in marksman competition and eventually win a national championship in 1963 at Camp Perry with a new national match record of 248-27V.

His civilian career began in the automobile business as a Chevrolet dealer in Bordentown, New Jersey in 1976. That involvement lead to the purchase of additional dealerships which created the Maguire Automotive Group, a company that sells 4,270 vehicles and earns $91 million in revenues annually.

In 1987, Bob Maguire was elected to the Board of Directors of the National Automobile Dealers Association representing 20,000 franchised new car and truck dealers that sell domestic and imported lines throughout the United States. NADA is the "voice of the dealer" on Capitol Hill and at regulatory agencies in Washington, D.C. The Association monitors legislation and regulation that affect dealers and works to minimize or eliminate any negative impact on the automobile industry. Positions on specific legislative and regulatory issues are presented as the collective view of dealers to Congress, the courts, federal agencies, and the public. NADA also stays abreast of regional and state issues that have the potential for national impact.

NADA's Industry Affairs Group is also the "voice of the dealer" to manufacturers and distributors. NADA representatives meet frequently with top-level industry executives to keep the lines of communication open and to be advocates for their dealers. NADA's own statistical resources produce forecasts and data in terms that anyone can understand. The Association analyzes industry trends, consumer behavior and changes in culture and technology to prepare dealers for tomorrow's challenges.

In January 2001, Bob Maguire became Chairman of the NADA. Automotive retailing is the largest retail sector of the U.S. economy, accounting for $646.8 billion or 22% of total retail sales. New car and truck dealers employ more than one million people.

Maguire's other activities include government service as Commissioner and Treasurer of the Mercer County Improvement Authority in New Jersey; Committeeman on the New Jersey Republican State Committee; Recipient of the Patriotism Award from Governor Thomas Kean.

He is a member of the Board of Directors of the National Marine Corps Scholarship Foundation, Princeton, New Jersey; co-chairman of the Marine Corps Leatherneck Scholarship Ball; president of the Ft. Dix Chapter of the Association of the United States Army; and major donor to the Major Thomas B. McGuire, Jr. Memorial, McGuire Air Force Base, New Jersey. In 2001, Bob Maguire was a Marine Corps Semper Fidelis Award Recipient.

Maguire is a Trustee of LaSalle Military Academy, Oakdale, New York and has been elected to the Duquesne University Sports Hall of Fame, as well as to the Duquesne University Century Club of Distinguished Alumni.

Bob and Marcy live in Princeton, New Jersey and their son, Michael, is a student at the University of Michigan.

SEMPER FIDELIS

Photo Credit (left photo) U.S. Army Photo.
Photo Credit (right photo) Pryde Brown Photographs.

John C. McCormack

"One thing the Marine Corps taught me is that just because you don't know anything about a job, is no reason not only to do it, but to excel at it."

Born: 2 June 1931 in Oak Park, Illinois
Service: United States Marine Corps, Enlisted, Artillery, Drill Instructor
Occupation: President and CEO, XiDEM, Inc.

Born in Illinois and raised in California, "Jack" McCormack was the product of a middle class family where both parents worked (not the norm in the 1930s and 1940s). During high school, Mac used a Triumph motorcycle to commute 30 miles each way to a high school offering agricultural courses. He rebuilt the Triumph for racing in his senior year and after graduation in 1950, he started racing on various dirt and pavement courses. Mac raced under the name of John McDermott since his parents refused to allow his participation in this activity. He led them to believe he prepared the bike and McDermott rode it. This was the first major sign of a person who had a great deal of determination and went to great lengths to achieve his goals.

McCormack joined the Marines in January of 1951 fully expecting to undergo Boot Camp and training and then go to Korea. After Boot Camp in San Diego, Mac was assigned to 105-howitzer training at Camp Del Mar, across from Camp Pendleton in California. He was then assigned to 12th Marines, 3rd Brigade (before it became a Division) under the command of Chesty Puller. Mac was first a gunner on a 105 and then made Battery Mechanic for Charlie Battery – because of his experience in engine mechanics. Battery Mechanic was a cushy job since most repair to the guns is handled by ordinance and the gun crews do much of the rest. Mac's only responsibility was to hand out bore cleaner and waste (cloth cleaning patches) to the gun crews and kneed grease into a few wheel bearings every now and then.

"While I was under going advanced training at Camp Pendleton, I was advised that the Corps wanted me to take tests for entry into Annapolis. While taking the test I rolled my parents' 1950 Buick Roadmaster three times coming out of Tent Camp One. I was going on liberty with five buddies. No one was hurt except me. I had the top part of my left ear cut-off and suffered a few scalp lacerations. While recuperating at the base hospital, I was advised that I could have the ear "fixed" by plastic surgery and was transferred to the Balboa Naval Hospital in San Diego. The attendant delays caused me to miss the rest of the Annapolis test.

"I was assigned to the plastic surgery ward where it took about three weeks to handle the process of fixing the ear. Three months later I was still in the Ward. In fact I was there so long that I had become the "Chief Gurney Pusher" for the main OR. Even the hospital commanding officer, a Navy Captain, knew me as Mac. During my stay in the plastic surgery ward I observed many wounded come back from Korea with some pretty ugly wounds, and watched the efforts of the Navy plastic surgeons in rebuilding those Marines.

After nearly four months orders arrived giving Mac the choice of going to a guard company or becoming a Drill Instructor. Mac chose the later and was transferred to MCRD San Diego. Here he was assigned to Charlie Company, 1st Recruit Training Battalion. These were the days before DI school and before the McClellan incident. Mac served an "apprenticeship" under three different Senior DI's and made Corporal during this time. After three platoons as a Jr. DI, Mac was made Senior DI and eventually made Sergeant.

"Becoming a DI and God to 75 people every 12 weeks was a wonderful, confidence building experience for a young man. It allowed practice of the various skills of leadership. It also taught me the differences in people and the various methods needed to successfully communicate with different personalities and individuals so that they would temporarily become one. The Marine Corps taught me that just because you don't know anything about a job, is no reason not only to do it, but to excel at it.

"The most beneficial lesson the Corps taught me as a Marine was the subservience of self to the welfare of your people and the entity you serve. If you are always first conscious of the welfare of the organization and the people who you work with or who you have responsibility for, you will be successful in accomplishing your goals."

Upon being discharged in 1954, Mac returned to motorcycles. He helped start American Honda Motor Co., and was credited as the "driving spirit" behind its surge to prominence. Mac is usually best remembered for the "You meet the nicest people on a Honda" campaign. Under McCormack's stewardship, American Honda achieved and maintained more than 50% of the then-expanding U.S. motorcycle market.

Mac co-founded the U.S. Suzuki Motor Corporation in 1964 (now American Suzuki), and received a 25% ownership in the U.S. operation. He led this enterprise from "ground zero" to second position in the industry, behind Honda. McCormack is credited with starting the surge in U.S. motorcycle sales that took the industry from a stagnated 50,000 annual new unit sales for the decade of the fifties, to approximately 1,300,000 annual units before the decade of the sixties was over.

In 1967, he founded McCormack International Motors, Inc., which was the first company to bring a wide range of motorized recreational vehicles together under one label (American Eagle). The company was the first to secure a private-label contract with a major Japanese motorcycle manufacturer (Kawasaki). The company established 925 dealers and ten overseas distributorships in less than three years.

Mac was a co-founder of Jacwal Corporation 1971, which successfully originated and distributed motorcycle aftermarket and accessory products for seven years, both domestically and overseas. He was also co-founder of Hirsch Electronics Corporation, which designed and developed access control devices. These systems are now used in the White House, FBI, Pentagon, British Secret Service, Lockheed's Skunk Works, IBM and GM as well as many others. He remains an active shareholder in this company.

Mac's passion for speed slowed down considerably when he established a tourist railroad. In 1985, he co-founded the Napa Valley Railroad and the Napa Valley Wine Train. He prevailed through a legal struggle that went to the California Supreme Court. Mac remained at the Train/Railroad, as CEO, for six years, and left after its success was assured. He is still a shareholder and is on the Board of Directors. The train continues to win four and five stars for its food and is a premier attraction in the Napa Valley.

In 1992, he founded McCormack & McCormack Consulting. In 1995 he was hired by one of McCormack & McCormack's clients as President and COO of Asha Corporation (a publicly traded company on the NASDAQ exchange). In 1998, he became its Chairman and CEO, and he presided over Asha's acquisition of McLaren Engines Inc., located in Livonia, Michigan. Mac retired in April of 1999 as the company announced revenues of $6,000,000 with earnings of 30%, or approximately $0.24 per share. ASHA Corporation changed its name to McLaren Automotive Group in April of 1999.

Mac and his wife, Gerry, went downunder, bought a large ranch and launched a Cow-Calf Operation in New South Wales, Australia. The Cattle Station is located in the northeast corner of New South Wales about 90 miles from the coast. It is a temperate climate about the same as California. They have approximately 1,300 acres with 2-1/2 miles along the Mann River. The property has a full time stream, a well and five springs. They presently run 200 head of hybrid breeders and 176 (at last count) calves. They maintain nine pure bred bulls.

In June of 2000, he returned to the states to head a new automobile company being started by Bob Lutz (Now Vice Chairman of GM and a profiled former Marine). Mac became Chairman & CEO of that company until it was reluctantly suspended due to legal challenges.

Currently Mac is President & CEO of XiDEM, a start-up company involved in intellectual property covering a new type of electric motor and generator for automobiles and wind energy. It has a patented approach to integrate computer technology with electric motor and generator technology to develop a highly efficient product that can be reconfigured in real time to adjust to varying load and speed requirements. This product has a huge market potential in both automotive and industrial applications. Research is currently being conducted on the motor to refine the hardware and software control of the technology.

Mac serves on the boards of the Marine Military Academy, Napa Valley Wine Train, and the McIntire Group. All of his companies, once mature enough to show profits, have been involved in local and national charities focused on the preservation of wildlife and wilderness.

Mac, his wife, Gerry, and his wolf, Yukon, four horses and a mule have a primary residence in Santa Ynez Valley, California. He also spends time in Draper, Utah where XiDEM is located and on the ranch in Australia. He is the proud father of six grown children from a previous marriage: Mike, Clare, Frank, John, Steve, Patricia, ten grandchildren and a stepson, Scott Settle.

SEMPER FIDELIS

RICHARD E. MILLER

"I owe whatever success I've enjoyed in my life to the values and behaviors instilled in me as a Marine."

BORN: 29 August 1946 in Oakland, California
SERVICE: United States Marine Corps, March 1965 – December 1973, Enlisted, Officer
OCCUPATION: Team Leader, Board Member, Credera

"Ric" Miller joined the Marine Corps as an enlisted recruit. In 1966 he was sent to Vietnam serving as an interpreter, and participated in the Marine Corps Combined Action Program. During his first tour he extended twice for two six-month periods. After being selected for OCS Ric returned stateside in 1967 and became a commissioned officer. In 1968 he returned to Vietnam as an infantry officer. He extended his tour for two six-month periods to serve as a platoon commander in the First Force Reconnaissance Company. During Ric's tours in Vietnam he earned and was awarded the Silver Star, Bronze Star w/V, and Navy Commendation w/V.

"Over the course of eight plus years on active duty, three of which were spent in the Republic of Vietnam, you're bound to have a treasure trove of memories. However there were three particular Marines who had a profound impact upon me.

"The first was Corporal Larsen in March of 1965. Corporal Larsen was the junior Drill Instructor for platoon 318 of which I was a member. He had a genius for leadership by example and drove us relentlessly in the pursuit of excellence. From him I learned the importance of living by the core values of courage, commitment, honesty and integrity. He became a much-needed role model for me and I absorbed those values along with the success generating behaviors of self-discipline, teamwork and taking care of my people.

"The second was Major Roger Simmons. As Commanding Officer of the First Force Reconnaissance Company at An Hoa in 1969, Major Simmons was in effect Corporal Larsen reincarnated as a Field Grade Officer. A man of uncompromising integrity and dedication to mission, Major Simmons first assembled and then led a team of unusually spirited and talented Marines. From Major Simmons I gained valuable insight into the challenges of leading the talented as well as the techniques for doing so successfully. That delicate balance required to maintain firm control without stifling creativity and initiative.

"The third was First Lieutenant Peters a Marine CH46 pilot. It was April 12, 1969 and I was leading an eight man recon patrol into NVA controlled territory. We'd taken fire attempting to land in two different landing zones the day before and were trying for a third time to get inserted. Upon exiting the helicopter we took small arms fire and the helicopter, riddled with holes, limped back to An Hoa. Surrounded by a company of NVA soldiers we successfully defended our position for several hours but were running low on ammunition with nightfall only a few hours away. The opinion of the Air Controller overhead in a small plane was that landing a rescue bird was risky to the point of being suicidal. In my opinion the chances of my small team making it through the night were slim at best. First Lieutenant Peters volunteered to take the risk; he had gotten to know us personally and understood the situation. Fearlessly he landed his helicopter and patiently waited while we boarded. While we boarded the bird was hit 38 times, miraculously nobody was seriously injured and we were extracted safely. From First Lieutenant Peters I witnessed the lengths to which Marines will go to help other Marines and possibly, I received the gift of continued life. First Lieutenant Peters was subsequently killed while in the process of helping other Marines."

Ric returned stateside in December 1969 and served as a Recon Company Commander, Recon Battalion Commander, and Infantry Company Commander. He left the Marine Corps in December 1973.

In May 1974, Ric obtained his B.A. degree in business from Chapman College and went to work for Michelin Tire Corporation in technical sales and service. In 1976, Ric went to work for Dunlop Tire and quickly assumed new responsibilities and rose to the rank of Company Senior Vice President. While serving in that capacity he also served as CEO of two Dunlop subsidiary companies. Ric stayed with Dunlop until 1993 when the entrepreneurial bug bit him.

In April 1993, Ric led the buyout of regional tire retailer, Dunn Tire Corporation. He assumed the role of CEO and transitioned the company from a family owned business to one professionally managed. He increased revenues from 17 million to 26 million. In 1997, he stepped down as CEO, but still retained an equity position in the company.

In October 1997, Ric was recruited by Pirelli Tire as CEO for North American operations. He worked to reduce their losses, conserve cash, and improve their relations with the unionized work force to enable them to maintain a presence in the U.S. market. Pirelli's manufacturing plant had sales of $120 million and 1,053 employees. In November 1998, Ric had achieved his goals including generating enough goodwill with the union to get a contract favorably ratified, so he took an early retirement and moved to Florida.

After four years of playing with his new toys in the ocean, Ric joined Credera, an IT Solutions and Services Company located in Washington, D.C. Credera works to implement systems integration, workflow automation and document management systems for its clients. As a shareholder, board member and team leader, he is working to achieve and manage this high growth potential endeavor.

Ric continues to serve the Marine Corps as a guest speaker at the DI School at Marine Corps Recruit Depot in San Diego as well as to NROTC and Naval Academy Midshipmen.

Ric and his wife, Kathy, have their permanent residence on North Captiva Island, Florida. They have two sons and two grandsons. Kathy is looking forward to the first granddaughter.

SEMPER FIDELIS

Zell Bryan Miller

"Everything that has happened to me, all of my success, has been at least an indirect product of my experience in the Marines."

Born: 24 February 1932 in Young Harris, Georgia
Service: United States Marine Corps, 1953 – 1956, Enlisted
Occupation: United States Senator from Georgia

Zell Miller's military experience began in Marine Corps boot camp in 1953.

"Our platoon was a microcosm of the entire United States of America, a little domestic melting pot housed in one crowded Quonset hut. We were all in it together, and it did not take us long to get over our mutual suspicions of each other and realize we were all going to swim, perish or survive together. If we had any doubts of that fact, the Drill Instructor dispelled them with his little welcoming speech. 'You people are whaleshit,' he bellowed, 'and it's the lowest thing on earth; it's the bottom of the ocean. If any one of you screws up, all of you will pay the same price for that one man's failure. When I speak, you will function as a team. You are all in this as a team. Do you understand?'

"At that particular time in 1953, not a one of us probably had any notion of who Dr. Martin Luther King, Jr. was. But even if we could not articulate the thought then, we would come to understand during the next twelve weeks what Dr. King meant when he later declared, 'We must live together as brothers or perish together as fools.'

"Nowhere on earth during that three-month period were there 74 more different individuals who learned so quickly how to suffer and survive together as brothers – sometimes admittedly, scared-to-death brothers. Platoon 311 was our world, and we became painfully aware that we would either endure its rigors collectively or be booted out of its ranks individually."

As an enlisted Marine, Miller's military occupations included artilleryman and combat correspondent.

He credits his USMC experience as the turning point of his life. Upon his discharge in 1956, Zell Miller returned to Georgia with his new wife, Shirley. At the University of Georgia he completed two history degrees and then stayed on teaching history.

Miller's public service career has spanned more than four decades. Beginning in 1959, he served as mayor of Young Harris, Georgia; then, a Georgia State Senator; Georgia's Lieutenant Governor; Georgia Governor; and now, United States Senator from Georgia. He was called the most popular governor in America by the *Washington Post*, and *Governing Magazine* named him Governor of the Year in 1998.

Currently, Senator Miller prides himself on representing all Georgians to the best of his ability and no single party. He bases every decision, every vote, on what's best for all of Georgia, even when it puts him at odds with his party in Washington. His term ends in 2004, at which time he is planning to retire giving him the opportunity and time to enjoy his family, friends and dogs.

Zell Miller, a man of many interests and accomplishments, has authored five books including, *Corps Values: Everything You Need To Know I Learned in the Marines*. He taught at Emory University, the University of Georgia and Young Harris College and has served several corporate boards.

His charitable interests are in education, religion and animals. He donates regularly to Young Harris College (his beloved alma mater and where his mother and father taught), to his Methodist Church, and to his local Humane Society.

Zell Miller and his wife, Shirley, have two sons, four grandchildren, four great-grandchildren, and two yellow Labrador Retrievers. The family resides in Georgia.

SEMPER FIDELIS

Carolyn A. (Howard) Minerich

"I always make sure my 'troops' are fed, they have all the tools they need to do their jobs, go to the dentist every six months, and I never forget to thank them for a job well done."

Born: 6 August 1952 in Mobile, Alabama
Service: United States Marine Corps, 1973 – 1978, Officer
Occupation: President, Carmin Industries

Carolyn has a degree in journalism and once dreamed of becoming an FBI agent, joining the Marine Corps as a stepping stone. Her first assignment was Officer in Charge of the Training Support Center, MCRD San Diego then on to Admin School. She became an Administration Officer and later Adjutant at MCAS(H) Santa Ana, California.

"I will never forget a very tall Major with a booming voice who made me write out the word A-S-S-U-M-E. Do I use the same 'mini-lecture' on young people today? You bet I do!!!"

Carolyn really liked the Corps and stayed in until she met and married a Marine pilot. They both left the Corps and Carolyn stayed at home with their two children. With an interest in gifted education, she worked with her own children and as support staff in elementary schools.

The family followed her husband's career making several moves until 1994, when they ended up in Jacksonville, Alabama. Without a job and with her children nearly grown, Carolyn was at loose ends. Her husband, Jon, had heard about a new technology and Carolyn headed to the library to research it.

Carolyn had no experience, no customers and no money, but the Marine Corps had taught her "not to think twice about doing things that had never been done or seen before." The Jacksonville Small Business Development Center, an SBA resource partner, helped her "put it all together" and she got a great deal of encouragement from the SBA. Finally in 1996, she launched Carmin Industries, a precision waterjet cutting and metal fabrication service.

At first Carolyn was Carmin Industries. She ran the machines, unloaded trucks and prepared products for shipment. Before long she had jobs for Estee

Lauder and Clinique, Lord & Taylor, Giorgio Armani, Neiman Marcus, Universal Studios, the Smithsonian Institute and the U.S. Air Force. They've even cut parts for the Patriot and Sabre missile systems and the Abrams tank.

The business grew quickly due to the enthusiasm Carolyn has for what she and her team do, and their willingness to tackle jobs that no one else will. The company's slogan is, "If you can dream it, we can cut it."

"Carmin Industries is simply a job shop where we cut things with high pressure water. Our company projects range from unique marble and granite inlaid floors to custom architectural signage to lots of military metal parts! Metal fabrication is the major portion of our business. Carmin's products primarily involve cutting, welding, painting and finish work. Our quality, safety, and environmental standards have been inspected by NASA, Marshall Space Flight Center. We are currently the only waterjet company certified for work at MSFC, Huntsville, Alabama.

"In 2002, we were honored by President Bush and the Small Business Administration as Alabama's Small Business of the Year. In 1999, we were selected for the Sam Walton Business Leadership Award. In 2003, I was again honored by President Bush, this time as one of America's Top 17 Women Entrepreneurs. This selection and honor coincided with the Small Business Administration's 50th Anniversary Celebration.

"Just as the Marine Corps taught me all those years ago, I always make sure my 'troops' are fed, they have all the tools they need to do their jobs, go to the dentist every six months, and I never forget to thank them for a job well done!

"As President of Carmin Industries, I am responsible for 22 employees. Since 1997, our first full year of production, the company has seen a 350 percent increase in sales and has an enviable client list. This year our company's growth area will be in defense related parts. In 2002, our company was at the $1,000,000 mark. It is my goal in the next year to triple our sales dollars!

"I am a believer in education! Our small company does everything it can to promote 'THE WORLD OF TECHNOLOGY' to young students, from plant tours to donations of scrap metal to local schools for welding classes. I serve on the Board of Directors of the Calhoun County Area Vocational Center, and have served the Chamber of Commerce and the Jacksonville Area Business Council."

Carolyn, who is known for her commitment to children and education in the community, always includes technology students in her workforce. "We want kids to be excited about technology, or ten years down the road, we won't have the skilled people we need to do this kind of work!"

The Minerich's reside in Jacksonville, Alabama a few hours drive from Mobile where Carolyn's family has lived since the 1600s.

SEMPER FIDELIS

Photo Credit (right photo) Studio One Photography, Inc.

Aaron Malachi "Mal" Mixon, III

"The Marine Corps taught me about tenacity, not giving up regardless of the obstacles."

Born: 22 May 1940 in Spiro, Oklahoma
Service: United States Marine Corps, 1962 – 1966, Artillery Officer
Occupation: Chairman & CEO, Invacare Corporation

"Mal" Mixon grew up in the small Oklahoma town of Spiro located 20 miles west of Fort Smith, Arkansas. In high school he was active in sports and played on winning football, baseball and basketball teams. His father, wanting to provide the best that he could for his son, filled out an application for Mal to attend Harvard College. Mal was accepted and with the help of scholarships (including NROTC), loans and jobs, he earned a B.S. degree in Physical Sciences. While attending Harvard, Mal met his wife, Barbara Weber, who was a Wellesley College student. After graduation, Mal was commissioned a 2nd Lieutenant and left for Quantico, Virginia.

"While in the Officer's Training program, we had a First Sergeant who used the 'F' word frequently and with flexibility as a noun, pronoun, verb, adjective or preposition which provided specific emphasis on what he had to say. While teaching us bayonet drills, the cleaned up version of what he explained to us was 'you first smash the enemy with the rifle butt, a slash with the bayonet, followed by a thrust.' His words were 'if you fail to get him on one of these three movements, drop your weapon and get out of there because you have a mean S.O.B. on your hands.'

"I learned management while at Harvard, but the Marine Corps taught me about leadership. Real leadership develops teamwork and motivation.

"After training, I was sent to Hawaii prior to being shipped to Vietnam. While there I had a Commanding Officer (CO) who made it mandatory for his lieutenants to join him at 'happy hour' every Friday. One day while seated at the bar I became excited during a conversation and using broad arm movements to emphasize my point and accidentally knocked over about three or four drinks. The next thing I know the officer in charge of the Officer's Club was alongside me seeking my name so that he could report me to my CO. Then I heard the voice, 'well you won't have to look very far – that's me.' My CO paid for the broken glasses and all was forgiven.

"I landed at Chu Lai, Vietnam in 1965 with the 1st Marine Brigade, 3/12. Once we were settled in, whenever possible we established a makeshift happy hour on Fridays with hors d'oeuvres. We had our families and loved ones ship us canned food and anything edible that would survive the postal journey. One day I had just returned from three hours of flight time as an artillery observer and was in dire need of a cold beverage and something to put in my stomach. I was given a cold beer and some meatballs that had just arrived from another Marine's wife. She was Mexican and knew the true meaning of hot and spicy. I ate one meatball and had a mouth on fire with increased perspiration for the next half an hour. They had gotten me. Being the good Marine that I was, I went out to share this treat with others. I passed the meatballs out and burned a few mouths myself that day. Then I came to a Marine who just said thank you, that was good, can I have another? Needless to say, he was from Texas."

After leaving the Marine Corps in 1966, Mal moved to his wife's hometown of Cleveland, Ohio. His first job was with Harris Corporation in finance, but soon he rotated into sales and eventually became their director of marketing.

Mal left Harris and worked for two small local companies prior to moving into the medical products field and accepted a sales position with Ohio-Nuclear, a subsidiary of Technicare Corporation. Mal excelled in the sales and marketing field and became a vice president.

In the late 1970s, Technicare began exiting non-essential businesses units in order to increase shareholder value and eventually sold out to Johnson & Johnson, Inc. One of the business units available for sale was a small wheelchair manufacturing subsidiary located in Elyria, Ohio. Mal saw the future value of this unit and made an offer to purchase it. This was a tough time to go out and raise capital, but being a former Marine, he did the impossible. Mal put together a $7.8 million financial package. Ten thousand was his own savings, forty thousand borrowed from friends and a one hundred thousand dollar loan from the company bought his 15% stake in the common stock. He raised $1.5 million in equity financing, sold and leased back the principal manufacturing facility for $2 million, and obtained a $4.3 million asset based loan at prime plus three, which within 6 months amounted to an incredible 26 percent annual rate.

Once the transaction was complete, Mal took stock of the company, its people and the market. They were in a stagnant position in a growing market with no innovations in the pipeline, a depressed sales team, and offshore competition moving in. However, Mal saw nothing but unlimited opportunity. When he led the leveraged buyout in 1979, sales were $19 million, but in 24 months, annual sales had climbed to $38 million. Through new product innovation, a dedicated and highly motivated sales force and strategic acquisitions, Invacare today has sales exceeding one billion dollars annually. Today Invacare has a 25 percent worldwide market share of their industry. The same opportunities abound that Mal first saw 20 plus years ago.

In addition to Invacare, Mal has been a prominent investor and mentor to many other Northern Ohio high growth companies including STERIS, a company that developed a unique process for sterilizing medical equipment and Royal Appliance Manufacturing makers of the Dirt Devil vacuum cleaners. Both of these companies, along with Invacare, went public.

Mal is also a founding partner in MCM Capital Corporation, a leveraged buyout firm focused on buying undervalued small and medium sized businesses in Northern Ohio.

Mal and his wife, Barbara, are active, prominent philanthropic citizens who have made a difference in the lives of many Northern Ohio residents. Through their personal and Corporate donations, almost every charity in the area has benefited from their generosity. The Mixons have made substantial contributions to the Marine Corps Heritage Foundation, Weatherhead School of Management, Harvard College, The Cleveland Clinic Foundation, and the Cleveland Institute of Music among others. In 1995, Mal was named "Outstanding Philanthropist of the Year" by the Greater Cleveland Chapter of the National Society of Fund Raising Executives.

Mal is an active Board Member of the Marine Corps Heritage Foundation, several public Corporations and is the Chairman of the Board of Trustees of The Cleveland Clinic Foundation and the Cleveland Institute of Music.

Mal and his wife, Barbara, live in Hunting Valley, Ohio. They have two children and four grandchildren.

SEMPER FIDELIS

THOMAS G. MURDOUGH, JR.

"Leaving college and entering the Marine Corps provided me with a huge dose of discipline and life style change that was far different from the previous four years of my young life."

BORN: 4 February 1939 in Tulsa, Oklahoma
SERVICE: United States Marine Corps, 1961 – 1965, Infantry/Counter Intelligence Officer
OCCUPATION: Chairman, CEO, Founder, The Step2 Company

Tom was born in Tulsa, Oklahoma, and graduated from high school in Evanston, Illinois. After graduation he attended the University of Virginia and earned a B.A. in 1961. He then made the decision to join the Marines prior to entering the workforce. He enlisted in the OCC program and went to Quantico, Virginia for training. After graduation, Tom was stationed at Camp Pendleton, California as an Infantry Platoon Leader.

"In the fall of 1962, the Cuban Missile Crisis occurred. President Kennedy immediately had a battalion of Marines moved to Guantanamo Bay, Cuba. Meanwhile a brigade of Marines and all of their tanks, combat weapons and equipment was loaded onto 29 naval ships. The day before our ships and men were to deploy, I was called into headquarters and informed that I was being removed from my unit. Since I was fluent in Spanish, I was being assigned as the Officer in Charge of duties of a 26-man interrogation/translator team. I was then dispatched with my new troops aboard the flotilla. The entire fleet passed through the Panama Canal and it took about ten days before we reached the Southern edge of Cuba."

"We arrived, prepared our weapons, received our ammo and were ready for the invasion. That order never came. Russia and Cuba had backed down and agreed to remove the missiles."

After Cuba, Tom returned to Camp Pendleton and was sent for counterintelligence training, finishing his tour with a CT unit.

After leaving the Marines in 1965, he joined the Wilson Sporting Goods Company as a salesman and was promoted to Vice President of Marketing for Wonder Products, a division of Wilson, in 1968. Wonder Products held the patent for, and manufactured, an American toy icon – the spring hobby riding horse that was attached to a metal frame. This gave Tom his first exposure to the toy market.

During his time at Wilson, Tom became aware of a new plastic molding process that he believed had wide applications in the toy industry. That process was called rotational molding. It allowed for the manufacture of large, thick-walled hollow plastic products and Tom envisioned the immediate weight, cost and consumer safety benefits this manufacturing process would provide for the toy market.

In 1970, Tom moved to the Akron area and founded The Little Tikes Company in a barn with nine employees. In 1984, he sold The Little Tikes Company to Rubbermaid as a wholly owned subsidiary and continued as its president and general manager until September 1, 1989. The company had grown to be one of the top toy manufacturers worldwide, with sales in 1989 of over $270 million.

In 1991, Tom re-entered the rotational molding market with the formation of his new company, The Step2 Company. The privately held company began operations in 1991 with 5 employees, grew to approximately 500 employees at the end of 1993, and presently has four manufacturing facilities and more than 800 full-time employees. The Step2 Company has a strong presence and brand identity in the toy and home & garden markets and is dedicated to going "A Step Beyond" in serving the consumer, its employees and the community. Current annual sales are approximately $100 million.

Like the company he heads, Tom has a strong commitment to serving his community. He is a founding member of the Marine Corps Heritage Foundation. He currently serves on the Board of Directors of the Baker McMillen Company in Stow, Ohio and is a former director of Universal Electronics Inc. and The Davey Tree Expert Company in Kent, Ohio. He is a former trustee of The Western Reserve Academy in Hudson, Ohio, the Akron Children's Hospital Foundation, and the Board of Managers of the University of Virginia (1991 – 1997). He is involved in many other church and community-related organizations.

Tom and his wife, Joy, live in Hudson, Ohio where they have raised four grown sons: Thomas, III, Marshall, Jody, and Peter.

SEMPER FIDELIS

Carol A. Mutter

"The youth of our nation are our future."

Born: 17 December 1945 in Greeley, Colorado
Service: United States Marine Corps, 1966 – 1999, Officer
Occupation: Business Consultant

Carol Mutter graduated from the University of Northern Colorado with a B.A. in Mathematics Education. She went to Officers' Candidate School in 1966 and was commissioned in 1967. During her 31 plus year Marine Corps career, she held various positions in logistics, data processing, financial management, personnel administration, and research, development and acquisition. Along the way she earned an M.A. in National Security and Strategic Studies from the Naval War College and has an M.S. degree. Carol also attended the Amphibious Warfare School and the Marine Corps Command and Staff College.

Capitalizing on her knowledge and expertise in both data processing and financial management, General Mutter was assigned as program manager for the development of new Marine Corps automated pay and personnel systems for active duty, retired and reserve Marines.

Next she joined the U.S. Space Command becoming the Division Chief responsible for the operation of the Commander in Chief's Command Center.

In 1990, General Mutter was assigned to the 3rd Marine Expeditionary Force in Okinawa, Japan as the Assistant Chief of Staff, Comptroller for both 3rd MEF and 3rd Marine Division. In 1991, she assumed duties as Deputy Commanding General, Marine Corps Systems Command and the Program Manager for Marine Air Ground Task Force Command and Control, Quantico, Virginia. She returned to Okinawa to command 3rd Force Service Support Group, U.S. Marine Forces, Pacific. She then served two years as the Commanding General of the Marine Corps Systems Command before being promoted to Lieutenant General when she became the USMC Deputy Chief of Staff for Manpower and Reserve Affairs.

Her medals and decorations include: the Distinguished Service Medal, Defense Superior Service Medal, National Defense Service Medal with Bronze Star, and the Sea Service Deployment Ribbon with four Bronze Stars.

"My entire tour as Commanding General of 3rd Force Service Support Group (1992 – 1994) was very special – from the discussion with then Commandant, General Mundy, about my desires to be considered for command of a major deployable unit, to my end-of-tour change of command while on a field exercise. I felt very keenly the responsibility to ensure all members of the command were able to effectively accomplish their mission safely in a deployed, operational environment. With the support of the other commanders in the Marine Expeditionary Force, the help of the staff and the hard work of all those in the group, we were able to deploy detachments in support of many successful operations including Sea Angel (Bangladesh) and Provide Relief (Somalia)."

General Carol Mutter achieved many firsts during her military career:

- She was the first woman to be qualified as Command Center Crew Commander/Space Director at U.S. Space Command.
- She was the first woman of General/Flag rank to command a major deployable tactical command.
- She was the first woman Marine Major General, and senior woman on active duty in all the services at that time.
- She was the first woman nominated by the President of the U.S. for three-star rank.

Upon her discharge she moved to Indiana and "recharged her batteries." Now as a consultant for contractors seeking to do business with the Department of Defense and other government agencies, she has provided "red team" and "black hat" advice on bids resulting in successful multi-million dollar contracts and more widely useful and operationally effective military equipment. She also has a contract that has been renewed for the third year to provide a two-day workshop to military chaplains on "Military Operations – How Religion, Culture & Other Factors Influence the Professional Religious Ministry of Chaplains."

Carol Mutter is currently a Senior Fellow at the Joint Forces Staff College, as well as the National President of the Women Marines Association. She serves as the Chair of the Defense Advisory Committee on Women in the Services. She's on the National Advisory Council of the Alliance for National Defense, on the National Academy of Sciences Committee on American Youth and Military Recruiting, and on the Advisory Boards for the Indiana Council on Worlds Affairs and the local VA Medical Center.

Carol and her husband whom she met and married in the Marine Corps support the youth of this nation because "they are our future." They have worked with the local Girl Scouts and as tutors at a local elementary school. They also provide leadership and ethics classes to 11 – 15 year old minority students every July at a summer enrichment camp in Piney Woods, Mississippi (*www.pineywoods.org*). Their financial support goes to the same organizations, as well as to military veterans groups (*www.womenmarines.org*) and The Young Marines (*www.theyoungmarines.org*).

Carol's non-military awards include the American Leadership Award from the state of Colorado, the 1992 Trail Blazer Award from The University of Northern Colorado, the Living Legacy Patriot Award from the Women's International Center and the Margaret Cochran Corbin Award from the Daughters of the American Revolution. In addition, she has two honorary doctorate degrees – one from the University of Northern Colorado and one from Salve Regina.

Obviously, education, leadership, vision, and daring epitomize the life and career of this truly remarkable person.

SEMPER FIDELIS

WARNER A. "DREW" MYERS

"The echoes of war can sound for decades and there is absolutely nothing we can do to silence them."

BORN: 22 August 1964 in Akron, Ohio
SERVICE: United States Marine Corps 1986 – 1993, Artillery Officer
OCCUPATION: President, RecruitMilitary, LLC; President, Recruit Marines

Drew graduated from high school in Hobart, Indiana in 1982 and in 1986 received his B.A. in Political Science from Indiana University. Upon graduating from IU, he was commissioned a second lieutenant in the Marine Corps. He graduated from Marine Corps Basic School in the top five percent of his class, and from the Artillery Officer's Class in the top 10 percent. Drew served as a platoon commander and later as an executive officer in charge of a 150-man unit in assignments at Camp Pendleton and during two different deployments to the Far East.

After his artillery tour, Drew was assigned to recruiting duty in Cincinnati. As an executive officer he supervised 40 recruiters. He planned and executed recruiting programs in 414 high schools in the attainment of 1,200 enlistments. Over three years, Drew ranked first among nine peers in the Eastern United States on numerous evaluations. He received the Navy Achievement Medal, the Navy Commendation Medal, and the Honorable Order of St. Barbara.

"As an artillery officer in Okinawa, I had the responsibility of negotiating with local inhabitants concerning the times we would use a firing range very near their village. The villagers were in no physical danger. Our howitzers were oriented so that we could not strike the village, and the range was carefully patrolled. But our firing clearly distressed the villagers. We did much of our firing during the night, and our rounds would shake the ground of the village. Even so, the villagers had almost no choice; the negotiations were very definitely one-sided. I remember the sad expression in the eyes of one particular village elder as he 'contemplated, discussed, and accepted' one of my proposals. He could well have been three times my age – I was in my mid-20s at the time. I felt respect for this gentleman, and at the same time I understood fully that I was jamming my proposals down his throat.

"I had never been in this kind of a situation. But long before this time, my education and training, as well as my own sense of justice, had led me to an understanding of the flow of historical events that had placed American military might on this island and was keeping it there. I knew that we had arrived in a just cause and after much bloodshed. I recognized that, as long as we held the line, there was hope for a better world. The activities of my artillery unit were part of holding the line and so, even as I tried to treat the old gentleman with kindness, I carried out my negotiating assignment with no mental reservation.

"I left the Marines as a Captain in 1993, joining a military-to-civilian recruiting company that is now one of my main competitors. I opened the company's office in Cincinnati and, as an account executive, I was the company's top producer among nine sales professionals producing 25% of the firm's gross revenues. In 1994, I joined Carew International, a Cincinnati firm that counsels the sales staffs of many of the nations largest Corporations on how to improve their performance. I was promoted from inside manager to national account manager to vice president of sales in just over two years, and in 1998, became senior vice president. Also in 1998, the Carew organization and I established a military-to-civilian recruiting operation, now known as RecruitMilitary, within the company. In 1999, while functioning as senior vice president of Carew International and president of the recruiting company, I received an MBA from Xavier University. I left the Carew firm in 2000 to join Perot Investments, reporting directly to Ross Perot. I served as vice president of business development for a project to explore the viability of an e-commerce business serving the military audience. Also in 2000, I became the sole owner of RecruitMilitary. In 2001, I completed my assignment with the Perot organization and began to devote all my efforts to RecruitMilitary. In 2003, I founded a branch–specific operation called RecruitMarines.com. This is the only recruiting Website built exclusively for transitioning and veteran Marines."

RecruitMilitary has grown every year. The field of military-to-civilian recruiting is populated with many companies, and the business is highly competitive. It is no secret that they have placed candidates with some of the best-known firms in the world, including Coca-Cola, Ford, General Electric, General Motors, CSX, Bally Total Fitness, and Merck. RecruitMilitary is frequently cited in magazine and newspaper articles dealing with the efforts of military veterans to find civilian employment.

Drew's business has three aspects: (1) working with candidates, (2) working with Corporate clients, and (3) information management. He supervises all operations and does a great deal of client work. Much of his supervisory work involves gathering information and suggestions from his staff. As in the military, the lines of command are clear, but his doors are always wide open for ideas that will help his company grow.

"RecruitMilitary is the only nationwide, full-service firm engaged in the business of military-to-civilian recruiting — finding civilian jobs for men and women who are leaving the armed forces. We are nationwide, rather than a combination of regional operations, in that we will match any job candidate with a job at any location in the United States, subject to the candidate's own preference. Our full-service approach is analogous to the strategy of the modern armed forces of the United States. We have a carefully defined mission: To facilitate the flow of employment information between specific job candidates and the specific firms that make up Corporate America. To accomplish this mission, we use a full range of tools and tactics. For example, a company can post jobs on our website for our candidates to view, buy a subscription entitling it to view information on our registered candidates, or use our contingency search service in which we do all the searching and screening of candidates for each job opening, then present our selected candidates for interviews."

RecruitMilitary contributed to the Pentagon funds established after 9/11 as well as to the police and firefighter funds established during the same time period.

Drew is married to a former high school classmate, Kim Stookey, who is a forensic psychologist. They have two children and reside in the Cincinnati area.

SEMPER FIDELIS

Jim Northrup

"The Marine Corps prepared me for the rest of my life."

Born: 28 April 1943 in Cloquet, Minnesota
Service: United States Marine Corps, 1961 – 1966, Enlisted, Infantry
Occupation: Author, Playwright, Poet, Actor

Jim spent the last 13 months of his enlistment with the Flaming "I," India Company, 3rd Battalion, 9th Marines, 3rd Marine Division in Vietnam.

When in combat, he learned "... the Marine Corps takes over. Breathe, Relax, Aim, Slack, Squeeze. The shooting is over in 5 seconds, the shakes are over in a half-hour, the memories are never over. The Marine Corps taught me about courage, about how to accomplish the mission even when scared. I was proud to serve as a warrior, a grunt in the Vietnam War."

Jim entered boot camp in California in 1961, then in 1962 went to Cuba with the 1st Marine Division during the Cuban Missile Crisis. Once the crises was diffused and he was rotated out, he went on a 13 month Wespac cruise. Upon returning he worked as an MP at Barstow, California until being sent to Vietnam as a Corporal where he joined a rifle company already there.

When discharged in September 1966, Jim started finding his career as a writer and actor.

"I have been a deputy sheriff, a city cop, a public defender investigator, ironworker, bingo caller, construction worker, editor and writer.

"I used to be known as a bullshitter but that didn't pay anything, so I called myself a storyteller, a little better, a little more prestige but it still didn't pay anything. I became a writer, a freelance writer. At first it was more free than lance, but I eventually started getting money for my words. When I became an author and playwright I could charge consultant's fees."

Jim has been a free lance writer for 18 years and has won various writing awards. He has two published books (so far): *Walking the Rez Road* and *Rez Road Follies*. Both are still in print. PBS is currently featuring his video *Jim Northrup: With Reservations*, and Jim has a newspaper column *Fond du Lac Follies* that has been in print for more than 14 years.

Jim is Anishenaabe from the Fond du Lac Band of Lake Superior Chippewa. The Ojibwe language is once again being used on his reservation and taught in their schools, starting with Head Start and continuing into the Reservation's Tribal and Community College. Ojibwe was once outlawed. Here is how Jim says his name in English and Ojibwe, his identity, his clan, where he is from, when he was born, and where he was born.

> Jim Northrup indizhinikaz zhaaaganashiimong (Jim Northrup is my name in the English Language). Chibenesi indigoo Ojibwemong (I am called Chibenesi in Ojibwe). Anishinaabe endow (I am Anishinaabe). Makwa niin nindoodem (My clan is bear). Naagaajiwanaang niin indoonjiba (I am from the Fond du Lac Reservation). Date of Birth: Ishkigamizige-giizis o'apii ningi dibishka (I was born in the sap boiling moon) Ishkigamizige-giizis niizhtana ashi ishwaaswi, ashi-zhaangaswi nimidana niswi (April 28, 1943). Place of birth: Mookomaanininingaming (Cloquet, Minnesota).

Jim's reservation now has two casinos and the tribe is no longer living in poverty. And although Jim participates in many charity functions, he states, "I don't know if it is charity or not, but it is my relatives who get most of my charitable dollars."

Jim and his wife, Patricia, have a blended family of nine children and numerous grandchildren. Living on the Fond du Lac Reservation in Northern Minnesota, they live their lives with the seasons.

SEMPER FIDELIS

Photo Credit (right photo) Media Mike Hazard.

William J. Peters

"I strongly believe that my Marine Corps experience taught me the leadership skills necessary to run an international ministry that is active on several different continents."

Born: 18 April 1945 in Livermore, California
Service: 1968 – 1971 Reconnaissance Officer
Occupation: Minister, President of Angel Fire Ministries International

Bill Peters was born and raised 40 miles east of San Francisco in the Livermore Valley. He attended San Francisco State University in the late sixties, where he was a star linebacker for their Far Western Conference championship football team. In 1967, Peters joined the San Francisco State football coaching staff and helped the nationally ranked team capture a post-season bowl bid.

"My father's advice to me two weeks before his untimely death in August of 1968, and just before I reported for active duty as a Marine Corps 2nd Lieutenant, set the course for my life. He pulled me aside privately and cautioned me saying, 'Don't forget God and don't forget your family.'"

Bill was commissioned in the Marines via Officer Candidate School. After completing the Basic School at Quantico, Virginia, in 1969, he was assigned to Vietnam as a Force Recon platoon commander, where he conducted 23 long-range patrols in enemy-controlled territory. His personal awards include a Silver Star, two Bronze Stars with combat V (for valor), and a Purple Heart.

In addition to a B.A. degree from San Francisco State University, Bill has a California Lifetime Credential in education, a masters of divinity degree, and a Ph.D. in psychology.

Bill has chronicled the valor of the men he served with in Vietnam in a very popular book he authored called *First Force Recon Company/Sunrise at Midnight* that was published by Random House Publishing in 1999. Bill believes there were seven days that changed his life during his year tour as a

Marine Corps combat officer. They were spent with Marine 1st Lieutenant Ric Miller and six other recon team members. Beginning on April 12 through April 18, 1969, he and Miller survived an experience that few Marines live to talk about. On April 12, Miller, Peters and their recon team had to be extracted off Hill 551 after a fierce three hour fire fight against about 200 North Vietnamese Army soldiers. The team's insert helicopter took more than thirty hits as it landed on 551. The extract helicopter also took an equal number of hits while the pilot also named, Bill Peters, patiently waited for the team to board while a hail of enemy fire raked the vulnerable chopper.

"Late the following day on April 13, our combined team was once again inserted into the same area about a thousand meters from Hill 551. As we exited the chopper we noticed our small landing zone was ringed with unmanned enemy bunkers and slip trenches. Moving swiftly into a tree line at the south end of the landing zone we observed a 14-man North Vietnamese Army squad run past us and take up positions in the bunkers and slip trenches. From April 13th until the early morning hours of April 17, 1969, we laid on our bellies in that tree line as hundreds of enemy soldiers passed by on a high-speed trail located 40 feet from our position. The team had managed to get into the base area of a regimental sized unit of the North Vietnamese Army. The enemy, not knowing our Marine Recon team was in the midst of them, merely went about business as usual. Although the enemy soldiers manned the landing zone and a trail monitor stood daily just 40 feet from our hiding place, the enemy soldiers failed to check out the tree line. Living among the enemy was an interesting and at times terrifying experience. Women walked by camouflaged Marines and bathed in the creek just below our position. The team was under strict discipline and did not eat for three days. A squealing pig tied on a pole and carried by two enemy soldiers caused the team to nearly open fire in the direction of animal's ear piercing protest. A dead tree blew over nearly falling in the middle of our position. Day and night long columns of enemy soldiers moved by on the high-speed trail that was just a few feet from eight Recon Marines. During the day we had the enemy trail monitor directing the long columns of soldiers to worry about, and at night we prayed someone wouldn't wander into the tree line for a head call.

"Finally on April 17, one day before my 24th birthday, at daylight the team stood to their feet for the first time in four days. Following orders from me, the team moved on a compass heading 200 meters to a bomb crater on the edge of the high-speed trail that the enemy had been using. Precisely at 6:00 a.m., while barely concealed in the crater, we had our quiet early morning sunrise shattered by the engine blasts of two Phantom jets. The planes screamed over our position and delivered thousand pound bombs on the tree line from which we had just escaped. The enemy fell for the diversion provided by the bombing. We could hear the enemy shouting orders as they moved to cover the landing zone adjacent to the tree line. They were probably expecting a recon team insertion. The diversion lasted long enough to give a CH-46 helicopter time to hover above our recon team and lower a 140 ft. cable ladder into the bomb crater. Our eight-man team climbed onto the ladder and was pulled trapeze style out of the enemy's grasp. The jungle beneath us, as we were suspended on the ladder, was aglow with the protective fire from the Huey gun birds. Within an hour, several B-52 bombers dropped a devastating amount of ordinance on the enemy base area. Force Recon team leader Lt. Wayne Rolling, (Major General Wayne Rolling, USMC, retired), counted nine 50 caliber machine gun positions that opened up on the helicopter that was trying to insert his recon team for a bomb damage assessment of the area after the B-52 run. Truly, our team had been delivered from the mouth of the lion. On April 18, just seven days after the beginning of the ordeal, I celebrated my 24th birthday with the team on China Beach. After those seven days, I ran 20 more long range patrols as a Force Recon team leader."

In 1971, Bill dedicated his life to Jesus Christ, left a promising Marine Corps career behind and went into training for the ministry. He states, "The miracles of those seven days in April 1969 and my father's last words to me not to forget God, got me thinking about why I was put on this earth." He was ordained in 1980. Bill and his wife, Barbara, co-founded Angel Fire Ministries International (*www.angelfire.com*), a 501 C-3 non-profit Corporation in 1990. Angel Fire's slogan is, "Winning the hearts and minds of the people of the nations with the love of Jesus Christ." Bill believes very strongly that helping disadvantaged people in nations at risk is key to winning the war on terrorism. Angel Fire has about 40 ordained ministers worldwide. In the United States, the ministry is busy planting new churches and training pastors to oversee them. Six such plantings are located in Southern California.

Angel Fire is also very active on the continent of Africa. In South Africa alone the ministry is presently completing ten daycare/church structures with a goal of building 100 of these structures in the poorest black townships of that nation. Angel Fire's overall goal is to build such structures in any nation that is open to their assistance. The Angel daycare centers allow mothers a safe place for their children while they work to help support their families. Funds for the project are raised from the private sector allowing benefactors to receive a tax deduction for their contributions to Angel Fire.

Barbara, a trained counselor, is also an accomplished and recorded gospel singer. The Peters are sought after as speakers for national and international Christian conferences. Bill strongly believes that his Marine Corps experience taught him the leadership skills necessary to run an international ministry that is active on several different continents. He maintains a close relationship with the men with whom he served in the First Force Recon Company. Bill is frequently asked to share his experiences with Marine units based in Southern California.

Bill lives in Southern California with his wife, Barbara, and their two sons, Tony and Paul.

SEMPER FIDELIS

QUANG X. PHAM

"The Corps represents what America is about – duty, opportunity, and ... a sense of adventure."

BORN: 27 September 1964, Saigon, Republic of Vietnam
SERVICE: United States Marine Corps, CH-46 Helicopter Pilot, 1987 – 1994 active duty, 1995 – 2002 Reserve
OCCUPATION: General Manager, QTC Medical Services

In April 1975, Quang X. Pham was a 10-year-old scampering with his mother and three sisters up the ramp of a U.S. military plane that sat with its engines roaring on a darkened airfield in Saigon. It was the night after the President of South Vietnam had resigned and departed the country. Within hours and with one bag of belongings, he was uprooted from familiar surroundings and became a war refugee in America. Quang's father, a former South Vietnamese Air Force pilot remained behind and was captured and sentenced to 12 years in Communist reeducation camps.

The Pham family first set foot on American soil when they arrived at the makeshift refugee camp at Camp Asan, Marine Barracks Guam.

Quang never forgot his dream of becoming a pilot. Duty, family, and honor remained on his mind as he began his new life in America. He struggled at first leaning English and making new friends while helping his mother with the money he earned from cleaning offices and delivering newspapers. While attending UCLA, he met a Marine Corps officer recruiter that would change his life forever.

Captain Douglas J. Hamlin, USMC, told Quang in 1985, "You can go into business anytime. But this is your only chance to pay back your country, as a Marine and a naval aviator." Those inspiring words led Quang to join the 10-week Combined Platoon Leaders Class also known as Officer Candidates School in Quantico, Virginia. He survived OCS and was commissioned a second lieutenant upon graduation.

As Quang began his Marine Corps career in 1987, his father was finally released from reeducation camps and allowed to return to the newly renamed Ho Chi Minh City (Saigon). Seven months after earning naval aviator wings, Quang received orders to Saudi Arabia as a replacement pilot with Marine Medium Squadron 161 (HMM-161 "Greyhawks") as part of Operation Desert Shield. Ironically, HMM-161 was also the squadron that his father had escorted (in a T-28) into hot LZs during the early days of the Vietnam War. Quang served in the operations department and trained helicopter door gunners. During the brief conflict, he flew medical evacuations, resupply, and trooplift missions and earned an Air Medal.

A year after Gulf War ended, Quang departed on his second deployment with HMM-161 as part of the 11th Marine Expeditionary Unit (Special Operations Capable) embarked aboard the amphibious carrier USS *Tarawa*. He returned to the Persian Gulf, took part in joint exercises with the Kuwaiti Air Force and other allied military, and flew United Nations personnel into Mogadishu, Somalia in September 1992. The 11th MEU was under the command of then Colonel now General Michael Hagee, currently the Commandant of the Marine Corps.

Quang served his final year on active duty as the aide-de-camp to the Third Marine Aircraft Wing Commanding General headquartered at El Toro, California. He was selected for augmentation amid one of the most competitive board for rotary wing pilots and was awarded the Navy/Marine Corps Commendation Medal for his aide tour. He chose to enter the private sector but remained active with the Corps as a reserve pilot with the HMM-764 "Moonlighters" until El Toro was closed in 1999. During his fours years with the "Moonlighters," Quang also received the Marine Corps Reserve Officers Association's Award for Professionalism and the Military Outstanding Volunteer Service Medal for his community outreach efforts.

"My Marine Corps experience changed my life for the better and exposed me to fine Americans from different generations and all walks of life. I am a better person today because of the people I've met through the Corps. The Corps represents what America is about – duty, opportunity, and ... a sense of adventure."

To his business ventures Quang brought three lessons imbued in him by the ethos of the Corps: (1) keep a cool head in hot situations, even if it means swallowing your pride; (2) always have a way out, a backup plan; never put all your eggs in a single basket; (3) and always lead by example. The final lesson was taught by father as he stood his post during the panic-stricken days of the Saigon evacuation.

"My father was finally released and came to America in 1992. He passed away on November 10, 2000, shortly after becoming an American citizen and voting in his first and only democratic election."

After resigning his commission, Quang joined the pharmaceutical sales ranks and spent five years in various roles with industry leaders Astra Merck, Immunex and Genentech. In 2000, he founded Lathian Systems (then known as MyDrugRep.com), a leading provider of technology-based sales solutions for life science companies, and served as executive vice president, chairman and CEO. He raised $14 million from leading venture capitalists, led Lathian's rapid growth into a marketplace leader, and successfully transitioned from the company after it had reached profitability and enjoyed triple-digit annual growth rate.

In August 2003, Quang joined QTC Medical Services as vice president and general manager. He currently heads the QMO Division which has medical examination facilities nationwide serving federal, state and local level disability businesses. Founded in 1981, QTC Medical Services is the largest private provider of medical disability evaluations and a pioneer in the development and implementation of software technology to improve the efficiency of conducting and managing disability evaluations.

Quang serves on the Boards of the Marine Corps Scholarship Foundation, the Orange County Forum, and the Chapman University George L. Argyros School of Business and Economics. He volunteered with the Vietnam War Memorial, Inc. of Westminster, California, and spearheaded the dedication ceremony in April 2003. The Memorial is the only one of its kind in the world, with two 11-foot tall bronze statues of an American G.I. and an ARVN soldier standing side-by-side representing their cooperative efforts during the long and bitter war.

In his spare time, Quang is completing a memoir about his family's transition after the Vietnam War and their eventual reunion in America.

Quang resides in Orange County, California with his wife, Shannon, formerly of Jacksonville, Florida.

SEMPER FIDELIS

Dale C. Pond

"When confronted with adversity or opportunity ... address it head on, with passion, confidence, commitment and ferocity – and you will prevail."

Born: 7 April 1946 in Spokane, Washington
Service: United States Marine Corps, 1969 – 1975, Active 6 months, Reserves 5 years, Enlisted, Public Information Officer
Occupation: Senior Executive Vice President, Lowes Companies, Inc.

Dale was working for an NBC affiliate in Denver, Colorado as a Regional Director of Sales when he took a 6 month leave of absence to serve his country by joining the Marine Corps Reserves.

"I think every Marine remembers their first night as a recruit. I received advice from a good friend and retired Marine just prior to my departure to San Diego. He advocated a simple survival philosophy – 'Stay in the middle and volunteer for nothing.' Upon arriving at the San Diego airport, a bunch of hapless young men were herded into busses for a short trip to MCRD San Diego, I among them. Because I was one of the first on the bus, I was therefore one of the last off. As others had already found the infamous 'yellow foot prints' and the only remaining ones were at the front of the ranks, I literally fought my way, as a 6' 3" over-weight college grad, into an occupied pair of footprints and stood my ground. Shortly thereafter the DI appeared for the first time. He immediately asked for volunteers to serve as squad leaders. Recalling the advice of my friend, I stood tall, but very quietly in the middle of the ranks. The DI's next sentence changed my life forever. 'Okay you lazy, good-for-nothing, (expletive deleted) ladies ... if there are no volunteers for this prestigious, honorable and highly revered job ... I'm going to appoint a few of you. I want the tallest recruits front and center and the shortest in the back.' I never felt so tall in my life ... and I became known that night, and for ever after as, Private Pound.

"The single biggest lesson I learned in the Marine Corps was: Life, like the weather is unpredictable. Encountering unexpected challenges is the norm, not the exception. When confronted with adversity or opportunity ... address it head on, with passion, confidence, commitment and ferocity … and you will prevail. Thirteen weeks of boot camp taught me that. And I've lived it every day since."

Following his 6 month active duty, Dale returned to the NBC affiliate he left prior to joining the Marines. Shortly thereafter he joined Bernstein/Rein Advertising, running their Denver branch office and servicing the regional McDonald's business. Over the course of nine years with the agency, he increased his responsibilities and eventually ran all the agency's branch operations and supervised the agency's McDonald's business in 13 states. In 1977 a McDonald's owner-operator in Boulder, Colorado and Dale created and developed the Happy Meal concept. Eventually the concept was tested in several markets served by the agency, and ultimately adopted as a national promotion (and subsequently as an international menu item) by McDonald's Corporation. In 1981, Dale was recruited by one of the agency's clients, Payless Cashways. He joined Payless as a Vice President of Advertising and was promoted over the course of his nine years with the company, to eventually assume responsibilities as the Chief Marketing and Merchandising Officer. Over the next few years he worked for both Montgomery Ward (as Chief Marketing Officer) and a division of Hechinger Company in various marketing-related senior management positions. In 1993, he joined Lowe's Companies as SVP marketing. In 1998. Dale was promoted to Executive Vice President, Merchandising & Marketing, and in 2003 he assumed the title of Senior Executive Vice President.

Lowe's Companies, Inc. is a $26.5 billion dollar retailer (2002 sales) of a complete line of home improvement products and equipment. The company serves more than seven million do-it-yourself and commercial business customers each week through it's more than 875 stores located in 44 states. Lowe's is the world's second largest retailer of home improvement products & services and the 12th largest retailer in the United States. Lowe's current prototypical store is approximately 116,000 square feet of sales area with a 25 thousand square foot garden center contiguous to the building. In 2002, the company was named Fortune magazine's Most Admired Specialty Retailer. In 2003, the company is opening a new store, on average, every three days. Lowe's employs approximately 130,000 employees and is headquartered in Mooresville, North Carolina, a northern suburb of Charlotte. Lowe's has been a publicly held company since October 1961, with it's stock listed on the New York Stock Exchange and shares trading under the symbol LOW.

Dale's current responsibilities at Lowe's include running both the merchandising and marketing functions of the company. His departments determine the products their customers expect and desire to find in their stores, source them by evaluating the capabilities and qualities of various manufacturing companies offering the products, and then decide how the products are to be presented, promoted and priced consistent with Lowe's corporate brand strategy. Within the merchandising and marketing areas, several hundred professional marketers and merchants work toward representing their customer's best interests in terms of quality, value and service in every product sold.

The Lowe's Charitable and Educational Foundation directs most of their resources to educational programs in the areas and neighborhoods served by our stores. Additionally, Lowe's has been a major funder of the United Way program, as well as the founder and principle supporter of the Home Safety Council, a national organization dedicated to promoting home safety through education.

In addition to Dale's participation in Lowe's corporate charities, he has been actively involved in a variety of philanthropic and professional organizations. These include board positions with Colorado Special Olympics, Kansas City Arts Council, State Ballet of Missouri, Home Safety Council, Texas A&M Center For Retailing Studies, The National Center For Small Communities, and the Home Improvement Research Institute. He currently serves on the board of directors for Bassett Furniture Industries, Inc. and is a member of the Washburn University (BBA, 1969) and Stanford University (SEP, 1985) alumni associations, as well as other social and civic organizations.

Dale and his wife, Susan, have been married for 37 years and currently reside in North Carolina. "We have a beautiful daughter, Ashli, and a wonderful son-in-law, Don, who have given us an extraordinary grandson, Christopher Guglielmo."

SEMPER FIDELIS

William D. Powers

"Second best in politics means you lost."

Born: 25 December 1941 in Rockville Center, New York
Service: United State Marine Corps, 1961 – 1966, Infantry Rifleman
Occupation: Senior Partner, Powers, Crane & Company, LLC

William Powers attended Fairleigh Dickinson University in New Jersey and the State University of New York at Albany. He has a degree in public relations from Albany Business College. He has been awarded an Honorary Degree of Doctor of Humane Letters – Honoris Causa by the New York College of Podiatric Medicine.

"I have five years of memories from the Marines, and a lifetime built on the foundation that time provided me. In those years I grew up quick, became a man, got married to my wife and sweetheart, Judy, and had the first of three sons (he was born at Camp Lejeune). I came up through the ranks, did my tours of duty and saw a fair share of blood, sweat and tears. Some joyous times and some difficult times – just as we all face throughout our lives. But that time in the Corps helped me understand both life's challenges and blessings. The Marines instilled in me a sense – almost an obligation – to work hard, face adversity and succeed in the mission at hand. I think that these traits are what make Marines a special breed. The ability to see success on the other side of challenge. The ability to remain unshaken – with level headedness, focus and determination. To me, memories of my active duty in the Marines are more of a playbook I can use and build upon everyday."

After leaving the Marine Corps in 1966, Powers moved to the upstate New York region. At first, he found work in building maintenance for General Electric in Pittsfield, Massachusetts. In 1967, Powers went to work for the Terminal Service Railroad in Selkirk, New York. Starting off as a general laborer, loading and unloading freight, he worked his way up to a regional Vice President. It was 1971 when the political bug hit. Powers had been getting increasingly involved in local political issues and developing a network through his job at the railroad. In 1972, he took a job offer to begin working for the New York State Assembly under the leadership of Assembly Speaker Perry Duryea.

That was the staring point for three decades of political, election and governmental service for Bill. "What I loved most were the challenges and the battles we had in politics. Keep in mind, every year there is an election. Depending on the race, there are elections in the spring and fall. The task at hand was to find the best people, organize them, create and execute a battle plan and realize that in each campaign there are only two possible outcomes ... victory or defeat."

Since his election as the Chairman of the New York Republican State Committee on January 14, 1991, Bill Powers demonstrated that Republicans could win in New York State. Prior to him taking over as State Chairman, the New York State Republican Party was in disarray and mired in debt. Focusing on the life-blood of the Republican Party, Powers worked with local leaders to ensure all of New York's 1,000 towns had an active Republican organization that would spread the GOP message. Republicans throughout the state enthusiastically embraced the former Marine Corps Sergeant's can do attitude and winning philosophy.

In 1993, Powers' rebuilt Republican organization was put to the test and defied all pundits to achieve what many thought was unattainable. With Powers' strong supporting grass-roots efforts, Rudy Giuliani was able to overcome a 6-to-1 Democratic enrollment advantage to become the first Republican Mayor of New York City in decades.

Then in 1994, Powers' leadership solidified the Republican's hold on the state. He worked with George Pataki to defeat liberal icon, Mario Cuomo.

Powers' winning habits and adherence to his rock-solid belief that all politics are local have made New York's State GOP what it is today. For his accomplishments, Powers was asked to serve as the Chairman of the Republican National Committee's State Chairman's Advisory Committee from 1993 – 1995.

On May 25, 2001, as a testament to all that he has done for his party, state, and Nation, President George W. Bush appointed Bill Powers to the Board of Directors for the Federal Home Mortgage Corporation (Freddie Mac). Powers was recently re-appointed to his third, one-year term.

Currently Bill is the Senior Partner at Powers, Crane & Company, LLC, which was formed in March of 2001 to provide governmental and business development consulting services to organizations, individuals and political subdivisions before New York State's decision makers.

Powers, Crane & Company's presence in New York State's Capitol enables it to monitor and assess the political impact of state and local regulatory and legislative activity for its clients. Its knowledge of the intricacies and inner workings of New York State government and deep personal understanding of and relationship with its participants enables it to provide its clients with unique counseling and insight.

Bill has been on the Board of Directors of Trustco Bank NA, for eight years, as well as serving as one of the three members on the Executive Committee. Trustco Bank is one of the top rated banks in America by financial performance and efficiency ratio's.

He supports The St. Jude Children's Research Hospital and the local U.S. Marine Corps Reserve, Fox Company, Second Battalion, 25th Marine Regiment, Marine Corps Coordinating Council, as well as the Arthritis Foundation and Hospice organizations in New York.

Bill and his wife Judith live in Old Chatham, New York. They have three grown sons and four grandchildren.

SEMPER FIDELIS

Joe Riggio

"My Marine flight call sign was 'Network' and the Marine Corps was my network training school, so it is only natural that my network of choice is Marines."

Born: 26 January 1951 in New York City
Service: United States Marine Corps, 1970 – 1997, Officer, Pilot/Financial Management
Occupation: President, Network by Images

Joe started college right after high school and attended the State University of New York (SUNY) at Farmingdale, New York. It was a two-year junior college. He graduated with an Associate of Applied Science degree in Aeronautics.

After earning his associate degree, Joe went into the Marine Corps in the Aviation Officer Candidate Scholarship Program. The program was offered to people with a two-year college degree and an aviation contract. After OCS, aviation candidates did not attend The Basic School. He went directly to flight school in Pensacola, Florida. TBS was done by correspondence for the aviation candidates.

After Joe's initial five-year tour, including flight school, he went back to college using the Marine Corps College Degree Program.

"After two years of being a full time student and Marine Captain with full pay and allowances, I graduated with honors (Summa Cum Laude) from Dowling College with a B.S., Aeronautics and Management. At the graduation ceremony I wore my uniform. After the ceremony another graduate came up to me and said, 'I knew Marines were tough, but I did not know they were smart.'

"After graduation, I went back to the fleet for a while then applied and was accepted to the Advance Degree Program. I went to the Naval Postgraduate School at Monterey California. After 18 months I graduated with an M.S. in Management. Once I career transitioned from the Marine Corps I earned my Ph.D. I was the first in my extended family to obtain these degrees and the Marine Corps helped make this possible!"

After 26 plus years, Joe retired from the Marine Corps. Since 1997, Joe has been an author, a business owner, a Corporate analyst and a trainer. He is now focusing on helping other Marines transition in a successful manner.

Joe is the ultimate networker. His company, Network by Images (*www.joeriggio.com*), represents a number of products and services that he himself uses and believes will make the lives of those around him better.

"I continue to develop an extensive pool of people to network with. Each day I help connect people to the people and organizations that will help them achieve their dreams. Connecting the dots to make a positive change in peoples lives is a natural high.

"I do a weekly newsletter about health and transition and a monthly newsletter for transition websites to include Corps Careers (*www.Corpscareers.tv*).

"Every day I network to help people get what they want using a number of different vehicles and organizations. If their need solution is not in my network I seek out a source the fill their need. It is fun and exciting, a marvelous journey through life.

"My mission is to help people find their life mission and provide them with a network to accomplish that mission. If I can help only a small percentage of the people who seek me out I believe the world will be a better place. If we had more people who found their mission and passion like Mother Theresa, Bill Gates, and Thomas Edison imagine how much better the world would be."

Joe is the author of *The Courage to Transition*. The book is to help people transition from the military back to the civilian world, and is the result of four years of transition experience. He has also written an ebook titled *How to Make a Successful Transition* and it is available on his website.

Joe's other passion is the homeless. Joe informs me "one third of all homeless are veterans. There will be 270,000 homeless veterans sleeping outdoors tonight." Veterans are homeless for the same reasons that others are homeless, plus an additional few. The downsizing of the military, a reduction in educational benefits, physical and mental ailments, drug and alcohol abuse problems, and war related mental illnesses, such as post traumatic stress disorder (PTSD), all contribute to the tremendous number of our nation's veterans who are homeless at any given time.

The Circle of Friends for American Veterans (*www.vetsvision.org*) is fighting back by actively supporting programs that help create jobs for motivated veterans who want to work. You can join this campaign and help us help those men and women who have risked all for America.

Joe is an active member of the Marine Executive Association (MEA) (*www.MarineEA.org*), and serves as Chair Emeritus 2003 and Information Webmaster for the organization. The MEA is a national volunteer, non-profit organization of Marines who provide assistance in the career process to Marines transitioning from active or reserve to retired status; leaving the Corps at the end of tour; or moving from one civilian position to another. In February 1982, six Marines, who were already part of the business community in the Washington, D.C. area, met to explore how they might help other Marines leaving active duty find suitable civilian employment. From this first meeting, the Marine Executive Association (MEA) evolved into the network it is today with hundreds of members around the country. In connection with the MEA, Joe is working with the Marine for Life program (*www.marineforlife.com*).

Today Joe resides in Aldie, Virginia. He is the proud father of two children, Joseph, Jr. and Michelle, and two grandchildren, Caitlin and Hunter.

SEMPER FIDELIS

Burton M. Sack

"The Marine Corps was a turning point in my life."

Born: 13 December 1937 in Melrose, Massachusetts
Service: United States Marine Corps 29 January 1955 to 28 January 1958, Enlisted
Occupation: Chairman/Partner, Classic Restaurant Concepts

Burton "Skip" Sack enlisted in the Marine Corps at the age of 17. During his enlistment his military occupation specialty designations included truck driver, post office worker, and security personnel among others.

"I have several memories of my time in the Corps, ranging from funny to tragic. When I was at Parris Island in boot camp, I had a tough time withdrawing from my daily sugar needs and was starving for candy bars ("pogey bait"). One night I had guard duty from midnight to 0400 in the administration building where there were candy machines. At about 0330 I started putting coins in the machine to get as many candy bars as I could carry. As I was loading the candy bars in my utilities, two of my drill instructors came into the room and saw what I was doing. They confiscated my candy and told me to report to their room at 0600 with my rifle. When I reported later that morning, they had me do deep knee bends with my rifle on my back and counting out loud. As they sat reading the Sunday paper, I did my deep knee bends. When I got to over 2200, I literally couldn't move my legs any more. My muscles had contracted and frozen. Friends in my platoon had to come to the DI's room and carry me away. They put me on the concrete laundry table and massaged my legs for an hour. I couldn't walk for three days until my leg muscles started to relax. It was about a week before I could start walking normally again.

"Another incident I remember well was when I was playing Judo in Japan. I got a 1st degree black belt and was in a match against a group of Japanese high school students. I figured it would take little time to win the match. Boy, was I wrong! My opponent was smaller than I was, so imagine my surprise when he threw me into the air. As I was falling to the mat, I was so shocked that he had thrown me that I forgot how to land properly. I landed on my shoulder, dislocating it and causing a lifelong injury that plagues me to this day.

"Yet another unforgettably shaping experience was when I was asked if I wanted to attend the Naval Academy. I said yes, and was sent to NAPS (Naval Academy Preparatory School) in Bainbridge, Maryland. I was there for about three weeks when I realized that engineering was not for me, and I asked to be transferred back to Quantico. When I got back, I was summoned to the base Commandant's office where I was severely chastised (reamed up one side and down the other) for wasting one of the few billets the Marine Corps received to send enlisted men to the Naval Academy. Within a week I found myself on an LST (flat bottom boat) crossing the Pacific to an 18-month tour in Japan. The LST trip lasted 32 days and I was seasick for 31 days!"

Having attained the rank of Sergeant, Skip was discharged in January 1958 with many Marine experiences under his belt and a new determination.

"While in the Marine Corps, I was fortunate to be stationed at Camp Upshur, Quantico. Camp Upshur was where all the PLCs went for training after graduating college and getting commissioned. Up until that time, I had no interest in going to college. My ambition in life was to become a restaurant manager. However, after spending considerable time with the officers at Camp Upshur, I saw that their standard of living was considerably better than mine. I was living in a squad bay with 65 other guys and they were living two to a room. They were eating at tables for four and I was eating at picnic tables for 12. I was saluting THEM! I realized the only difference between us was the fact that they had a college education. I decided to go to college and applied to several schools before my discharge. My discharge was scheduled for 0800 on January 28. By January 27 I had not been accepted to any school. On the afternoon of January 27, I stopped by the post office to pick up my mail for the last time. My car was packed and I was planning to leave the next morning for Boston where my parents lived. In the mail, on the afternoon of January 27, was an acceptance letter to the Hotel and Restaurant School at Cornell. I was to start classes on February 4. Obviously, my acceptance was a last minute thing but I didn't care. I called my parents and told them I wasn't coming home, but was driving to Ithaca, New York to start at Cornell. Within weeks of starting school I got a job with the Campus Police as a full time patrolman. I worked my way through school as a deputy sheriff of Thompkins County, assigned to the Cornell Campus Police. Since I was full time I worked through the summers and went to summer school enabling me to graduate in three and a half years. I earned a Bachelor of Science degree with Distinction and graduated in June of 1961."

With his bachelor's degree in hand, Skip began work as an advertising assistant for Howard Johnson's. Twenty-two years later in 1983, he bought a division of the company with a partner. In two years time, they sold those restaurants and he began an association with Applebee's. Skip bought the franchise rights for New England for Applebee's Neighborhood Grill & Bar and in the next ten years built 16 Applebee's restaurants. He sold those restaurants to Applebee's International in 1994. Applebee's is the largest casual dining chain in the country with more than 1,500 locations (more than Friday's and Chili's combined). Since 1994, Skip has been the largest individual shareholder in the Applebee's system. In 2002 Applebee's had more than $3 billion in sales.

Skip founded The Sack Family Charitable Foundation and has given more than $1.5 million to numerous organizations including The Wellness Community, Cornell University, American Cancer Institute, Dana Farber Cancer Institute, Greater Boston Association for Retarded Citizens, and a number of civic, cultural, and charitable organizations in the Sarasota, Florida area. With the passing of a family member due to cancer in 1983, Skip is partial to organizations working to cure cancer as well as those that are supportive of cancer patients.

In addition to being Chairman and Partner in Classic Restaurant Concepts, Skip serves on the Applebee's Board of Directors, and is on the Board of the National Restaurant Association as Treasurer. He will become Chairman of the Restaurant Association Board in May 2004. TIBERSOFT, a software company for the food service industry also benefits from Mr. Sack's restaurant experience with his input on their Board of Directors.

Burton "Skip" Sack was honored recently when he was asked to be part of the Founders Group of the Marine Heritage Museum to be built outside of Quantico.

Skip and his wife, Gail, now reside in Longboat Key, Florida.

SEMPER FIDELIS

John A. Scarsella, Jr.

"The Marine Corps taught me leadership, self confidence, a strong sense of a team effort to attain goals, and a belief that anything can be accomplished."

Born: 3 March 1942 in Youngstown, Ohio
Service: United States Marine Corps, 1964 – 1967, Communications Officer
Occupation: President & CEO; Durham Furniture, Inc.

John Scarsella entered the United States Marine Corps via the Platoon Leaders Class attending the Junior course in the summer of 1961 and completing the Senior course during the summer of 1963. Upon graduation from Youngstown State University in June of 1964, John was commissioned a 2nd Lieutenant and reported to The Basic School in Quantico, Virgina in August 1964. John achieved the rank of captain in March of 1967.

His Military Occupational Specialty (MOS) was 2502, Communications Officer. During the early Vietnam build up in 1965 there was a shortage of CommOs so the Marine Corps developed a short course in Communications in Quantico, Virginia.

"My first assignment in the Fleet was to 8th Engineer Battalion as the CommO. Interesting year 1965 to 1966; 8th Engineer Battalion was assigned to go to Guantanamo Bay, Cuba to remove the mine fields that were put in during the Cuban missile crisis. We put a platoon in every four to six weeks to remove mines and all hands received hazardous duty pay. We had a good number of casualties during this time. My best friend, at the time, was a great basketball player in college and was going on to teach and coach after the Marine Corps, lost his foot at the ankle during that operation. Jerry Daniels was a platoon commander and Officer in Charge (OIC) of the operation at the time of his injury."

"Upon my return to the United States in the late summer of 1967 after completion of a tour of duty in Okinawa and Vietnam, I was stationed at the

Naval Air Station at El Toro in Southern California for a period of time prior to being released from active duty.

"This was a troubled time in our country and most of my peers had gone overseas early in the Vietnam conflict and weren't familiar with all of the demonstrations going on at home and we had certainly never seen a "hippie." It was the summer of 1967 with major social changes taking place in our country. Music like "Whiter Shade of Pale" and "If You're Going To San Francisco (Be Sure to Wear Some Flowers In Your Hair)" was all over the "transistor radios." The great "Love In" was scheduled for San Francisco late in the summer of 1967 and "flower power" young people were everywhere in Southern California.

"As a group of Marines just returned from combat operations in Vietnam, we weren't too popular in the civilian world that summer. There was, however, a terrific 'night spot' in Laguna Beach called The Sand Piper which, for the most part, was a Marine hang out. Every night the place was filled with young men with high and tight haircuts. As all Marines do, we stuck together and avoided the civilians like the plague, with the exception of the local and transient female population who seemed to really enjoy hanging out at The Sand Piper.

"One particular evening a strange incident took place in The Sand Piper which showed the locals that having a group of highly trained, fearless Marines around could prove very beneficial.

"On the evening in question a long haired fellow walked in and tried to work his way up to the front of the bar to order a beer. He was obviously not from the area because no one ever came into The Sand Piper with long hair and an unkempt appearance. The stranger was scruffy, unshaven, in need of a bath, and swathed in very dirty, multi-colored serape. During the 1960s virtually everyone smoked, in fact every package of C-Rations had a small package of cigarettes included, and unfortunately someone must have brushed up against the newcomer's serape with a lit cigarette. Instantly the poor stranger's serape was on fire with flames climbing up his back into his long hair.

"At that point in the crisis a number of vigilant Marines, seeing the apparent danger the stranger was in, threw the flaming stranger to the floor and immediately doused the flames with their beer rations saving the man from injury. It was a tremendously selfless and brave act."

After three years in the Marine Corps, John returned to Youngstown, Ohio where he opened a small retail furniture store and served in the Marine Reserves for a period of time. After 15 years in retail John made a transition from furniture retail to wholesale as an independent sales representative. Ever interested in learning new things, John spent a good deal of time in the factories of the companies he represented learning the product development and manufacturing side of the business. He ultimately became a vice-president of sales and marketing for Jamestown-Sterling Corporation, a solid wood furniture manufacturer located in Jamestown, New York.

In 1993, John started his own marketing company working with Canadian furniture manufacturers in developing solid wood furniture and marketing their products in the United States. John took his principal client, Durham Furniture, Inc., from a $6 million company in 1993 to $91 million in 2002, making Durham Furniture the eleventh largest furniture manufacturer in Canada.

Upon the untimely death of Durham's president in 2002, the Durham Board of Directors asked John to assume the position of President and CEO. John accepted. Currently Durham Furniture employs 763 people and is in the midst of a $50 million dollar expansion program building a new 250,000 square foot manufacturing plant, which will employ another 250 people.

Durham is a vertically integrated company manufacturing everything associated with their product except metal hardware and mirrors. They start with raw green lumber, directly from the sawmills, and do their own grading, kiln drying, and assembly through to the final finishing.

They manufacture solid wood bedroom and dining room furniture using cherry, maple, ash, and hickory. Durham produces products to sell in upper middle price points and their styles range from very traditional to contemporary. They sell to more than 500 home furnishing retailers throughout the U.S. and Canada, and the company maintains a permanent 16,000 square foot showroom in High Point, North Carolina. Sales for 2003 exceeded $100 million.

"The Marine Corps taught me leadership, self confidence, a strong sense of a team effort to attain goals, and a belief that anything can be accomplished. I apply this Marine Corps acquired knowledge, skill, and self confidence to my work and life everyday."

John has recently returned to his Marine Corps roots. He is a founding member of the Marine Corps Heritage Foundation and has taken an active role in the organization's fund raising efforts.

The Scarsella family supports a number of charitable causes but devotes most of their energy to the Order of the Ursuline Sisters of Youngstown, Ohio. The Ursuline nuns are dedicated to abused women and their AIDS ministry. The Ursuline Beatitude House provides homes, education, and childcare for battered and abused women with children, enabling the victims to build lives for themselves and their children. The Ursuline AIDS ministry assists families, particularly women and children, affected by this horrendous disease and its far reaching social implications through every walk of American life by providing housing, child care, and education for afflicted families.

John and his wife, Jean, reside in Canfield, Ohio. They have four sons: John, III, a Durham Sales Representative; Paul, an Assistant District Attorney; Mike, the Director of Marketing for Durham; and Nick, a high school football player.

SEMPER FIDELIS

Thomas Schweizer, Jr.

"I learned the importance of effective communications, leading by example and taking care of your troops while leading my men into combat, I have also learned the importance of applying those same leadership skills in Corporate management."

Born: 21 December 1943 in Baltimore, Maryland
Service: United States Marine Corps, 1966 – 1969, Infantry Officer
Occupation: President, Brown Advisory Securities

Tom entered Vanderbilt University under the NROTC program. During his junior year he took the Marine Corps option. Upon graduation in 1966, he was commissioned a Second Lieutenant.

In 1967, Tom was sent to Vietnam and his first billet was as Platoon Commander of Echo Company, 2nd Battalion, 1st Marines, 1st Marine Division. This was the same platoon that his father had led in 1945 in the South Pacific.

"One of my first night patrols south of Da Nang I got hopelessly lost. Sticking to the proper radio protocol, I tried to tell my Company Commander of my problem. The next thing I heard over the radio was 'Schweizer, get your damned compass out and head south.' Needless to say, every Marine listening on the radio net that night heard the same thing."

During Tom's tour of Vietnam, he was awarded the Bronze Star with combat V, two Purple Hearts, and a Presidential Unit Citation.

After leaving the Marine Corps in 1969, Tom went to work for Alex, Brown & Sons, America's oldest investment banking firm, founded in 1800, and a leader in financing growth companies. They were a full service brokerage service prior to being acquired by Deutsche Bank in 1999. He was first employed as a financial advisor and during his 33 year career with them became a managing director and a member of their Board of Directors.

Brown Advisory Securities, LLC was created in 1993 as a separate, focused group within Alex, Brown & Sons. From the very beginning, they created and sustained independent research and trading capabilities and an independent Board of Directors.

In 1998, they separated from Alex, Brown & Sons by purchasing the business in a management led buy out, in the belief that their clients' interests would best be served by independent ownership. Brown Advisory's mission was then and is now to serve a small number of institutions, Corporations, and high net worth investors by providing the insight and sophistication that their complex financial circumstances demand.

In September 2002, Tom started a second career with Brown Advisory Securities, LLC (*www.brownadvisory.com*) in Baltimore, Maryland. He is President and a partner in the firm.

By virtue of their employees' substantial equity interest in the firm, each employee has a vested interest in forging lasting client relationships based on integrity, loyalty and trust. In a world of financial supermarkets, their independence means that each client benefits from their individual attention and expertise.

Tom and his wife, Barbara, currently reside in Brooklandville, Maryland. They have two sons, Nicholas and Anthony and three grandsons.

SEMPER FIDELIS

Carlton Sherwood

"When asked about the 'healing' qualities of the Vietnam Veterans Memorial, Marine combat hero Jim Webb spoke for many veterans with this: 'No, damnit, I don't want to be healed! There are some wounds that must remain so we never forget.' Amen brother Webb."

Born: 16 December 1946 in Camden, New Jersey
Service: United States Marine Corps, 1964 – 1968, Enlisted
Occupation: Executive Vice President, WVC3-Group

As a schoolboy, Carlton was particularly interested in the Civil War, enthralled by tales of gallantry like those depicted in such works as Stephen Crane's *Red Badge of Courage*. However, he was always left with the question: What could possess thousands of men to willingly march to their deaths, leaning into a maelstrom of bullets and shells as those around them were ripped and torn in ways too horrible to imagine? What power could cause normally sane men to ignore all their instincts for flight and survival, to knowingly participate in the equivalent of mass suicide?

"Those thoughts shot through my mind in late September 1967 when I heard, for the first time since arriving in Vietnam several months before, the command to 'fix bayonets.' At the time I was a Scout Sniper for the Second Battalion, Fourth Marine Regiment (2/4) which had already suffered massive casualties patrolling the DMZ north of Con Thien. On this day I was assigned to Golf Company which was urgently dispatched to extract another infantry company that had been ambushed and pinned down by a dug-in, reinforced NVA battalion. It was a rare, beautiful day — clear, deep blue skies, cool and dry — in stark contrast to the surreal, otherworldly landscape of the DMZ, a true dead zone whose soil had already been saturated by the blood of thousands of Marines killed and wounded in heavy fighting over the preceding months.

"As we flanked the beleaguered rifle company, the only sounds heard were sporadic gun fire in the distance and the drone of a 'bird-dog' spotter plane over head as it dropped red smoke pellets identifying enemy positions and visible NVA (North Vietnamese Army) troops. A dozen or more streams of wispy red smoke seemed to engulf us — to our front, to both sides of our column, even to our rear. It was only then that the sound of a human voice rang out, repeating up and down the line, 'Turn to the left ... fix bayonets!' I forced back the urge to heave the C-ration I ate earlier, and looked in disbelief at the men to my right and left – 'please tell me I didn't hear that.' I implored them. Both just stared at me, more with a look of resignation than disgust as they snapped their bayonets on their rifles. Before another word was said, I was doing the same, hands shaking, my entire body trembling, adrenaline flooding every cell and fueling the fierce argument raging in my head. 'This is insane!' the inner voice screamed. 'This is 1967 not 1864. Where are the tanks, the jets, the flame-throwers? You're not really going to do this, are you? You will die!' As I looked at the pathetic little black knife on the end of my rifle, trying desperately to think of some way to stop this, the G Company Commander's voice boomed again. 'Stay on line Marines ... at a walk ... CHARGE!' The inner-voice shouted 'What? You've got to be joking.' But slowly and, at first quietly, I advanced across the open terrain with the rest of the men of Golf Company. We walked a hundred yards or so, through a couple hedgerows, before the first NVA machine gun opened up, down to my far right. All two hundred weapons of Golf Company ripped the relative silence with a gut-splitting roar. But, instead of stopping and taking cover as we normally would have, the line of Marines continued to move forward, at a much faster pace, screaming things I only thought came form the mouths of Hollywood actors. 'Come out and get some, you Commie Bastards!' ... 'Die you mothers!' Others just screamed as loud as they could, some even bellowed Rebel Yells, a chilling sound when it's for real ... on a battlefield ... rising from the throats of men who expect to die. My inner voice shouted as well ... 'this is absurd, this is absurd, you will die, you will die.' Nonetheless, I continued on, firing my rifle, throwing away empty magazines, reloading and yelling something unintelligible, caught up in the unleashed fury of the Marine rifle company. It was then I first began to realize I wasn't moving of my own will, not even by my own legs. I was moving forward, to be sure, but I was being carried, almost floating on a wave of something, pushed on by a force I could not identify. When the NVA guns opened up on my small piece of the battlefield, the initial shock of men being hit and killed — a couple even vaporized — sent me to the ground, drenched in their blood. But like those who managed to survive that first volley, I got up and sprinted forward again ... my inner voice finally quieted by the din of gunfire from all sides.

"I rank that day among some of my worst in Vietnam. We did not 'win,' far from it. We were lucky just to relieve the Marines who had been pinned down and Golf Company took far more casualties in its rescue efforts than those it was sent to prevent. Indeed, the fire was so intense that many of the dead had to be left on the battlefield, their bodies recovered several days later. But the experience did answer my childhood question. There is a force in the human spirit that compels men to completely ignore their own survival, to resist the deep-rooted instincts to live and cast aside any consideration for self-preservation. Some might suggest it's a form of mass hypnosis or hysteria or even group insanity, but the power I felt that day was none of that. It was, as best as I can describe, the force of Brotherhood, a compulsion to risk everything for the sake of others. That quality may be as rare as a cloudless day in Vietnam but among combat Marines it is ever-present, waiting to be awakened. And, God help those who must face it!"

After mustering out of the Marine Corps in 1968, Carlton began what would turn out to be a rather blessed career as a journalist. Initially, he worked as a reporter for several newspapers in and around the Philadelphia area. As his investigative skills gradually become known, he was recruited by the Gannett newspaper chain to join their news staff in Washington, D.C.

In 1980, while working as a national investigative reporter for Gannett News Service, Carlton was awarded the Pulitzer Prize for a two-year investigation of a Vatican financial scandal. A number of other national honors followed for his investigative series on such things as drugs in the military, organized crime, medical malpractice and nursing home abuses.

In 1983, Carlton was again named as a finalist for the Pulitzer Prize for a newspaper and TV investigative series on institutional child abuse in Oklahoma's state-run, federally subsidized institutions. That story earned TV's equivalent of the Pulitzer Prize, the George Foster Peabody Award, which, resulted in his transition to TV news. For several years afterward, until the late 1980s, he worked variously for CBS, ABC and CNN networks producing several award-winning news documentaries. When, in 1994, friend and fellow Vietnam veteran, Tom Ridge, became Governor of Pennsylvania, he joined his staff as Broadcast Communications Director.

After nearly eight years as Pennsylvania Governor Tom Ridge's Broadcast Communications Director, Carlton was hired by the WVC3-Group in Reston, Virginia, to be their Executive Vice-President for Communications and Public Affairs. The WVC3-Group provides a variety of services to Government and private sector clients from antiterrorism, security and counterintelligence issues, to product technology, advanced technology placement and force protection. They are currently engaged in work for the Department of Homeland Security, the Justice Department, CIA and several other federal agencies. Carlton is the project manager for a new Homeland Security website currently under development, the first-ever dedicated to the nation's first responder community due out in 2004.

After conducting many investigations involving non-profits, Carlton prefers to shy away from being involved with them. The only non-profit he currently has any involvement with is the Salvation Army.

Carlton has one daughter, Melinda, from his first marriage. Mindy is currently the business editor for the Princeton Packet newspaper in New Jersey. Carlton currently resides in Dillsburg, Pennsylvania, with his second wife, Susan, and her two sons, Spencer, 16, and Devon, 10. Susan is a former TV news reporter and an executive for the Pennsylvania Public Television Network.

SEMPER FIDELIS

Richard A. Simon

"The instant you meet another Marine in business, esprit de Corps takes over and usually you not only end up doing business together but also making a friend."

Born: 27 November 1950 in Chicago, Illinois
Service: United States Marine Corps, 1967 – 1970, Enlisted, served in Vietnam as a Forward Observer
Occupation: President and CEO, United Service Companies

While in high school Rick worked part time at a company which is now called United Service Companies in Chicago. At the age of 17, Rick decided that he was not college bound and enlisted in the Marine Corps. He was sent to Parris Island for boot camp, to North Carolina for ACT and then to Camp Pendleton as a base for a series of schools.

"It was the late sixties, and I was at the north end of Camp Pendleton for about a year of training prior to going to Vietnam. During the time that I was off base, I spent every evening and weekend that I could in the Laguna Beach area. Much of that liberty time was spent with my friend Jeff Schilling in a fine establishment called the 'Sandpiper.'

"Since we made about 90 dollars a month, we had more consumption ability than funds would allow. But, being resourceful Marines even though we were all of 18 years old, we knew that befriending the bartender was a good idea. So after a few visits, 'Tommy, the bartender' was our new best friend and each night that we went there we would order pitchers of whatever Tommy was making. The fact that some nights we went there with about ten dollars between us didn't matter. Tommy always made sure that we were well watered.

"Being men of the world, we always tipped at least two bucks after a full night of festivities with a tab of less than five dollars. This went on for about a year of my advanced training until I had completed the final lesson (cold weather indoctrination in Fallon, Nevada). I returned to Pendleton from

Fallon and got orders to I Corps in Vietnam the same day. With my new cold weather parka never to see the Sandpiper again (or so I thought), I departed for Vietnam.

"About 25 years later, I was in Los Angeles on business and the next stop was San Diego. I decided to take the day and drive down the Pacific Coast Highway rather than fly or use the freeway. About half way to San Diego, I passed through Laguna Beach, and on the west side of the Pacific Coast Highway there it was – the Sandpiper – just like it was a lifetime ago. I pulled over my car and parked, and stood outside for a long time. It was about four in the afternoon, and the Sandpiper was open, but I really didn't have a reason to go in. Something, however, made me walk into this mostly dark bar that was empty in the middle of a bright sunny afternoon.

"As I walked in and my eyes adjusted to the light I could see 1968 again. The walls were covered with the same Marine Emblems from a hundred Marine units, and the booths were still made of black imitation leather with black tape holding them together, just like always. As I looked toward the bar I thought, 'this is not really happening.' The bartender was Tommy. He was older, heavier and grayer, but so was I. He was the same person who so many years ago took care of a couple of kids who were far from home, just like they were his family.

"He recognized me instantly, not by name but I could tell he knew me. The next two hours went by in a flash as we talked about a lot of different people – some I remembered and some I didn't. Some people had come back to see him and put their business card on the wall, and some people never came back. When I had to leave, I added my card to the wall. And, even though I knew I didn't have to, I left money on the bar and asked him to use it to take care of the next kids who come in as Marines.

"I got back in the car, turned on the oldies station and headed south on the Pacific Coast Highway, feeling like I was 18 years old, 30 pounds lighter and bulletproof. Thanks, Tommy."

In 1970, Rick was discharged and returned to Chicago and to the job he had prior to enlisting in the Marines. He took the exam to become a Chicago Police Officer, passed the exam and was hired. He enjoyed a 20 plus year career with Chicago's Police Department, but continued to maintain his part time position at United Service Companies.

United Services was established in 1965 as a janitorial company. In nearly 40 years, United Services Companies has grown to encompass all aspects of staffing solutions for businesses across the country, from stewards and housekeepers at hotels to security officers for properties and special needs. United Service Companies offers a diverse range of customized staffing and business solutions to its clients through an integrated group of businesses that include: United Maintenance Company, United National Maintenance, United Temps, United Temps-Professional Employer Organization, United Security Service and United Supply Services. The United Services website is located at *www.unitedhq.com*.

In the 1990s the founder of United Services passed away. Rick took an early retirement from the Chicago Police Department as a Sergeant. While doing double duty at the police department and United, he expanded the company and its geographical service area. The company now has a strong presence across the U.S. and has the ability to serve their client base nationwide.

"The opportunity to eventually own the company I worked at part time in high school is the American dream. I learned in the Marine Corps that whatever your mind can conceive, you could achieve."

As CEO Rick continues to focus on continued expansion and enhancing the company's technological infrastructure. "With United I have traveled the U.S. on business and have met former Marines everywhere. The instant you meet another Marine in business, esprit de Corps takes over and usually you not only end up doing business together but also making a friend."

Rick serves on the Board of The Marine Corps Scholarship Foundation. "This is a way to help repay the USMC for putting me and many others on the correct road in life and making us believe that the key to achieving our goals is believing we can do anything." He is Chairman of the Board of the Chicago Convention and Tourism Bureau. He also supports the Maryville Academy.

Rick currently resides in Chicago, Illinois with his wife, Debbie, and his son Richard.

SEMPER FIDELIS

James A. Skidmore, Jr.

"The Marine Corps instilled in me my management philosophy of 'Action not Promises, Results not Excuses.'"

Born: 30 June 1932 in Newark, New Jersey
Service: United States Marine Corps, Reserves 1952 – 1964; Active 1954 – 1957; Officer 1954 – 1964
Occupation: Chairman, President, CEO, Science Management Company, LLC

After receiving his B.A. in Economics from Muhlenberg College in 1954, Jim married Peggy one week later, and the following week left as a Marine Corps Reservist for Officer Candidate School at Quantico, Virginia. After receiving his commission, he started his three-year stint of active duty at the Marine Corps Air Station in Miami, Florida and Guantanamo Bay, Cuba.

"Upon arriving before midnight on my designated reporting date for Officer Candidate School the Staff Sergeant who logged me in was impressed with my blue suit so much so that he decided I should run the obstacle course in the dark, which of course I did. Somewhere along the way I lost my right loafer and was not allowed to find it. The following day while awaiting the issue of my uniform I was forced to march with my new platoon with only one shoe on, and of course dressed in my blue suit stained with mud and grass. My Marine Corps buddies never let me forget this historic event."

In 1957, Jim left active duty and accepted a position with New Jersey Bell Telephone Company. He started as a Customer Service Representative and rose to become the Division Marketing Manager responsible for training and supervising more than 500 sales people. Meanwhile, he continued to serve in the USMC Reserves.

In 1965, Jim was elected President of the United States Junior Chamber of Commerce, which is headquartered in Tulsa, Oklahoma. He and his family lived in the Chamber's Tulsa "Little White House" for the year that he served as President.

At the end of his term as Jaycee President in 1966, Jim went to work for PepsiCo as an assistant to the President for Public Affairs. He served as Chairman of ACTT (America's Christmas Train and Trucks) which raised 100 million for the people of South Vietnam. Then in 1967 he took a leave of absence.

Jim left PepsiCo to work on Richard Nixon's original campaign staff as National Field Director of Citizens for Nixon-Agnew. After their successful election campaign he served as Assistant to the President on the White House Transition Staff.

After the transition was complete Jim accepted a position as Vice President with Handy Associates. In 1972, after being elected as President of Handy, Jim was recruited for the position of President and CEO of Science Management Corporation (SMC), a public company listed on the American Stock Exchange. In 1975, he was elected Chairman of the Board at SMC a leading international professional services firm.

For more than 50 years SMC has provided quality professional services to clients in every major industrialized nation, and in virtually all business and institutional sectors. SMC serves its clients through three major operating groups: consulting, business information services and healthcare systems and services. SMC Consulting provides comprehensive restructuring and reengineering programs designed to change culture, improve quality and customer service, improve profitability and instill a continuous improvement mentality. It has served clients throughout North America, Europe and Africa.

SMC Business Information Systems offers information systems and professional services for all matters related to business recovery and facilities management (outsourcing). Through its business partner relationships it supports the development and/or management of client facilities and personnel.

SMC Healthcare Systems and Services assists Healthcare institutions to become more financially stable and self-reliant by seeking out and providing them with the most economically effective solutions.

Jim is very active in many charities in New Jersey and nationally and has received numerous awards for participation and achievement. Most of this activity has been focused on education and scholarship programs. He currently serves as a Trustee for The Scholarship Fund for Inner-City Children, Rutgers University Graduate School of Management and Muhlenberg College.

He also serves on the Board of Directors of major Corporations including several Horizon Healthcare companies and HMO Blue – Blue Cross & Blue Shield of New Jersey.

Jim has three brothers, Elmer, Gerry, and Robert, who also served in the United States Marine Corps.

Jim and his wife, Peggy, divide their time between their residences in New Jersey and Longboat Key, Florida. They are the proud parents of two children, Jacqueline Sue Skidmore and James A. Skidmore, III. They also have three grandchildren, Colin, Jessica, and Amanda.

SEMPER FIDELIS

Frederick W. Smith

"The indelible lessons about leadership, taking care of one's troops, focusing on the mission, and dealing with adversity were invaluable lessons taught me by the Marine Corps."

Born: 11 August 1944 in Marks, Mississippi
Service: United States Marine Corps PLC 1963 – 1966, Active duty 1966 – 1970, Platoon Leader/Company Commander and Forward Air Controller
Occupation: Founder, Chairman, President, CEO, FedEx

While an undergraduate at Yale, Fred made two life-altering moves. He wrote a significant term paper and joined the Marine Corps' Platoon Leaders Class. Upon graduation in 1966 with a B.S. in Economics, he entered active duty as a second lieutenant.

"When I first joined the Platoon Leaders Class in 1963, I could not imagine what a profound effect it would have on my life. The indelible lessons about leadership, taking care of one's troops, focusing on the mission, and dealing with adversity were invaluable lessons taught me by the Marine Corps. These were the foundations upon which I built FedEx.

"While I have greatly enjoyed business, nothing compares to the pride and honor I feel having been privileged to lead Marines in Vietnam. That experience, while bittersweet, transcends all others in my professional life. My Marine comrades, both here and lost, occupy a unique place in my heart. I am indebted to all of them for their outstanding service, the support they afforded me, and their friendship then and now."

After two tours in Vietnam, Fred was discharged in 1970. He immediately acted on the business plan/term paper that he wrote in 1965. The term paper proposed an airfreight system that could accommodate time-sensitive shipments such as medicines, computer parts, and electronics. He realized that in order for a next day delivery organization to be effective his operation would have to function at night. Federal Express officially began operations on April 17, 1973 with the launch of 14 small aircraft from Memphis International Airport.

Today FedEx has annual revenues of $20 billion and is the premier global provider of transportation, e-commerce and supply chain management services. The company offers integrated business solutions through a network of subsidiaries operating independently, including; FedEx Ground, North America's second largest provider of small-package ground delivery service; FedEx Freight, a leading provider of regional less-than-truckload freight services; FedEx Custom Critical, the world's largest provider of expedited time-critical shipments; and FedEx Trade Networks, a provider of customs brokerage, consulting, information technology and trade facilitation solutions.

"As I reflect on my business career, I take great pride as the founder of FedEx in its growth from a startup in 1971 to one of the largest global companies, employing more than 200,000 people. Our wonderful employees – as our advertising says – 'changed the way the world works.'

"A key factor in the success of FedEx, often noted by others, is our unique employee culture and commitment to customer service. Far less known is that the genesis of the FedEx emphasis on its people was directly derived from my service in the U.S. Marine Corps.

"I will be forever grateful to the Marine Corps."

Fred has served on the boards of several large public companies and is co-chairman of the U.S. World War II Memorial Project. He is also a director of the Business Roundtable, CATO Institute, Library of Congress James Madison Council and the Mayo Foundation, and he serves as vice chairman of the China and French American Business Council. He is also the former chairman of the U.S. Air Transport Association and International Air Transport Association.

Fred and his wife, Diane, currently reside in Tennessee.

SEMPER FIDELIS

Doug Stone

"If it's worth doing in the Marine Corps, it's worth doing with class!"

Born: 21 April 1950 in Santa Monica, California
Service: United States Marine Corps, Reserves 1969 – 1973; Active 1973 – 1978; Reserves 1978 – present, Officer
Occupation: Scientific Applications International Corporation, Senior Vice President; USMCR, Brigadier General

Doug Stone graduated from the U.S. Naval Academy in 1973 with a Bachelor of Science in Analytical Management and General Engineering. Immediately following he was commissioned in the USMC.

"My favorite Marine story is thanks to General Charles Krulak, who was my Company Officer at the U.S. Naval Academy while I was a Midshipman there. The then Captain Krulak got all of us Midshipman who were 'would be' Marine Officers in the Company wardroom, and gave us a test. 'He said, what do you do if, as a Second Lieutenant, your new Company Commander tells you; 'Lieutenant, there is a 100' pole over there and a two foot hole in the center of the battalion grinder. I want you to have that pole standing straight up in an hour when I will be back to inspect it.' Of all the answers there was only one right one, and it wasn't one that any of us gave. The answer was, 'Gunny, get that pole in the hole and standing straight, I will be back in 45 minutes to inspect, right before the Company Commander shows up!' In a terse story it has always said the most about the Corps, our Officer and enlisted relationships, and the confidence and trust in the lynchpin of our Corps, the NCO's, who frequently accomplish the seemingly impossible."

Upon discharge from the active Corps in 1987, Stone began his civilian career with Hewlett Packard. Continuing his education, he earned a Masters in Human Resource Management from Pepperdine University that same year.

Continually pressing forward, Stone became General Manager at Rolm Corporation, then President/CEO of Personal CAD Systems. By 1992 he received a Masters in Public Administration from the University of Southern California and a Masters in Business Management from Stanford University.

In the work force, Stone moved to President/CEO of GammaLink, a pioneering technology firm he grew and sold. Next came yet another Masters degree in International Security from the Naval War College in 1995. As President/CEO of Decisive Technology, he provided strategic direction taking the entrepreneurial firm far beyond its projected growth. Moving on to Qwest Communications, a Fortune 500 Company, Stone again led business and strategic development. By 2001, he finished a Ph.D. in Political Science at the University of Southern California.

Since the last quarter of 2002, Stone has been Senior Vice President of Scientific Applications International Corporation, one of the largest international systems integration and engineering consulting firms.

Over the last twenty-plus years General Stone has led an increasingly demanding life. Through diligence and determination he has dramatically advanced his civilian career, earned five post-graduate degrees and steadily moved upward through the ranks of the Marine Corps Reserve.

General Stone's military awards are numerous: the Vietnamese Service Medal in 1969, a Navy Commendation Medal in 1986, a Meritorious Service Medal in 1991, a Legion of Merit award in 2001, and a Defense Meritorious Service Medal in 2003, just to mention a few.

No less than 28 organizations have benefited from Stone's enthusiasm and dedication as he has served on their board of directors or as an advisor over the last several years. Currently, General Stone is the USMC Designee to the Army Science Board and is on the National Board of Directors of Toys for Tots Foundation.

Now, back on active duty as the Senior Defense Representative in Pakistan, General Stone is the Senior U.S. Military official in that country. He also functions as liaison with Centcom LNO (Central Command) regarding regional policy and operational matters. As Deputy Commander, Combined Joint Task Force – Afghanistan, Stone's operational focus is along the Pakistan/Afghanistan border.

Doug and Kathy have been married 31 years and have two married daughters and a handful of grandchildren. One son-in-law works with Stone in the civilian arena and their other son-in-law is a Major in the USMC, a highly decorated veteran of the liberation of Iraq.

The Stones live on a working cattle ranch in California where they also have a vineyard that produces Stone's Crossing wine, an award winning Italian variety.

SEMPER FIDELIS

James H. Stone

"The values we learned in the Marine Corps are valuable in running a business."

Born: 20 December 1925 in New York City, New York
Service: Unites States Marine Corps 1943 – 1946, 1950 – 1952, Officer
Occupation: Chairman of the Board, Stone Energy

James H. Stone spent five years in the United States Marine Corps during World War II and the Korean War. He was an infantry officer and attained the rank of Captain.

"On reporting to Parris Island, the drill instructor said he was signing everybody up for a war bond which cost $18.75. We were being paid $21.00 a month. I suggested that I would like to pass on the opportunity and he told me he couldn't make me buy the bond, but could make me wish I had bought the bond! I signed up immediately and he said I was a quick learner."

"The values we learned in the Marine Corps are valuable in running a business." James Stone founded Stone Energy Corporation in 1952 as a gas and oil exploration company. Most of their work is in the Gulf of Mexico region, but they also actively drill in the Rocky Mountains. Stone Energy is one of the leading independent producers of gas and oil in the United States.

Stone Energy Corporation is listed on the New York Stock Exchange as SGY and Mr. Stone is still active as Board Chairman. The company employs more than 200 people and has revenues approaching $300 million a year. In addition to running his own company, Stone currently serves on the Marine Board of Toys for Tots, and the Marine Corps Heritage Foundation.

As a successful company, Stone Energy Corporation contributes to many charities including The Marine Corps University Foundation, the Marine Corps Heritage Foundation, Marine Corps Toys for Tots, and the Marine Military Academy.

The Marine Corps continues to be an important and influential factor in James Stone's life.

SEMPER FIDELIS

ROBERT D. STOREY

"The Marine Corps is one of the great institutions of America."

BORN: 28 March 1936 in Tuskegee, Alabama
SERVICE: United States Marine Corps, 1958 – 1961, Officer
OCCUPATION: Partner, Thompson Hine LLP

Bob Storey is a Harvard alumnus, having received his A.B. in 1958. Upon graduation he joined the United States Marine Corps and served as a communications officer where he attained the rank of Captain.

Bob remembers a "brush with history" as he reported for duty with the 1st Marine Air Wing in Atsugi, Japan. His assignment there began about the same time as Cpl. Lee Harvey Oswald was leaving.

"Another Marine memory involves a 'mystery plane!' On the base, aviators occasionally spoke of a 'mystery plane' on the premises, flown by persons unknown. But after Francis Gary Powers' U-2 aircraft was shot down over the former Soviet Union, Japanese protesters rioted outside our main gate over the apparent presence of a similar plane at our base. Evidently, they had better information than we did about this 'top secret' aircraft."

Law school was Bob's goal following his discharge from the Marine Corps in 1961. He attended Case Western Reserve School of Law, graduated in 1964, and began a job in the legal department of a natural gas utility serving Northeast Ohio. Next he applied his legal skills as the Assistant Director of the Legal Aid Society of Cleveland where he and Burt W. Griffin (former lawyer-investigator for the Warren Commission inquiring into President Kennedy's assassination) established one of the nation's first Neighborhood Legal Services Programs. For the next 25 years Bob was a partner with a prestigious Cleveland law firm. In 1993, he joined Thompson Hine LLP as a partner in the Corporate and securities practice area. Bob focuses his practice on general Corporate and organizational matters; Corporate authority; duties and liabilities of directors/trustees/officers; and educational issues.

"Established in 1911, Thompson Hine LLP is among the largest business law firms in the United States, and has been nationally recognized as one of the Best Corporate Law Firms in America. Thompson Hine has offices in Cleveland, Cincinnati, Columbus, Dayton, New York City, Washington, D.C., and Brussels, Belgium. The firm's clients include such major Corporations as Verizon, Procter & Gamble, Ford Motor Company, KeyCorp, and Sherwin-Williams.

Bob Storey serves on the boards of several Corporations, major educational institutions, and public entities; Case Western Reserve University, Spelman College, The Kresge Foundation, and The Center for Strategic & International Studies just to name a few. He is a former Trustee of Phillips Exeter Academy and Overseer of Harvard.

Bob has been married to Juanita for 43 years and they are the proud parents of Charles, Christopher, and Rebecca. The Storeys reside in the Cleveland area.

SEMPER FIDELIS

Photo Credit Mort Tucker Photography.

Arthur Ochs Sulzberger

"Many of the lessons I learned from my experience in the Marine Corps played a major role in my future education. As we look ahead to the mission of The Marines, it seems a terrible waste not to use this educational asset as one more card in the complicated deck we all are served."

Born: 5 February 1926 in New York City, New York
Service: United States Marine Corps, 1943 – 1951, three years active and five years reserves, Enlisted, Officer
Occupation: Chairman Emeritus, The New York Times Company

Arthur Ochs Sulzberger, better known as Punch, was the sole male in a family of three older sisters. To him this was as good a reason as any to join the Marines. He was a miserable student and quit school at the age of 17 to enlist. He became a communications specialist – ending up in General McArthur's headquarters in the Philippines, initially as a Naval Intercept Operator.

When the Japanese heard Punch was coming, they surrendered and after some months in Tokyo, he had enough points to come home.

A moment of glory came when he shared a hospital manifest list with the ex-premier of Japan – Hideki Tojo. Punch had a variation of athlete's foot. Tojo had sucking gunshot wounds. After a few days Punch went home. Tojo didn't.

Sulzberger was discharged on April Fool's Day, 1946. He remained in the reserves because he was married and needed the money. Punch did sufficiently well on his high school proficiency exam to enter Columbia University. Toward the end of his junior year he was recalled to active duty, but was permitted to complete his senior year and graduate as a Second Lieutenant. Following officer's training in Quantico, and a course in public information at Fort Slocum, he was sent to Korea as the Assistant P.I.O. of the First Marine Division. Some months later Punch returned to the USA and was assigned to the office of the legislative assistant to the Commandant. This office was what President Truman must have had in mind when he accused the Corps of having the finest PR in the world. Run by a wonderful historian, Brig. Gen. Don Hittle, to make sure that the interests of the Corps were quietly brought to the attention of the Congress and other government agencies. It was an eye opening experience for Sulzberger. When his time ran out he was once again discharged and submitted his retirement. New challenges lay ahead and he needed full time to address them.

The job that called was the family business: The New York Times Company. The newspaper, from which the company derives its name, had been purchased in 1896 by Sulzberger's grandfather, a newspaperman from Chattanooga, Tennessee. Prior to his death in 1935, he put the company into a trust which operates to keep the newspaper free and independent. In 1963, Sulzberger became the publisher, following in his father's footsteps, and then his brother-in-law's.

Today The New York Times Company is a vastly different company from the one it was in 1963. Here's the current description:

"The New York Times Company (NYSE: NYT), a leading media company with 2002 revenue of $3.1 billion, includes The New York Times, The International Herald Tribune, The Boston Globe, 16 other newspapers, eight network-affiliated television stations, two New York City radio stations and more than 40 web ites, including *www.NYTimes.com* and *www.Boston.com*. For the third consecutive year, the Company was ranked No. 1 in the publishing industry on Fortune's 2002 list of America's Most Admired Companies. In 2003 the Company was named by Fortune as one of the 100 Best Companies to work for. The Company's core purpose is to enhance society by creating, collecting and distributing high-quality news, information and entertainment."

In 1992, Sulzberger turned the publisher job at The Times over to his son Arthur, Jr., and in late 1997, retired from the business side, took the title Emeritus and asked the Board of Directors to name Arthur, Jr. Chairman of the company, as well as publisher of The Times.

The New York Times Company Foundation manages four philanthropic programs. First is its own program of grants and matching gifts, to which in 2002 it devoted about $7.6 million, $4.5 million in New York, plus $1.4 million through the Boston Globe Foundation.

Grants are made to organizations in the fields of education, culture, journalism, service and environment. In 2002, there were 378 grants. In addition, 1,050 Times employees and officers made charitable gifts which were matched by the Foundation, $1.50 for every $1 contributed. The totals for the year were $1,314,000 in Foundation matching funds added to $875,722 in employee contributions.

The Foundation each year conducts The New York Times Neediest Cases Fund. The 91st annual campaign ended January 31 with $8.8 million, which has now been distributed to seven social agencies with long experience in reaching people in distress.

Since 1999, the Foundation has also administered The New York Times College Scholarship Program. Each year, it selects 20 students from exceptionally deprived circumstances in New York and gives them four-year college scholarships, along with summer jobs and mentoring. The Foundation devotes about $250,000 a year to the program.

On September 12, 2001, the Foundation launched a special New York Times 9/11 Neediest Fund. Through 2002, it raised $62.4 million, almost all of which was committed within six months of the 9/11 disaster. Participating agencies estimate that the funds have helped 20,000 individuals and families affected.

The family makes its charitable contributions through the Sulzberger Foundation. Together Arthur and his three sisters give approximately $2.5 million to some 100 causes in which they have an interest.

Sulzberger has been married to Allison Cowles for eight years. Each lost their spouse about the same time and the four had been friends for years. Between them they have six married children and a dozen grandchildren.

The Sulzbergers have homes in New York, Southampton, Spokane, Coeur d'Alene and a flat in London, so all of their plans spell travel.

SEMPER FIDELIS

Patrick F. Taylor

"I used to think that it was the Marine Corps training that made former Marines such an extraordinary group, I have now come to realize that the Marine Corps attracts an extraordinary type of individual to undergo their training."

Born: 17 June 1937 in Beaumont, Texas
Service: United States Marine Corps 1958 – 1959, PLC
Occupation: Chairman, President and CEO of Taylor Energy

During his sophomore year at Louisiana State University, Patrick Taylor joined the Platoon Leadership Course for the USMC. Upon joining the Marine Corps, Mr. Taylor was slated to become an infantry officer. During training, he noticed that the future officers in aviation were afforded time in a military jets. During his second year of PLC he made the decision to become a Marine pilot. However, the aviator's program required another set of physical examinations. During this aviator series of physicals a heart condition was detected. This not only precluded Mr. Taylor from becoming an aviator but also concluded his career as a Marine. As his second year concluded, he was honorably discharged.

"When the condition was first discovered, I disagreed strongly and appealed to everyone inside and outside of my chain of command. But the Commanding Officer of OCS had made a decision and it was to remain final. This decision immediately changed the course of my life and planned career goals. I was no longer going to continue my career as a Marine or become a pilot. So, I put this incident behind me and moved forward with my life. In 1999, I commissioned five large bronze statues of Marine General Lejeune. In November 2001, one of the statues was placed at Quantico and I returned to the base for the first time since being discharged for its dedication. During that visit, I was given a base tour that included the hall containing the portraits of former academy commanders. Each portrait contained the name of the commander and their years of reign. Imagine my surprise when I discovered that the commanding officer who forever changed my life by discharging me from the Marine Corps was Lieutenant Colonel Louis H. Wilson, Jr., Medal of Honor Recipient and later Commandant Marine Corps. As destiny would have it, I later met him."

Upon being discharged, Mr. Taylor went on to obtain his degree in Petroleum Engineering from LSU. After graduating, Mr. Taylor began his career in the oil fields. While working in this industry, he made his biggest and most profitable find in October 1963. It did not happen in a promising patch of oil, it happened at a trade show. There he met Phyllis Miller, and they were married in December 1964.

During the years from 1961 to 1966 he worked in a number of positions in the oil exploration industry. In 1967, while working for John Mecom, Sr., he was fired for his out of the workplace pursuits (skydiving), which Mr. Mecom adamantly opposed.

Being degreed, experienced, young, confidant and unemployed, there was only one thing to do; go out on his own. Mr. Taylor founded his own consulting company, Circlebar Consulting. In 1974, he received an offer from Mr. Mecom to rejoin him as his exploration partner. In 1979, that profitable enterprise was sold. Mr. Mecom retired and Mr. Taylor established Taylor Energy Company. Today Taylor Energy Company has over 100 offshore wells and is the only individually owned company to explore and produce oil and gas on federal lands.

After recently discovering some very significant high yield fields in the Gulf of Mexico, Mr. Taylor commissioned the building of a 690 foot 15 port drilling platform. This is believed to be one of the largest structures ever built for a single individual. When completed, the structure will weigh approximately 8,700 tons and rest in 665 feet of water. When additional equipment and structures are added to the main structure, it will rise 85 feet above sea level. The platform (named Simba) is expected to be completed, sunk and have 12 operating wells tied into its ports by the end of 2004.

In 2003, Mr. Taylor became the only businessman from Louisiana to be included on the Forbes "400 Weathiest Americans" list. And although he is a very succesful businessman, some of his greatest achievements and recognitions have been in education.

In March 1988, Mr. Taylor met with 183 students at Livingston Middle School in New Orleans. Every student in this group had already been held back at least one year, some had behavioral problems, and others planned to drop out. Mr. Taylor asked these students if they would like to attend college. Every student responded with a yes. He quickly realized that within each of these students was the desire, but their families did not have the means. He offered each of the students a fully paid college education if they went on to graduate while maintaining a B average. One half of the kids from this troubled group graduated and one half of those who graduated went on to college.

Mr. Taylor then concentrated his efforts on the rest of Louisiana's students to insure a college education for everyone regardless of their families' economic status. The state of Louisiana signed into law the first "Taylor Plan" (now referred to as TOPS) on July 10, 1989. It provided for state-paid college tuition for academically qualified students from families with less than $25,000 annual income (cap has since been removed). Applicants must also complete an advanced high school core curriculum, achieve a 2.5 grade point average, and a minimum score of 18 on the American College Test. Since then the "Taylor Plan" has been implemented in some format in 20 states. Mr. Taylor is working to implement his TOPS program nationwide.

Mr. Taylor has been involved in many other charities supporting the arts, museums, United States Marine Corps, law enforcement, and to better the quality of life for the people of New Orleans and Louisiana.

Patrick and Phyllis divide their time between their residences in New Orleans, Louisiana and their ranch in Mississippi.

SEMPER FIDELIS

RONALD E. TUCKER

"You can take the man out of the Marines,
but you can't take the Marine out of the man."

BORN: 11 July 1951, Spartanburg, South Carolina
SERVICE: United States Marine Corps, 1971 - 1992, Enlisted, Warrant Officer, Officer
OCCUPATION: President/CEO, Sandbar Productions, LLC

After graduating from high school, Ron worked for two years prior to enlisting in the Marine Corps.

During his military career he served in many enlisted and officer positions which included infantryman, platoon sergeant, administrative clerk, Adjutant, Personnel and Legal Officer, and served as a Protocol and Public Affairs representative on numerous occasions. His career was highlighted by over eight years of service with the Recruit Training Regiment at Parris Island, South Carolina and an assignment with the 4th Marine Expeditionary Brigade during Desert Shield and Desert Storm.

"I've got many memories of my time in the Corps … both good and bad. I've traveled the world and met many interesting people.

"As the Officer of the Day (OD) you're likely to encounter lots of strange things. One evening while on duty as the OD in Iwakuni, Japan, I noticed a slightly inebriated Marine walking across a field toward his barracks. I went to give assistance and to make sure he got back OK. While in his room I notice several M16 clips (also called magazines) in his wall-locker. When I asked why he had so many he told me they were issued when he checked into his unit. I called the OD at his unit and asked if they issued magazines to the new troops when they checked in. He told me no … they don't issue any kind of reading material when troops check in.

"I was serving aboard the USS *Iwo Jima* as part of the Marine amphibious assault force. Since leaving Morehead City, North Carolina in mid August 1990, we had become used to shipboard life. We drilled often ... man-overboard, general quarters, etc. We drilled so often I believe the Marines had become a little complacent. These drills were regarded more as a Navy function. All the Marines were expected to do was, 'go to your quarters and stay out of the way.' I should state at this point that I have the highest respect for the sailors who serve aboard ship. The sailors serving aboard the USS *Iwo Jima* were among the hardest working people I've ever known.

"On the morning of October 30th at about 7:45 a.m., the announcement came ... 'General Quarters, General Quarters ... All hands man your battle stations ... THIS IS NOT A DRILL ... THIS IS NOT A DRILL.' Shortly after the announcement, the ship lost power and went into total darkness. After weeks of practice drills you would think that all would be orderly and without chaos, but this was the first time we had to do it in the dark. This time there was a greater since of urgency ... we didn't know what was happening. All we knew was ... IT WAS NOT A DRILL. Many times in the previous weeks we had donned our MOPP gear (chemical protective clothing) as part of the practice exercises, but probably never as fast as we did that morning. We sat in our quarters for hours not knowing what had happened. Ironically, back in the states, the news networks were announcing that a steam accident aboard the USS *Iwo Jima* had occurred and there were casualties. All this time the embarked troops still didn't know what was going on. It would be mid afternoon that day before we would hear that 10 of our shipmates had perished. A short while later I was standing on the hangar deck as the bodies of our comrades-in-arms were carried off the ship. I will never forget that sight. Nor will I forget the Sailors and Marines standing side by side, tears rolling down our cheeks, as we said farewell to these brave men.

"Just as we never forget our casualties of war, let's also remember those who made the ultimate sacrifice while training for war."

During his time in the Marine Corps, Ron graduated from the University of South Carolina and earned a Masters degree from Webster University, St. Louis, Missouri. Ron retired from the Marine Corps in 1992.

"For the longest time, I felt like a fish out of water. Things just didn't feel right. I missed putting on the uniform everyday and most of all I missed my Marines. The bond that Marines form with each other is really known only to those who have worn the eagle, globe, and anchor. It can't fully be explained to those who were not initiated at Parris Island, San Diego, Montford Point, or Quantico. In time I began to adjust to a life of neckties and wingtips, but there was a void. I needed to be involved in some capacity with the lives of Marines. Making matters worse was that I lived within 10 minutes of two Marines bases … Parris Island and MCAS Beaufort."

In 1993, he founded Sandbar Productions, LLC (also does business as Good-To-Go Video), a coordinating production company, established to provide location management and scouting services to motion picture companies, major catalog companies, and other film and still photography professionals. Since that time, Good-To-Go Video has earned more than 20 national and international awards for video production excellence.

"When I told my wife what I was going to do, she was somewhat surprised, since I knew nothing about the video production business and didn't own a video camera. I told her, 'I don't need to know how to do it, I just need to know how to get it done.'"

In 1995, his first program titled *The Making of a Marine* was completed and released to the general public. The video was well received by Marine Corps public relations officials, veterans groups, youth organizations and most appreciative were the Marine Corps Recruiters. Since that time they have gone on to produce eight other titles about our fabulous Marines. All of these great Marine Corps videos can be previewed at *www.goodtogovideo.com*.

The Good-To-Go Video crew has traveled the world to document the stories and capture the images of Marines. From the historic parade grounds at Marine Barracks, Washington, D.C., "Oldest Post of the Corps," to the hallowed battlefields of Vietnam, they have provided a rare look at where Marines have trained and fought. Their productions have been applauded by educators, veteran's organizations, at-risk youth groups and even members of the other services for providing an up-close look at the more intriguing aspects of Marine Corps life.

Ron is actively involved in many professional organizations. He is a member of the International Documentary Association in Los Angeles, the Association of Independent Video and Filmmakers in New York, and is a Charter Member of the Carolina Film Alliance.

He is proactive with many Marine Corps groups such as the Marine Corps Association, Marine Corps League, Marine Corps Mustang Association, Veterans of Foreign Wars, the Second Marine Division Association, the Marine Corps Heritage Foundation, and the Marine Corps Combat Correspondent's Association.

Ron and his wife, Sandy, currently reside in Beaufort, South Carolina. They have two children, Christopher and Nicole and two grandchildren, Allison and Logan.

SEMPER FIDELIS

Rod Walsh

"Have a plan and a backup plan; and know all the rules."

Born: 22 August 1944 in Brooklyn, New York
Service: United States Marine Corps, 1963 – 1966, Enlisted
Occupation: President, Blue Chip Inventory Service, Inc.; Partner, Semper Fi Consulting

Rod Walsh enlisted in the Marines during the Vietnam War, performing various military occupations. Originally he was assigned to motor pool, but at his first duty station in Iwakuni, Japan, he was "volunteered" for the Military Police, and then ended his tour of duty with an office administration assignment.

"While I was stationed at Camp Lejeune, I decided to visit my older brother who was going through Army boot camp at Fort Jackson, South Carolina. Another Marine and I took a bus and had a nice visit with Tommy. We decided to save some money on the trip back to Lejeune by hitching a ride. Well, it took all night and we were unable to get closer than about 50 miles. We contacted the police, they woke a taxi owner and he drove us the rest of the way. The tab for the taxi was about $50; a bus would have cost us $10 or $15. When we got to the base and told our story, our NCOIC told us we could have called and let them know we'd be late. Learned two lessons from that: have a plan and a backup plan; and know all the rules."

During his Marine Corps experience Rod attained the rank of Sergeant, completed his enlistment and was discharged in September of 1966.

Rod worked some entry level jobs such as clerk and inventory counter over the next couple of years. His counting job at Washington Inventory Service is where he caught the "inventory bug" and then the boot! A draftsman job for Rapistan led to work in sales and administration, and encouragement to start his own inventory service. With energy and determination, Rod started Blue Chip Inventory Service, Inc. in 1970. His then boss, Bob Peacock, urged Rod on with Blue Chip and creatively offered ways for Rod to continue with

Rapistan while Blue Chip got established. By 1973, his business was beginning to click and Rod went into it full-time.

"My company performs about 3,000 inventories a year for other companies. We primarily work in California and Washington, but have done inventories in about half the states, and in 2002, we counted a few commissary inventories in Germany. We're a pretty lean organization; we have five people on salary and about 125 hourly inventory employees. I guess we're in the top 25, but many of my competitors think, because I have a big mouth, that my company is much larger than it really is. While we currently use the National DataComputer line of handheld terminals to accumulate data, we will soon deploy a new device. Recently, I joined six other inventory services and helped design a keypad that allows for very rapid entry of data into selected Palm and Handera PDA devices. Our new product – PalmQuest – is extremely innovative and about half the cost of competing products."

As company president, Rod looks toward the future to try to ensure Blue Chip Inventory is ready to be there.

Rod Walsh and Dan Carrison wrote *Semper Fi: Business Leadership the Marine Corps Way* in 1998. It has sold well and is now also available in Japanese, Korean, and Mandarin. In addition, Rod and Dan do leadership presentations to business and government organizations. From book royalties and presentation honorariums, they donate generously to the USMC Reserve Toys for Tots Foundation.

Rod Walsh contributes to several other charities and organizations: Cardinal Hayes High School in the Bronx, American Red Cross, Disabled American Veterans, The Yosemite Fund, Marine Corps Heritage Foundation, Marine Corps Scholarship Foundation, Vietnam Veterans Memorial Fund, Pacific Legal Foundation, United Negro College Fund, Los Angeles Mission, Paralyzed Veterans of America, Priests of the Sacred Heart, USO, World War II Memorial Fund, Pacific Lodge Boys' Home, and the Republican National Committee.

Rod is married to Linda and they make their home in sunny, southern California. Rod has a daughter from his previous marriage and two stepsons.

SEMPER FIDELIS

Thomas P. Walter

"If you want to be the best, you have to do the things no one else wants to do."

Born: 7 August 1942 in St. Louis, Missouri
Service: United States Marine Corps 1961 - 1964, Enlisted, Radio – Telegraph Operator
Occupation: Senior Vice President – Investments, Stifel Nicolaus & Company

Tom left for boot camp in San Diego on December 15, 1961. This provided him with a holiday period unlike any others he had previously experienced.

"Prior to boot camp, I had never climbed a rope. On my first try I must have looked like a one legged man in a butt kicking contest. I was not able to climb it. That evening the Drill Instructor took me aside to teach me how to climb. The following day wearing a pack and rifle, I made it to the top. Being so proud after slapping the wood, I let go with the other hand and fell all the way to the ground. I was met there by the Drill Instructor who explained to me that I had fallen on my gear and that was considered destruction of government property. That shocked me, I jumped up and ran back, feeling no body pain (the fall probably killed most of my brain cells)."

In 1962, Tom was dispatched to the Caribbean Sea aboard the USS *Henrico*, APA 45 in response to the Cuban missile crisis. While there, the 1-1 conducted a live fire practice assault at Viaques, Puerto Rico. With a field transport pack, rifle, PRC-10 radio, spare battery and 100 plus degree weather, they had their share of problems keeping Corpsmen busy.

"Stopping back at base camp afterwards for cold cuts and additional training, someone handled the food and forgot to wash their hands. Battalion diarrhea broke out. In true Marine Corps tradition, training continued. We were told to blouse our boots when climbing up the wet nets. Several days later on Thanksgiving, the battalion once again suffered the same fate. The Corpsmen ran short of paregoric so everyone was issued their own roll of toilet tissue. That was my Marine Corps vacation on a Puerto Rican beach."

After leaving the Marine Corps in 1964, Tom worked at Emerson Electric in Research and Development assisting engineers in developing new products. During his entire time at Emerson, Tom read the discarded copies of the Wall Street Journal developing a strong interest in business and finance. In 1965 while reading a discarded copy, he noticed an ad from a Wall Street financial services firm new to the St. Louis area. He applied for the position, was called and interviewed. He was informed that they do not hire 23 year olds with a limited night college education. He replied "I was an NCO in the Marine Corps and I am capable of accomplishing anything that I set my mind to." He was called back the next day and hired. That Wall Street financial services firm was Walston and Company.

In 1979, after stints with Pain Webber and Reinholdt and Gardner, he joined R. Rowland and Company. This company was purchased by Stifel Nicolaus Inc. in 1988. They are a full-service regional brokerage and investment banking firm established in 1890 and currently headquartered in St. Louis, Missouri. The company provides securities brokerage, investment banking, trading, investment advisory, and related financial services to individual investors, professional money managers, businesses and municipalities.

Tom's duties include serving institutional clients, managing over 50 million dollars in assets and as a producing manager for high net worth clients. Personalized service for Tom's clients includes helping them with all financial decisions including mortgage, banking, insurance and general planning information.

Through Stifel Nicolas, Tom supports many charities including Cardinal Glennon Hospital, St. Patrick Center for the Indigent, Sunshine Mission, and the St. Louis area food banks.

Personally, Tom co-founded a golf tournament more than 20 years ago. The original focus of the tournament was to provide scholarships for children of Marines and former Marines. In those early years the tournament raised more than $2.5 million dollars.

The organization evolved and has provided $10,000 scholarship bonds to dependent children of all the services: Army, Navy, Marines Corps, Air Force, and Coast Guard for those who served in Granada, Panama, Lebanon, and Desert Storm. After 9-11, they provided scholarship bonds to children of all parents killed in the terrorism attack on the Pentagon, even civilians. Recently they presented bonds to the 12 children of our fallen astronauts of Space Shuttle Columbia.

Most recently the children of parents killed in Afghanistan and Iraq will be presented with $20,000 scholarship bonds including the children of British, Polish and Australian troops.

Tom has recently become very active and involved in the Marine Corps Law Enforcement Foundation.

Tom and his friends also work to make military life enjoyable for the recruiters stationed in St. Louis. They provide them with tickets to baseball and football games in addition to occasional dinners "with the guys." It helps the recruiters relax during the sparse evening time they have away from their jobs.

"None of these many charity functions would be possible without the continued support of my very tolerant wife, Linda." Tom and his wife Linda have two children, Lindsay and Mary Clare, and currently reside in the greater St. Louis area.

SEMPER FIDELIS

James H. Webb, Jr.

"Only those who were in the middle of any battle can ever fully understand it."

Born: 9 February 1946 in St. Joseph, Missouri
Service: United States Marine Corps 1968 - 1972, Officer
Occupation: Former Secretary of the Navy, Author, Film Maker, Business Consultant

James Webb grew up on the move, attending more than a dozen different schools across the U.S. and in England. He graduated from high school in Bellevue, Nebraska, and started his military career by first attending the University of Southern California on an NROTC academic scholarship. Leaving after one year for the U.S. Naval Academy, he graduated in 1968, one of 18 in his class to receive the Superintendent's Letter of Commendation for outstanding leadership, and elected to take his commission as a Marine Corps officer.

2nd Lieutenant Webb was first in his class of 243 at the Marine Corps Officer's Basic School in Quantico, Virginia. He then served with the 5th Marine Regiment in Vietnam, as a rifle platoon and company commander in the infamous An Hoa Basin west of Danang, where he was awarded the Navy Cross, Silver Star, two Bronze Stars, and two Purple Hearts. He later served as a platoon commander and as an instructor in tactics and weapons at Marine Corps Officer Candidates School, and then as a member of the Secretary of the Navy's immediate staff, before leaving the Marine Corps in 1972.

"As a young second lieutenant, I was pulled aside by a senior officer while lecturing a platoon about drill and ceremonies. 'What are you doing?' he asked. 'Look at your men.' I looked at them and saw nothing unusual. 'Their faces are in the sun,' he said. 'Turn them around. You are the officer. When you talk to your troops, your face should be in the sun.' This small point is emblematic of Marine Corps leadership.

"Americans, and particularly Marines, fight for many reasons. We are proud to fight for our country. We are impelled by accountability to our traditions and to those who have gone before us to fight for the honor of our Corps. And we are bound by the sanctity of our very motto, Semper Fidelis, to fight against all odds if necessary on behalf of one another.

"And what was given to one another is probably the most profound. Friends are found on the battlefield, and unfortunately friends are also lost. And where do we find the measure of the sacrifice? How can we account for the value of that loss? Sometimes we can find an answer in our sense of country, at other times in our Corps. But clearly we can see it in the lives that were able to continue due to the acts of others who were not so fortunate. This is our Marine Corps heritage."

Both sides of Mr. Webb's family have a strong citizen-soldier military tradition that predates the Revolutionary War. Family members have served during the Revolutionary War, the War of 1812, the Mexican War, the Civil War, the Spanish-American War, World War II, Korea, Vietnam, and the Gulf War. Mr. Webb's father was a career Air Force officer who flew B-17s and B-29s during World War II, cargo planes during the Berlin Airlift, and was a pioneer in the United States missile program.

Mr. Webb spent the "Watergate years" as a student at the Georgetown University Law Center, arriving just after the Watergate break-in in 1972, and receiving his J.D. just after the fall of South Vietnam in 1975. While at Georgetown he began a six-year pro bono representation of a Marine who had been convicted of war crimes in Vietnam (finally clearing the man's name in 1978, three years after his suicide), won the Horan award for excellence in legal writing, and authored his first book, *Micronesia and U.S. Pacific Strategy*. He also worked in Asia as a consultant to the Governor of Guam, conducting a study of U.S. military land needs in Asia, and their impact on Guam's political future.

Mr. Webb has written six best-selling novels: *Fields of Fire* (1978), considered by many to be the classic novel of the Vietnam war, *A Sense of Honor* (1981), *A Country Such As This* (1983), *Something To Die For* (1991), *The Emperor's General* (1999) and *Lost Soldiers* (2001). He taught literature at the Naval Academy as their first visiting writer, has traveled worldwide as a journalist, and his PBS coverage of the U.S. Marines in Beirut earned him an Emmy Award from the National Academy of Television Arts and Sciences.

In government, Mr. Webb served in the U.S. Congress as counsel to the House Committee on Veterans Affairs from 1977 to 1981, becoming the first Vietnam veteran to serve as a full committee counsel in the Congress. During the Reagan Administration, he was the first Assistant Secretary of Defense for Reserve Affairs from 1984 to 1987, where he directed considerable research and analysis of the U.S. military's mobilization capabilities and spent much time with our NATO allies. In 1987, he became the first Naval Academy graduate in history to serve in the military and then become Secretary of the Navy. He resigned from that position in 1988 after refusing to agree in the reduction of the Navy's force structure during congressionally mandated budget cuts.

Among Mr. Webb's many other awards for community service and professional excellence are the Department of Defense Distinguished Public Service Medal, the Medal of Honor Society's Patriot Award, the American Legion National Commander's Public Service Award, the VFW's Media Service Award, the Marine Corps League's Military Order of the Iron Mike Award, the John Russell Leadership Award, and the Robert L. Denig Distinguished Service Award. He was a Fall 1992 Fellow at Harvard's Institute of Politics.

Mr. Webb travels extensively, particularly in Asia, as a journalist, business consultant and screenwriter-producer. He speaks Vietnamese and has done extensive pro bono work with the Vietnamese community dating from the late 1970s. In 1989, he met with key Japanese government and industrial officials as a featured guest of the Japanese Foreign Ministry. He has worked on feature film projects with many of Hollywood's top producers. His original story *Rules of Engagement*, which he also executive-produced, was released in April 2000 and starred Tommy Lee Jones and Samuel L. Jackson. It was the number one film in the U.S. for two weeks.

His fifth novel, *The Emperor's General*, was purchased by Paramount pictures as the largest book-to-film deal of 1998. He is writing and producing the film version of *Fields of Fire*, which will be filmed in Quang Nam Province, the same area of Vietnam where the 5th Marines fought. He is also writing a nonfiction book that traces the evolution of the Scots-Irish culture from its origins in Scotland, and its impact on American culture and politics.

James Webb currently resides in Virginia.

SEMPER FIDELIS

Francis J. "Bing" West

"The Marines are an organization which has refused to compromise its standards."

Born: 2 May 1940 in Boston, Massachusetts
Service: United States Marine Corps, 1962 – 1967, Infantry Officer
Occupation: President, GAMA Corps, Author, Former Assistant Secretary of Defense

In 1962, Bing graduated from Georgetown University, joined the Marines and went to Quantico, Virginia for Officer Candidate School. Upon completing OCS, he served as a platoon commander in the 7th and later the 9th Marines. He then attended graduate school at Princeton and also served on the G-3 staff at the Marine Amphibious Force in Da Nang, where he was sent to join various units in contact and write about the nature of the fighting.

"In July of 1966, five of us on Force Recon Team Primness were stuck west of The Rockpile just south of the DMZ. We had stayed too long calling fire on an North Vietnamese Army battalion and they had cut us off. Over our PRC-25 radios we were calling any station on the net to lend us a hand. An Air Force Forward Air Controller (FAC) in a single-engine Piper Cub-type plane came buzzing overhead and we thought, oh, great, he's got about four smoke rockets. No help here. Then this little guy tells us to get our heads down and we're wondering which part of his anatomy his head is in, when we are knocked off our feet and boulders and tree limbs start falling around us. It was a good ten minutes before any of us could hear well enough to get on the radio and scream at the son-of-a-b for bombing us. The pilot calmly told us to stop cursing. The problem had been taken care of. Sure enough, the Vietnamese didn't continue to chase us and we were later extracted.

"It turns out the FAC had fired a marking rocket for a Marine F-8 which had been heading north with two 2,000 pound bombs. The Marine F-8 pilot, Captain Orson Swindle, refused to release with us so close to the mark until the FAC told him we were going under anyway, so he might as well try. Swindle later said those were the longest ten minutes of his life until we came up swearing on the net. The next week Swindle was shot down and spent seven years in the Hanoi Hilton, a 'roommate' of Senator McCain. Swindle said one positive thought he often had while in captivity was that at least he had gotten us out before he went down. In 2002 I met Swindle's wing mate at a dinner and somehow we made the connection of who he was. It turned out that Swindle then was serving as Federal Trade Commissioner and had coordinated several presidential campaigns. We had lunch and I was able to offer my thanks, 37 years later."

After leaving the Marine Corps in 1967, Bing finished his master's degree at Princeton and went to work for RAND Corporation, returning often to Vietnam. He then went to the Pentagon in the office of Systems Analysis. In 1971, Bing started his teaching and academic career at the Naval War College. He started as a Professor of Economics and Decision Making and finished his time there as Dean of Research. While working full time at the Naval War College, he also was employed as a visiting professor at Tufts University from 1977 – 1978, and from 1978 – 1981 as Adjunct Professor at the Center for Strategic and International Studies.

In 1981, he was called upon to serve as Assistant Secretary of Defense under President Ronald Reagan. He was responsible for International Security Affairs. After two years he left government and returned to the civilian sector and took a position as Vice President of the Hudson Institute. In 1985, he left Hudson and formed his own company, named GAMA Corporation. GAMA provides services in war gaming and in decision making under stress in combat situations.

Bing was a CNN commentator during Desert Storm and writes regularly for national defense and international security publications. Bing has served on various boards, including the Secretary of State Commission on Foreign Aid, the Brodlio Center for International Security and The Center for Naval Analysis.

In March 2003, he accompanied the lead Marine units from Kuwait to Bagdad.

"I am grateful for the time I was able to spend with today's generation of Marines. The Marines are an organization which has refused to compromise its standards. It attracts a certain kind of recruit – someone who wants to be challenged and expects discipline. It then molds the fighting force into the finest fighting force which exists today."

His most recent book is *The March Up: Taking Baghdad with the 1st Marine Division*, Bantam Books, September 2003. Bing West and Major General Ray Smith, one of the most decorated Marines since World War II, traveled with 18 Marine units and saw combat on 16 days. His other books include *The Pepperdogs*, *The Village*, and *Small Unit Action in Vietnam*.

Bing currently divides his time between Newport, Rhode Island and Washington, D.C. He is the proud father of four children: Owen (former Marine), Patrick, Alexandra, Kaki and two grandchildren.

SEMPER FIDELIS

Owen West

"Filled with patriotic men drawn into the guild from across the socio-economic spectrum, the Corps breeds the conclusion that gains are only made through sacrifice."

Born: 24 September 1969 in Washington, D.C.
Service: United States Marine Corps, 1991 – 1996, 2002 – 2003, Infantry Officer
Occupation: Vice President, Energy Trading, Goldman, Sachs & Company

Owen attended Harvard University on a ROTC scholarship and rowed for the varsity crew team. After earning his degree in 1991, he left for training at Quantico, Virginia.

"When I arrived at Camp Pendleton, the battalion I was scheduled to join was still afloat. My group of fledgling lieutenants passed the time working out and reconnoitering the bars, giggling at our new schedule. We were swapping stories in the lieutenant's hooch one day when a major—who seemed to be 50 ranks above us – strode in, sending us rocketing to our feet. 'Which one of you is West?' he asked. I raised my hand and he tossed a manila folder at me. 'There's been a helicopter crash. You're the CACO. Get your Alpha dress uniform on.' So my first real job was as a Casualty Assistance Call Officer. I twice served that painful, breathless notification wherein a young woman became a widow because of what we said. In the Marine Corps, you grow up fast."

During Owen's first tour he led a rifle platoon, a rifle company, and a reconnaissance platoon. In 1996, he resigned his commission and attended Stanford Business School to earn an MBA While there, he served as CEO for MBA Challenge for Charity, benefiting the Special Olympics.

After Stanford, he took a job trading commodities with Goldman Sachs, one of the leading investment banks in the world. "Wall street 'teamwork' will never compare to the Corps version, but Goldman does its best to emulate the value system."

In 2002, Owen took leave from Goldman Sachs and joined First Force Recon in Operation Iraqi Freedom. During his 4-month tour in Iraq, Owen's first child was born.

When First Force's mission ended, Owen returned to Goldman Sachs. Today he runs the Canadian natural gas trading business, taking proprietary positions in the extremely volatile energy futures market. "It's a daily war between risk and reward in a zero sum arena. Still, it's not life and death."

Owen's Marine Corps experience with discipline and fitness provided a pent up need to continue in civilian life. He found his outlet in the world of endurance sports. As a recon Marine he tried out for the Eco Challenge, a 400-mile endurance foot race in which he competed six times, finishing as high as second. One team consisted of Marines, in another he ran with three Playboy Bunnies. He also attempted Mount Everest from the north side in 2001, but fell some 1,000 feet short.

In the civilian sector Owen sought intellectual challenge as well as physical challenge. He has written two books, *Sharkman Six* and *Four Days to Veracruz*. Both are action packed novels featuring Marines. In addition, he is a term member of the Council on Foreign Relations to fill the foreign policy debate vacuum created by his discharge.

Owen has been an active supporter and participating member of the Marine Corps Law Enforcement Foundation. The Marine Corps Law Enforcement Society pays out 100% of its donations to family members who have lost loved ones in the line of duty. Very few charities pay out 75% of revenues, let alone 100%. Leave it to the Marines to run the best charity in town.

Owen, his wife Susanne, and their son Gavin, currently reside in New York City. Owen has this to say about having a son, "My father, Bing West, never forced the Corps on me and I won't force it on my own son, but I hope like heck he'll follow the call of the wild that drew all of us. The Marine Corps remains the most important experience in my life."

SEMPER FIDELIS

DALLAS RANDOLPH WHITE WING

"I have always looked to my Marine Corps experience for guidance and inspiration."

BORN: 10 April 1946 in Mauston, Wisconsin
SERVICE: United States Marine Corps, 1968 – 1971, Enlisted, Radio Operator – Force Recon
OCCUPATION: Ho-Chunk Nation Senior Legislator

"Most of my family live in a small area called Pochee Nuk, which in our language means Little Forest. This is where I grew up. It is land that our ancestors before us settled long ago. Many generations of White Wings have lived there and they are buried there. That is the way of our people. The wild forests and sparkling rivers in northeast Wisconsin still have a very strong hold on us."

Dallas attended grade school and high school in nearby Wittenberg. During high school he played football and was named to the second all state team. He also wrestled in high school and placed fourth in the state wrestling tournament during his senior year. He was recruited by several college football teams and decided against going to college at that time.

"From the time of my boyhood, like nearly every other Native American boy, I longed to be a warrior. This 'Warrior Worship' has been part of our culture since time began and young Indian boys start early emulating their hero warriors. My cousins and I would play day after day in the forest surrounding our homes with sling shots we made ourselves out of inner tubes and other cast off materials. All day long we would attack and retreat. War was about the only game we played. So when Vietnam became part of the national news we were ready to go. I enlisted and was sent to San Diego. My family had a prayer service for me before I left for boot camp. I took my Medicine Bag with me as all Native American warriors do and it wasn't long before I found myself heading to Vietnam – a long, long way from home.

"I was serving as a radio operator in a force recon unit near An-hoa. I have many vivid memories of my time in Vietnam – many of them I would like to forget, but I think that will never happen. One especially indelible event happened near the time I was to be sent back to the states. I had about seven days left when I was told one Sunday morning that I was to get ready to leave. A small team was going to be sent to place sensor devices near enemy trails. Seven men were going and since I was the only radio operator available, I had to go. It was about 7:30 on a hot Vietnam morning as our chopper left base. We headed out to an area called Antenna Valley. As we neared our destination and began to set down, almost immediately we started taking enemy fire. Quickly our pilot aborted and we flew further up the floor of the valley where we found a place to land in an area of elephant grass that must have been about nine feet high. I was the first guy out the tail gate exit and in another moment I spotted two enemy Viet Cong practically right in front of me. I can still see them today in my mind. I signaled in sign language to Sergeant Ayres and by then the enemy was running and must have climbed into their tunnel holes. These were everywhere and they could hide pretty well in them. It was about then I realized we were pretty nearly surrounded by the enemy. Sergeant Ayres signaled for me to call the helicopter back. In a few minutes the chopper came back taking fire all the while. In the meantime, Marine Cobra gun ships were supporting us. The Aerial Observer in a Bronco OV-10 told us that there was enemy all around us and we were soon in a wild and bloody fire fight. The Cobras were racking (strafing) with their mini guns to keep the enemy down, but all around me I heard popping sounds that I realized was gunfire and I was praying as intensely as I knew how clutching a small New Testament that I carried with me and making all sorts of promises to the Creator about becoming a preacher some day if we could just get out alive. Shortly, the helicopter ran out of ammunition, but thankfully, we were relieved by two Army Huey gun ships.

"After what seemed an eternity, we headed out and I thought with great relief that we were going back to our base camp, but that wasn't the case. We exchanged helicopters and headed up near the Que-son Mountains watching for enemy all the time. Once again we circled and landed in the high grasses. Suddenly I heard enemy voices; I signaled Sergeant Ayres. We went up to some high ground with Sergeant Williams and myself staying in the rear behind some trees. The next thing we know – one enemy came through an opening and suddenly, all hell broke loose. Sergeant Ayres had signaled for me to call the 'bird' back. As I was heading up the hill at first I thought the popping, snapping sounds I was hearing were leaves on the trees, but in another instant I realized we were in the middle of another hell of a fire fight. One of the best sights I have ever seen was that chopper heading toward us. 'Let's' get out of here,' Sergeant Ayres yelled and as the chopper landed we buckled ourselves to the S.P.I.E. and all seven of us lifted up. We were taking fire all the time, but miraculously none of us were hit and at last we headed back to our base. We were successful in our mission and still alive. We later learned that we had walked right into a N.V.A. regiment. We left 12 of those soldiers dead before we got out of there. Just another day in the Marine Corps?

This warrior had had enough of war for that day. Promising the Lord I would be a preacher another day, I hurried to the lounge to get very drunk."

After Vietnam, Dallas played football for the Marines in Quantico prior to leaving the Corps in 1971. He returned home to Wittenberg, Wisconsin and soon found work as a beef boner in a Milwaukee meat-packing plant and also worked for several years as a heavy equipment operator. Dallas then spent several years as an over the road truck driver.

In 1990, Dallas was elected to the Ho-Chunk Legislature. He has been re-elected in every election held since then. After becoming a legislator for his Nation, Dallas' first task was to oust the group of non-Indians who had taken over their tribe as well as their gaming enterprises. Dallas and others felt that if this group had been successful, they would have made millions of dollars from their tribal casinos while sharing very little with tribe members. It was Dallas' vote that put the Native American people back in place. It was a difficult and dangerous time, but he is proud to say, "After nearly a decade, we are not only the largest employer in the county where our tribal offices are located, but also employ thousands of people at two other very successful casinos in the state." As part of Ho-Chunk's legislative efforts, they have built health care facilities, hundreds of new homes, Head Start Centers and acquired hundreds of acres of land that once was the land of the Ho Chunk people, but had been confiscated by white settlers in the past century and a half.

"None of this has come without a monumental struggle, but during these years, I have always looked to my Marine Corps experience for guidance and inspiration. I feel certain that the 'do or die' attitude, I gained from being a United States Marine has led me down the right paths."

Today Ho-Chunk's gaming enterprises, generate more than $300 million of revenue each year, provide each of our more than six thousand members a yearly payment of $12,000. They also offer employment for any member willing to work and have helped raise living standards in all of their areas for Indians and non Indians as well.

"While my Vietnam experiences happened more than 30 years ago, many of the sights and situations I witnessed will never be forgotten although I have prayed constantly for them to leave my head—and heart. There is not a day that passes I haven't felt a sense of guilt for surviving that war when so many of my comrades didn't make it back home. It seems I can never really enjoy a day without these thoughts. Any good times or events that should be happy ones are always covered by the shadow of my guilt and pain. I have been diagnosed with Post-Traumatic Stress and have had help dealing with it, but it only seems to fade slightly. The only time I really feel OK is when I am doing something for someone else. Maybe that's why I take my legislator job so seriously – there I know I can make a difference and justify that my life was spared in Vietnam while so many others paid a far greater price. These days, my prayer is that our leaders will search much harder for peace because war is just too costly in every way."

The Ho-Chunk tribe contributes generously to the American Cancer Society, Children's Miracle Network, Special Olympics, Homeless Shelters in the area and many other worthwhile efforts such as funding life-saving equipment for area fire departments and emergency needs for communities in the state.

Several years ago after witnessing "The Wall" in Washington D.C., Dallas was bothered that there was nothing to commemorate the many Native Americans who had fought so bravely and died in many wars, and he vowed to change that. He set about planning and designing such a memorial. The result is a beautiful and moving Vietnam Native American Memorial at the High Ground in Neilsville, Wisconsin. The High Ground is located on a large tract of land with many statues and other memorials that have been created and built to honor veterans from the wars of the past century. Thousands of people visit each year and many believe that they can feel the intense emotions that seem to hover over this ground. The Native American memorial at the High Ground is a beautiful bronze statue of a Native American soldier carrying a staff with eagle feathers. Surrounding the figure are the names etched in black stone of all Native Americans who lost their lives in Vietnam, the dates and the tribes they represent.

Dallas was married and later divorced and has remained single. He currently resides in Wittenberg, Wisconsin and is the father of one daughter, Natanha and uncle to 16 nieces and nephews.

SEMPER FIDELIS

Guy P. Wyser-Pratte

"The worst plan, if executed aggressively, can succeed."

Born: 21 June 1940 in Vichy, France
Service: United States Marine Corps, 1962 – 1966, Reconnaissance Officer
Occupation: President, Wyser-Pratte and Company

Guy Wyser-Pratte immigrated to New York with his family at the age of seven. He quickly learned English through sports, and was so successful in school that he received a Naval Reserve Officers Training Corps scholarship for college. Upon graduation in 1962, Wyser-Pratte began his four-year active duty obligation, following his brother into the Marine Corps.

After a tour of duty as a platoon commander in the 3rd Marine Division with the 3rd Reconnaissance Battalion, Wyser-Pratte was assigned to guard duty in the Brooklyn Navy Yard. He had requested an assignment to use his fluency in French, but took advantage of his New York assignment to begin a master's program at a local university.

"While on a joint exercise with the Republic of Korea Marines in South Korea in March 1963, we were hit by a typhoon. Having taken one course in meteorology at the university, I felt roughly conversant with the situation. When the battalion commander asked my advice about the storm, I told him, "We're in the eye," and that we'd soon be smacked by the other side of the typhoon. The colonel moved the entire battalion, rolling stock and all, into concrete hangars. Within minutes of this maneuver, the sun shone brightly and did so for many weeks to come. The 'We're in the eye' has followed me to this day amongst those with whom I have served."

In 1966, Captain Wyser-Pratte made an extremely tough decision to leave the Corps and work in the family business, Wyser-Pratte and Company, originally founded in Paris, France in 1929. The company was re-opened on Wall Street in 1948 by Guy's father Eugene. "I began as an analyst with Wyser-Pratte and Company in June 1966 while attending night school to finish my MBA in finance. Wyser-Pratte and Company was purchased in July 1967, by

Bache and Company, which was in turn acquired by the Prudential Insurance Company of America in 1982. In 1991, I left Prudential to reconstitute the family firm of Wyser-Pratte and Company and am currently President of the organization."

Transitioning from the Marine Corps to the civilian sector was a shock to Guy, he could not understand a civilian's "frame of reference." "I expected the same caliber of individual in civilian life, particularly on Wall Street, that I encountered in the Corps, I was gravely mistaken. They didn't have the same values, the same commitment to integrity or sense of honor. Whatever it is that you find within an organization like the Marine Corps, you don't find in the civilian world and certainly not on Wall Street. Everyone is out for themselves … if someone can take advantage of you they will, because they get the upper hand and benefit somehow.

"As constituted today, WPC is an investment firm specializing in event driven strategies including merger arbitrage and Corporate governance, and is reputed to be one of the leaders in both of these markets. Its Corporate governance activities have taken it from the United States into a number of European countries where WPC has forced a number of companies to create value for their shareholders."

Guy Wyser-Pratte serves on the board of Vivarte SA. He is a former board member of Comsat Corporation, Prudential Bache Securities, and Bache & Co.

In addition, Wyser-Pratte serves on the Board of Directors of the International Rescue Committee, the oldest and largest non-governmental refugee organization in the world, Center for Humanitarian Cooperation, and The Congressional Medal of Honor Foundation and a member of the Council on Foreign Relations.

Wyser-Pratte is President of the U.S. Marine Corps University Foundation, which oversees the professional military education of Marines throughout the world.

He and his wife, Vivien, and their son, Jamie, live in New York City and Bedford, New York. He also has two grown daughters, Joell and Danielle, and three grandchildren.

SEMPER FIDELIS

Gregg A. Yetter

"The Marine Corps taught me to persist against adversity, persevere against odds, and possess patience to oversee it all."

Born: 13 May 1966 in Kansas City, Missouri
Service: United States Army Reserves 1985 – 1986, Marine Corps 1987, 1992 – 2003, Officer
Occupation: Owner/Driver, Yetter-Campbell NASCAR Weekly Series Racing Team

Major Gregg Yetter's military career spans 18 years with 14 years of service in the United States Army Reserve and the United States Marine Corps. During this time, he served as a medical records specialist, adjutant, and legal officer.

He began as a Private First Class in the United States Army Reserve and affiliated with the 12th Special Forces Group (Airborne) as a medical records specialist. PFC Yetter drilled with the reserve unit while awaiting his orders to recruit training. One day while in the student union at William Jewell College, he saw a Marine Officer Selection Officer (OSO), and after a 20 minute conversation decided that "I want to be like him." He then initiated the paperwork to transfer to the Marine Corps Platoon Leaders Class (PLC).

"I have one distinct memory from my experience at PLC Jr.'s that has stayed with me throughout the years. Prior to going to Officer Candidates School (OCS), I was a second year student at William Jewell College and had applied for transfer from the Army Reserve to the Marine Corps PLC Program. I had a mediocre academic record up to that point and the Marine Corps kept deferring my acceptance until my grades improved. I was down on myself because my grades were not indicative of my abilities. In May 1987, I received orders to attend PLC Jr.'s, which surprised me. I didn't question the reason why because now I knew that I had the chance to prove myself. As I was preparing to go to OCS, my recent hernia repair ruptured, but I went anyway. When I arrived at Quantico, Virginia, the doctors gave me an amended physical that didn't include the usual hernia check and I wasn't going to tell them! But then a Major called me over, looked at my records and asked if I was 'Trotnic's kid' (1st Lt. Trotnic was my OSO). Taken aback, I told him 'Yes.' He then informed me that I shouldn't even be at the PLC course because of my grades, but somehow my application ended up in the accepted pile and orders were cut. He said he didn't find out about the error until it was too late and let the orders stand. I was so mad at this officer for telling me that I wasn't good enough to be there, and not good enough to be a Marine. Right then, I then made a pact with myself that I was going to leave PLC Jr.'s in one of two ways: with my graduating class or in a body bag. I graduated and validated to myself what I already knew – that I had what it took to be a Marine – hernia and all."

Gregg returned to William Jewell College in the fall of 1987, only to find out that because of his poor academic history he was disenrolled. To stay in the Marine Corps Officer Candidate Program he had to be at least a part-time student, but it was too late to enroll elsewhere. At the moment he signed his letter requesting release from the PLC Program, Gregg made another pact with himself, that he would pursue a Marine Corps commission the same way he had finished OCS.

He spent the next 18 months working, at one point three jobs at once, getting his priorities realigned. He then enrolled part-time at Penn Valley Community College and then subsequently applied to the University of Missouri at Kansas City (UMKC). His cumulative grade point average from William Jewell College was a 1.7 (on a 4.0 scale), but his average at Penn Valley and UMKC was over a 3.0.

"I was now getting the grades that I knew I could get all along. I was waiting tables at night and going to school during the day and would go for months on end without having a day off from work or school. After years of that routine, it can take a toll on you. There were many times when I felt like quitting, but I refused to quit. I had done that once already."

In his last college semester, he reapplied to the Marine Corps Officer Candidate Program and returned to OCS in June 1992. Gregg was commissioned a Second Lieutenant on August 14, 1992.

"That was the happiest day of my life, because five very long years of extremely hard work since disenrolling from the PLC Program had finally came to fruition. You can't imagine the extreme joy I felt, and continue to feel, because I know that I had truly earned those gold bars. When others were faced with my challenges, they might have given up because it was too hard and took too long. I've been accused of being stubborn and hardheaded, so doing things the hard way seems to suit me."

"April 19, 2001 is the day my life changed forever." While stationed at Marine Aircraft Group 41 in Fort Worth, Texas, Gregg enrolled in the racing experience offered by the Richard Petty Racing School and attended a two-day course at Texas Motor Speedway. He achieved the fastest speed in his class of 163.28 mph.

"As we were nearing the end of the second day, the speeds were beginning to really pick up, I remember coming off of turn four and onto the front-straight. Right after I passed the start/finish line I remember a feeling that I had never experienced before. I can best describe it, as a 'moment of clarity' for what seemed like a minute, was only a brief moment; I had a feeling of calmness, and a sense of belonging that I had never felt before. It was as though at that moment in time, I intuitively knew that driving a racecar was where I was supposed to be. That 'moment of clarity' is as vivid now, as it was the moment it happened."

Gregg made the decision to pursue a career as a professional racecar owner/driver.

Gregg and fellow Marine Captain Derek Campbell started Yetter-Campbell Racing (*www.yc-racing.com*), in May 2002. YCR raced in the Legends Car Series in northern Virginia in 2002 and had planned on moving up to the NASCAR Weekly Series in 2003 but the plans were put on hold when Derek was sent overseas for Operation Iraqi Freedom. YCR will move to North Carolina and race at Concord Motorsport Park in the NASCAR Weekly Series in 2004. Some of the team sponsors for the 2004 season are: Coors Light, The Employer Support of the Guard and Reserve, Bilstein Shocks, Y3K Grafix, Big Image Graphics, Motova8 and Web-Emerse. By 2005/6, YCR plans to be in a national touring series full-time and by the end of the decade, field a competitive car in the NASCAR Winston (soon to be Nextel) Cup.

"My long term racing goal is to one day be standing on pit road getting ready to race in the Daytona 500. I fully realize that the odds of a 37-year-old man, with a couple years racing experience under his belt, making it to NASCAR's highest tier are slim at best, but that's fine with me. I gladly accept the challenge.

"In a May 1961 speech, President John F. Kennedy stated that the United States would be landing a man on the moon before the end of the decade: 'That we chose to do these things, not because they are easy, but because they are hard.' His words sum up my determination to reach the NASCAR Nextel Cup.

"I've loved my time in the Corps, and I love being a Marine, but it is time for me to move on. I feel very lucky and fortunate, humbled to be quite honest, to be able to pursue my dream. I tell my family and friends that it's like being six years old on Christmas morning. Remember the excitement, the anticipation, the joy and waking up your parents at 5:00 a.m. because you just couldn't wait any longer to open your presents? That's the way I feel everyday!"

Gregg has a personal interest in two foundations: The Cystic Fibrosis Foundation (*www.cff.org*) and The Multiple Sclerosis Foundation (*www.msfacts.org*). Craig Allen, a childhood friend, passed away from cystic fibrosis. "Growing up, I remember seeing how Craig struggled with his disease and not once did I ever hear him feel sorry for himself or ever complain.

Whatever challenges I may face in my life pale in comparison to those he endured." A good friend and fellow racecar driver, Kelly Sutton, has RRMS (Remitting and Relapsing Multiple Sclerosis). "She is a remarkable woman who has lived with her disease for 15 years, and has been able to achieve success as a mother, wife and racer. She is very successful in a male dominated sport, and does so with a fierce determination and gentle kindness. She's a hero of mine."

In addition to being an owner/driver, Gregg also serves on the Board of Directors for Sport Coins, Inc.

Gregg is single and lives in Charlotte, North Carolina.

SEMPER FIDELIS

Profiled Marine Corps Non Profit Organizations

Marine Corps Heritage Foundation

Established in 1979 as the Marine Corps Historical Foundation, the MCHF is a non-profit, 501(c)(3) organization dedicated to the preservation and promotion of Marine Corps history and traditions. We directly support the historical programs of the Marine Corps in ways that might not otherwise be available through appropriated funds. The Foundation is governed by a member-elected Board of Directors, comprised of former Marines. There is a very small paid staff located at the administrative offices in Quantico, Virginia.

Foundation support comes in many different forms:

Education: Funding for the study of Marine Corps history through Internships, Research Grants, Masters and Doctoral Fellowships; and development of lesson plans for middle and high school teachers on John Brown's raid at Harper's Ferry, the Boxer Rebellion in China, and the Battle for Iwo Jima.

Awards: Annual program to recognize superior achievement in literature, art, photography, videography, and museum exhibits. The Foundation also sponsors a Marine Corps History Prize in conjunction with the National History Day contest.

Special Projects: Additions of battle honors to the base of the Marine Corps War Memorial in Arlington, Virginia as well as the installation of wayside panels to inform visitors to the Memorial about the battle for Iwo Jima, the men who raised the flag and a brief history of the Marine Corps; rehabilitation and maintenance of the Commandant's House in Washington, D.C.; special funding support for the United States Marine Band (the Foundation recently sponsored the appearance of world renown composer, John Williams, as guest conductor at the Band's 205th anniversary concert at the Kennedy Center in Washington, D.C.).

Preservation: Acquire documents, works of art, artifacts and memorabilia for display in the Marine Corps Museum. From time to time, certain desired and rare artifacts come on the market, which must be purchased promptly if they are to be acquired at all. The Foundation moves quickly to facilitate these purchases. We have purchased rare scrapbooks owned by former Marine Band director, John Philip Sousa; a desk that belonged to the 18th Commandant, Alexander Vandegrift; and one of only 6 Civil War Brevet Commissions granted to Marine officers for gallantry during the attack on Fort Sumter in 1863.

Gift Shop: Operate retail, mail order and online gift shops in Quantico, Virginia.

Marine Corps Band: The "President's Own" U.S. Marine Band and the Marine Corps Heritage Foundation share a long and distinguished relationship of teamwork and support. As the nation's oldest professional musical organization, the Marine Band has often relied upon the Marine Corps Heritage Foundation's financial support in presenting concerts and events as well as producing special projects that enhance the image of the Marine Corps as a whole. Whether it's commissioning new works for wind band by up and coming American composers, or acquiring historical artifacts that rightly belong in the Band's archives, the Heritage Foundation has provided invaluable support to the Marine Band.

Examples of such support include the commissioning of a new work for wind band by American composer David Holsinger, acquiring a collection of John Philip Sousa programs to be added to the Band's library, and providing exchange gifts for an historic visit by a Russian military band to the United States. The Heritage Foundation was also responsible for purchasing a new grave marker at Washington's historic Congressional Cemetery for the Band's 14th Director, Francis Scala.

More recently, the Heritage Foundation produced and sold two recordings that have helped in furthering the Band's reputation of musical excellence throughout the world. The latest collaboration between the Band and the Heritage Foundation was the July 12, 2003 celebration of the Marine Band's 205th Anniversary. Legendary conductor and film composer John Williams conducted the Band in a concert of his own music at the Kennedy Center. In addition to handling all travel and lodging expenses surrounding Mr. Williams' trip, the Heritage Foundation hosted a gala reception for the Commandant and his guests prior to the concert.

Many of the truly special moments in the Band's history would not have been possible without the Marine Corps Heritage Foundation. All members of "The President's Own," both past and present, share a deep respect and admiration for the unwavering support and dedication of the Marine Corps Heritage Foundation.

National Museum of the Marine Corps: The Foundation, in partnership with the United States Marine Corps, is developing a Marine Corps Heritage Center at Quantico, which will be the home of the new National Museum of the Marine Corps. It will be a campus of buildings to include the museum, an armory, auditorium, outdoor demonstration area, conference center and artifact storage and restoration facilities. Site development is underway and groundbreaking occurred in September, 2003.

In a message to the American people, General Michael W. Hagee, Commandant of the Marine Corps said,

"Creation of the new Marine Corps Heritage Center, with the inspiring National Museum of the Marine Corps as its centerpiece, turns the dreams of thousands of Marine veterans into reality. This magnificent place represents our heritage and timeless esprit de corps and finally allows us to tell our story as we would have it told – through the eyes of Marines."

The building design inspired by the heroic Flag Raisers at Iwo Jima, the Museum's tilted mast soars 210 feet above a massive canopy of steel and glass. The dramatic design of this state-of-the-art Museum creates an immediate and powerful impact, one that evokes an enduring symbol of the Marines' contribution to the American people. The image of unity, clarity, and strength reflects Marine values and invites visitors to share in the Marine experience and its legacy for the future. The Museum will be the shining centerpiece of the preeminent center where the public, the military, and scholars can research and understand the history of the Marine Corps.

General Charles C. Krulak (Ret.), 31st Commandant of the United States Marine Corps stated:

"From the approach to Quantico on I-95, the Museum's soaring atrium will be seen over the trees from any direction. This spectacular first impression is of such awe-inspiring magnitude that visitors will surely carry it with them for a long time."

The vision for this state-of-the-art museum is for visitors of all ages to immerse themselves in the story of the Marine Corps. From the dramatic Central Gallery to the multimedia and interactive exhibits, visitors will be able to walk through the history of the Marine Corps through chronological exhibits that depict pivotal battles, achievements, and the Marines' vital contribution to the nation and the preservation of America's freedom.

Membership in the Foundation is open to anyone with an interest in preserving the history of the Marine Corps. Individual, corporate and institutional memberships are available. The Foundation publishes two quarterly newsletters: *Sentinel*, which informs the membership of events, programs and publications; and *Legacy*, which gives progress updates on the development of the Marine Corps Heritage Center.

Marine Corps Heritage Foundation
307 5th Avenue
Quantico, VA 22134
(800) 397-7585, (703) 640-7965
www.marineheritage.org
E-mail: info@marineheritage.org

Marine Corps Law Enforcement Foundation

It was a gathering of a few former Marines and one guest, new to the New York metropolitan area, who did not serve in the Corps. In common to all was their very modest approach about the success each earned in life – pride in their families, whom they loved so dearly, passionate about the United States of America, the U.S. Flag, and the United States Marine Corps.

Of course the food and drink was good, but not as good as the stories told and shared. With their enthusiasm and energy you would think they all were still serving on active duty in their beloved Corps, but in fact they got together to serve others on active duty and their families.

Their civilian experience was extensive as they were leaders with law enforcement, finance and law. Their lives were very busy because of the demands of job and involvement in many charities – helping those in need, especially children. This evening they were forming the Marine Corps – Law Enforcement Foundation. They spent many years helping children of Marines with education and medical assistance and each knew they could do more by doing it in a different way. The marching order was to help the children of Marines who lost their life while on active duty and those law enforcement officers who also gave the supreme sacrifice. It was very easy to include law enforcement officers as many entered the FBI and DEA after a hitch with the Marines. The brotherhood of federal law enforcement officers includes former Marines and many others who did not choose the U.S. Marines

These former Marines established the Marine Corps Law Enforcement Foundation in January 1995 and the first donations came from them. They all knew the enormous amount of hard work that it takes to raise funds and set up a charitable Internal Revenue Service recognized 501(c)3 with contributions to the Foundation as tax deductible. If there is such a thing as a "perfect" charity, it's quite probable that the MC-LEF is it. The MC-LEF touts the fact that they incur absolutely no operating expenses so that every dollar donated gets funneled directly to the scholarship funds. It relies 100% on volunteers and private donations. Donors have the assurance that every penny goes to the children.

Members of the Marine Corps – Law Enforcement Foundation believe that our nation's most precious resource is its youth. Their educational development is of primary importance to become meaningful members of their families and society. What we try to do is make the world a better place.

The current war in Iraq has certainly illuminated America's commitment to freedom. We are reminded that freedom is not free. The price is great. No one knows that better than the left-behind sons and daughters of America's fallen heroes. Though these precious children will live in a safer and more secure world because of the sacrifice and bravery of America's fighting best, they face a future without a Mom or a Dad to love them and be by their side.

Nothing can ever replace the loss of a parent; however, thanks to the Marine Corps-Law Enforcement Foundation, these little ones will not be forgotten or forsaken. Formed in January 1995, the MC-LEF seeks to make the future a little brighter for each and every eligible child of a coalition forces member killed in the line of duty in Iraq. The Foundation does this by awarding scholarship bonds for the future education of these sacred children.

In addition to the Marine Corps and various Federal law enforcement agencies, these scholarships apply to eligible children of members of the U.S. Army, Navy, Air Force and Coast Guard. Due to the current conflict in Iraq, the Foundation has decided to also include children of our nation's coalition partners fighting alongside our American military. Currently, these include England, Poland, and Australia.

Here is a summary of some of the Foundations previous funding actions:

> $9,200,000 to those who died in Operation Iraqi Freedom – to all children of U.S. Service personnel killed, Marines, Army, Navy, Air Force, and our nation's collation partners.
>
> $240,000 to the twelve children who lost a parent on the space shuttle Columbia.
>
> $1,400,000 to children whose parent was murdered on 9-11-2001, specifically the attack at the Pentagon and Flight 77.
>
> $290,000 to the children of Marines and federal law enforcement employees murdered at the bombing of the Murrah Building in Oklahoma City, Oklahoma in June 1995.

Since the formation of the Marine Corps – Law Enforcement Foundation in January 1995 to October 2003 – maturity value bonds and assistance has been made to qualifying children amounting to $14,000,000, which is only possible though the dedicated work of its many volunteers and donations made by very compassionate, and generous and grateful people.

Marines, law enforcement personnel, friends, foundations, private businesses and corporations make financial contributions to support our important work. The Foundation also benefits from annual scholarship galas in New Jersey and New York, and golf tournaments in Missouri, New Jersey, New York, Ohio and Pennsylvania. Contributions made in memory or in honor of individuals are also gratefully accepted. The Internal Revenue Service recognizes contributions to the Marine Corps – Law Enforcement Foundation as tax deductible. Contributions of any amount are gratefully accepted by the Foundation. 100% of all donations, and the net proceeds from special events, go toward scholarships, with no administrative costs whatsoever.

If you would like to make a tax-deductible gift to the MC-LEF or learn more about the Foundation, including upcoming events, you can call, mail or visit the MC-LEF on the web.

Marine Corps – Law Enforcement Foundation
PO Box 37
Mountain Lakes, NJ 07046
(877) 606-1775, (973) 625-9239 fax
www.mc-lef.org
E-mail: info@mc-lef.org

Marine Corps League

The Marine Corps League is the outgrowth of Marine Clubs established by Marines returning to the United States from the trenches of France in 1918. The Marines who served in France during World War I organized local groups for the purpose of maintaining the comradeship that developed while serving actively with the United States Marine Corps.

As these clubs grew in size and number they became more active in the pursuit of objectives of interest to their members and in support of the Corps. It was not until November 1923 that Major General John A. Lejeune, the Commandant of the Marine Corps convened the first all Marine Conference in New York City. Out of this conference came the first nationwide organization of Marines in support of the Marine Corps. The conference elected a National Commandant and other officers to run the organization. In addition, the conference provided for the meeting of the group on a regularly scheduled basis.

As this first all Marine association grew in size, it was apparent that there was a need for a formal organization. Association officers drew up plans and petitioned the Congress of the United States to grant a Congressional Charter to the group. Congress complied with the request, establishing the Marine Corps League as the only Congressionally Chartered Marine Veterans Organization on August 4, 1937.

The Marine Corps League today has a membership in excess of 58,000 members and that membership is comprised of honorably discharged, active duty and retired Marines and members of the Reserves who have earned ninety days creditable service or more. They also accept Associate members that have the desire to work consistently with and for the United States of America and the United States Marine Corps. The League has forty seven Departments with eight hundred forty four active local detachments. In addition, the League is supported by an Auxiliary with a membership in excess of 3,500 members.

The League has a network of accredited Service Officers providing assistance to all Veterans of the Armed Forces. A full time National Director of Veteran's Services works out of the National Headquarters. The workload of the Service Officer has increased considerably with appeals to the Department of Veteran Affairs. The Department of Veteran Affairs accredited the Marine Corps League in 1945 thus allowing the League to represent Veterans of all branches of the Services in their appeals.

The National organization granted 341 scholarships in 2003 to assist the children of Marines in the furtherance of their education. Many of the local

Detachments and Departments also have educational assistance programs including scholarship programs. The MCL's Chesty Puller Scholarship supports a student at the Marine Military Academy in Harlington, Texas.

The Department of Veterans' Affairs Volunteer Service Program is supported by members of the League. These dedicated volunteers are accredited by the Department of Veteran Affairs and go into the Veterans' Administration Medical Centers to provide free personal service and assistance. This supplements what cannot be provided by paid medical staffers. In their National Veterans' Administration Volunteer program they have logged many volunteer hours during the past year. Their members working in the Veterans' Administration Medical Centers are doing a great job.

The League does not ignore the needs of America's youth. The League supports an established program called the Young Marines of the Marine Corps League. This program is open to all youths ages 8 – 18. The youths enrolled in this program must maintain passing grades in school. They are evaluated by their parents for conduct at home as well. The Young Marines are given training in physical fitness, life saving techniques, swimming, and are taken camping. They are taught to be self-reliant and prepared to take their place in American society for they are the future of America. The Leagues support of the Boy Scout program is making tremendous strides to becoming a vital part of our support of the Youth of America. Leaguers are also gaining new experiences in this program.

The MCL's Youth Physical Fitness program has been adopted by many schools all over the United States from Elementary to High School and is even being used in some college programs. Awards were presented to students at each level of accomplishment. In connection with this program they have not forgotten the musical talents of our youth. Awards for this program are presented through school bands and orchestras.

The League provides representation to the United States Congress in legislative matters affecting the United States Marine Corps, National Security, and Veterans' Benefits through its work with the Veterans' Organizations in the United States Government.

To find out more information about the Marine Corp League and locate detachments in your area, make a donation for any of the many worthwhile MCL programs or to obtain additional information, contact them by mail, phone, or visit their website.

Marine Corp League
Mailing Address
PO Box 3070, Merrifield, VA 22116
Street Address
8626 Lee Highway, Suite 201, Fairfax, VA 22031
(703) 207-9588, (800) 625-1775, (703) 207-0047 fax
www.mcleague.org
E-mail: mcl@mcleague.org

Marine Corps Scholarship Foundation

More than four decades of helping the Marine Family

Brigadier General Mike Wholley, executive director of the Marine Corps Scholarship Foundation, tells about attending one of the gold tournaments sponsored by the foundation.

"A number of scholarship recipients had been invited to help the volunteers and to talk with the supporters and let them know how much they appreciated the opportunity to go to school. Shortly after General Wholley had been introduced and made some remarks to the participants, a young man approached him.

"'General Wholley, my name is — and I would appreciate it if you would thank all of those involved in helping me with this scholarship.' Wholley responded that he would be happy to pass on the young man's appreciation, and thanked him to taking the time to seek him out. Wholley could see, however, that there was something more in the young man's demeanor, something more he wanted to say."

"'I don't think you understand what a difference this scholarship has made in my life, general. My dad served in Vietnam. I am the oldest of five children and my dad has been an alcoholic for as long as I can remember. I have been working to help my mom support the family since I was thirteen years old. Because of that, I never had a lot of time to devote to studies or to extracurricular activities at school. I was just one of the crowd at school, getting by with average grades.'

"'You know how it's always the same kids being recognized in school, sir? Well, I certainly wasn't one of them. But I knew that I could outwork any kid in that school. I never thought that I would get to college. I didn't have super grades – mostly B's with some C's sprinkled in there – and my family situation ruled out the money to make it.

"'I was lucky, though. I had a counselor who was a Marine veteran and who knew my family situation and had taken an interest in helping me. He told me about the Marine Corps Scholarship Foundation and said that I was the kind of kid that the foundation would help. You see, I did volunteer work at my church on the weekends. At his urging, I filled out the application and applied to a state school.

"A few months later at the graduation assembly, they were recognizing all the students who were receiving scholarships and honors, and were announcing what schools they were going to. When they called my name and announced that I had received an $1,800 scholarship from the Marine Corps Scholarship Foundation, heads turned around to see who they were talking about. You see, for four years I was just a bump on the log in that school, and very few knew my name. At that point, I had to stand up and everyone applauded me as they had the other students. Sir, that was the first time in my life I had ever been recognized, and it felt real good.

"I'm now a junior at Texas Tech, and I'm carrying a 3.8 average in Electrical Engineering. I want you to thank everyone for giving me this chance. I will help this foundation when I graduate, sir, and I will make all of you proud of helping me.'

"General Wholley looked at the young man and could only say, 'You already have made us proud … you already have."

An Organization with a Tradition

In 2002, the Marine Corps Scholarship Foundation began its fifth decade helping Marines and their families. The foundation's motto … youth, education, and values … shines through in everything that it does.

Founded in 1962 by a handful of Marines over Sunday lunch at a New York restaurant, the Marine Corps Scholarship Foundation has now grown into a nationwide organization with hundreds of committed volunteers who organize the golf tournaments, scholarship balls, and other fundraising events that take place across the country.

The primary focus of the foundation is to help the sons and daughters of our nation's Marines to achieve their dream of higher education. For the 2003 – 2004 academic year, the foundation awarded more than $1.55 million in scholarships to 982 great young men and women. It marked the twelfth consecutive year that the Marine Corps Scholarship Foundation has exceeded the million dollar level of scholarship assistance, and pushed the total of scholarships awarded over $21 million! In addition, the foundation awarded $10,000 education bonds to every child who lost a parent in the 1983 Beirut Barracks terrorist attack or in Operation Desert Storm, regardless of the branch of service of the parent.

"We want our Marine warriors to know that we will be there for their families," said retired Lieutenant General Jeff Oster, the current chairman of the foundation. "We want them to know that we care and that we are here to help."

The Foundation's Response to Terrorism

After the terrorist attacks on 9/11, the board of the Marine Corps Scholarship Foundation stepped up again, as it had in the past, and pledged $10,000 in scholarship assistance to the children of veteran and Reserve Marines who lost their lives in the attacks. The board has also pledged to provide scholarship assistance of at least $10,000 to every child of a Marine, or of a Navy Corpsman serving with the Marines, whose parent is killed in combat in the ongoing war on terrorism.

Marine Corps License Plates

Through the efforts of some great volunteers, the Marine Corps Scholarship Foundation has also been able to get legislation passed for Marine Corps license plates in Florida and Illinois. The Florida license plate, which has been available for several years now, has allowed the foundation to support not just its regular scholarship program, but also the four Veterans Nursing Homes in Florida, the Young Marines program in Florida, and the fourteen Marine Corps Junior ROTC programs in Florida high schools. The Illinois license plate, which became available in 2003, will be used exclusively for scholarships for Illinois students. Further information on how these Marine Corps license plates can be obtained is available at the website.

Commitment to the Future

More than 16,000 scholarships have been awarded by the Marine Corps Scholarship Foundation in the forty-one years that it has existed. From an average of thirteen scholarships a year during its first decade to an average approaching a thousand a year in the decade ending in 2003, the foundation has continued to grow and to be responsive to the needs of Marine families. While the support from the Marine Corps and the Marine community has been tremendous, there is also tremendous support from the public. "Even people who have never served in the Corps, or in uniform, recognize how very special the Marine Corps is and how much Marines sacrifice for this country," remarked Oster. "Many of these patriotic Americans want to help. When they learn who we are and what we do, they step up in support."

How You Can Help

You can learn more about the Marine Corps Scholarship Foundation by visiting its website. Golf tournaments and scholarship balls are conducted across the country and your support as a participant is encouraged! Contributions can also be made online. The foundation participates in the Combined Federal Campaign and its number is CFC-2111. Donations can also be made by sending a check to the address below.

Marine Corps Scholarship Foundation
PO Box 3008
Princeton, NJ 08543-3008
(800) 292-7777, (609) 452-2259 fax
www.marine-scholars.org
E-mail: mscf@marine-scholars.org

Marine Corps University Foundation

The mission of the Marine Corps University Foundation (MCUF) is to provide resources that enhance and enrich Marine Corps Professional Military Education and leadership development for all Marines.

Mrs. Vincent Astor, daughter of Major General John Russell, 16th Commandant of the Marine Corps, and her son, Ambassador Anthony D. Marshall, were instrumental in the establishment of the original Command and Staff College Foundation in June 1980 with a $100,000 grant from the Astor Foundation. The purpose of the grant was to enhance the professional education and leadership development of the Command and Staff College students and staff when government funding was not available. Ambassador Marshall served as the Foundation's first Chairman, succeeded by General Robert H. Barrow, 27th Commandant of the Marine Corps, in 1993. General Carl E. Mundy, Jr., 30th Commandant of the Marine Corps, was elected as the Chairman in 1995 and continues to lead the Foundation today.

The Marine Corps University (MCU) was established in 1989 to serve as the focal point for the Marine Corps' Professional Military Education programs. Like any university, it is made up of various schools that educate Marine leaders from corporals to colonels. On November 10, 1996, to better reflect the Foundation's mission, the Foundation's name was changed to the Marine Corps University Foundation.

Colonel Charles J. Goode, Jr., USMC (Ret) was the Foundation's first Executive Director. Colonel Goode guided the creation of many of the Foundation's current MCU programs such as the Russell Leadership Conference, The Oppenheimer-Stein Marine Corps Scholarship at Harvard University, The Basic School Reflections Series, The General Graves B. Erskine Distinguished Series, The Brigadier General Harold C. Oppenheimer Chair of Warfighting Strategy and The Major General Matthew C. Horner Chair of Military Theory. The Foundation's premier award, The General Leonard F. Chapman Medallion, was also established during Colonel Goode's tenure.

The Foundation continues to move forward under the capable leadership of Major General Donald R. Gardner, USMC (Ret), Chief Executive Officer since 1999. Under General Gardner's leadership, the Foundation has added The Robert A. Lutz Distinguished Chair of Military Studies, of which General Gardner is the chair holder, and two Donald Bren Chairs, one focusing on ethics and leadership and the other on innovation and transformation. The other endowed chair is The Guy P. and Vivien Wyser-Pratte Humanitarian Operations Chair, established in 1998.

The Foundation's continued success depends on the Board of Trustees. These volunteers, many of whom are current, former and retired Marines, guide the Foundation and give unselfishly of their time and money. The Trustees provided the Foundation with a new building in February of 2001 by setting up and contributing to the Building Fund. As influential leaders, they give the Foundation prestige and focus, as well as being prime examples of the adage, "Once a Marine, always a Marine."

Three fundraising events are held each year: The Major General John H. Russell Leadership Award Luncheon in New York City, The Semper Fidelis Award Dinner and The Semper Fidelis Golf Classic, both held in northern Virginia.

The Major General John H. Russell Leadership Award, established in honor of Major General John H. Russell, USMC, 16th Commandant of the Marine Corps, is presented annually to a former Marine whose commitment to personal and professional excellence embodies those qualities of leadership and character uniquely associated with the United States Marine Corps.

The Semper Fidelis Award was first presented in 1985. In every year since, the Foundation has recognized a distinguished American leader whose commitment to personal and professional excellence embodies those qualities of leadership and character uniquely associated with the United States Marine Corps. Vice President of the United States Dick Cheney was the 2003 award recipient. This prestigious award dinner is the Foundation's largest fundraiser.

Today, the Foundation's funding programs continue to focus on the schools of The Marine Corps University located at the Marine Corps Base Quantico in Virginia. In 2003, the various schools will receive more than $600,000 in support of academic chairs, symposiums, seminars, guest speakers, staff rides, battlefield studies and student and faculty research.

An example of the Foundation's support for MCU schools includes the School of Advanced Warfare's annual three-week European campaign ride. In 2003, the students visited battle sites in Italy and France, as well as NATO commands. The Major General Matthew C. Horner Chair of Military Theory endowment also provides funds for an annual trip for students of the Command and Staff College. In 2003, the chair holder, Dr. Ian Beckett, guided students through the battle sites of South Africa. In previous years, students have visited Korea, Vietnam and Gallipolli.

In addition to MCU funding, the Marine Corps University Foundation provides support for Professional Military Education (PME) for Marine operating forces and separate commands throughout the world. The Foundation provides funds for battlefield studies to historical sites throughout the world, as well as guest speaker lectures, where Marines gain knowledge of warfighting techniques and battlefield lessons.

Another aspect of PME funding for Marine units is the Professional Library Program. The Foundation provides books from the U.S. Marine Reading List to Marine operating forces and separate commands in order to promote education and leadership throughout the Corps. Marines and Sailors in the operating forces and separate commands will receive more than $80,000 for battlefield studies, staff rides, visiting scholars and books.

Through the generosity of Foundation friends and members, revenue from fundraising events, active duty support through the Combined Federal Campaign (CFC), the Corporate Member Program and The Eagle, Globe, and Anchor Society planned giving program, the Foundation continues to carry on its mission of enhancing and enriching Marine Corps Professional Military Education and leadership development.

To inquire about the Marine Corps University Foundation or to give a donation, please contact Lieutenant Colonel John R. Hales, USMC (Ret), Chief Operating Officer.

Marine Corps University Foundation
PO Box 122
Quantico, VA 22134
(703) 784-6835, (888) 368-5341, (703) 640-6177 fax
www.mcuf.org
E-mail: jhales@mcuf.org

The Marine Military Academy

The Marine Military Academy is the only College Preparatory Military Boarding Academy in the nation that is based on the traditions and ideals of the U.S. Marine Corps. Over 95% of the graduating classes are accepted to the college of their choice and in the last 12 years, 73 graduates have been accepted to one of the Military Service Academies and 70 have received a Navy, Air Force or Army ROTC Scholarship.

The profile of the Cadets that attend MMA varies from one young man to another. There are Cadets at MMA who made the decision to attend and there are Cadets whose parents made the decision for them.

Prior to attending the Marine Military Academy, cadet Tommy Duff from Corpus Christi Texas was 80 pounds overweight, bright but not living up to his talents and abilities. In his own words he stated, "I was hanging out with the wrong crowd, not going to class and failing four subjects." His father, a pediatric heart surgeon decided that his son needed the structure and discipline that the Marine Military Academy provided. Cadet Tommy Duff graduated after three years at the Marine Military Academy and served as the Delta Company Commander his senior year. Cadet Duff was also the recipient of the General Vernon E. McGee Award and Commandant of Cadets Award. He earned his private pilot's license, became an Eagle Scout and was a member of the National Honor Society. Upon graduation, he accepted an appointment to the United States Naval Academy with the goal of becoming a Marine Corps officer.

In 2000, Mrs. Georgia Duff, Mother of Cadet Tommy Duff, gave thanks to the Marine Military Academy with the following comments: "Before Tommy enrolled in the Marine Military Academy, he was practically failing the 9th grade at his local public high school. He lacked motivation to study and while he was never a discipline problem, he began cutting classes and staying out late. Additionally, he was overweight and out of shape. After visiting MMA, Tommy agreed to enroll 'for a year.' By May, he was making all A's to earn a spot on the President's list , he became a Sergeant, and he lost 80 pounds. The physical and mental self-discipline that our son acquired from the MMA program has transformed his life."

Cadet Ivan Radcliffe from Houston, Texas had three brothers who were all high achievers but unlike his brothers he lacked the drive necessary to be successful. He knew that he needed an environment that would challenge him and he made the decision to attend MMA. After graduating from MMA cadet Radcliffe graduated from Harvard and is currently a member of the U.S. Bobsled team. What he found at MMA was the academy's ability to instill respect and pride in himself through self-discipline.

The Marine Military Academy is committed to helping each cadet develop into a whole man. Special attention is paid to the mental, physical, and spiritual development of each cadet. It is this focus on developing a well-rounded and accomplished individual that makes the Marine Military Academy truly unique from many other exemplary academic institutions. Marine Military Academy cadets are prepared for life beyond secondary education.

In the early sixties an Arizona rancher and former Marine, Bill Gary, wanted to send his son to a private military school that embraced the same ideology as the U.S. Marine Corps. He found none. Politics of that period were tumultuous, causing a decline in all military schools. Captain Gary wanted a school that focused on college preparation while concurrently teaching the responsibilities of leadership, teamwork, individual accountability and moral values. Through this vision the Marine Military Academy was born.

The doors of the Marine Military Academy opened in September 1965, with an initial enrollment of 58 cadets; six would compromise the graduating class of 1966. The founders of the Marine Military Academy knew firsthand the value of an educational program based on the Marine Corps concepts of focus, fraternity and esprit. Therein lies the philosophy of the Marine Military Academy.

The philosophy that Captain Gary was striving for when he founded the Marine Military Academy is best exemplified by the following statement from Dr. Michael T. Jones, MMA Class of 1974. "From 'screaming around the sky' in a jet aircraft with over 3,000 precision flying hours as a USAF weapons officer, to grueling academics of pharmacy and medical school and now as a clinician administering the best possible medical care to our mentally ill population, MMA has provided me with the integrity, leadership, organizational skills, perseverance and what my DI called just plain, ordinary 'guts' to accomplish what I have and to succeed in life. Take these influences out of a young man's life and you have a very hollow shell indeed."

Providing a solid college preparatory education is the primary purpose of the Marine Military Academy. Small classes, mandatory evening study periods, a focused core curriculum and balanced course offerings in math, literature, science, history and written communications prepare our students to be successful for the competition they will experience at the university level. The Marine Military Academy is a Naval Honor School. As such, the Academy is one of the nation's recognized preparatory schools for the U.S. Naval Academy, U.S. Air Force Academy and the U.S. Military Academy (West Point). The Academy's graduates have taken their experiences in to the best schools in the world such as: Stanford, Princeton, MIT, University of Texas, Rice, Texas A&M and all the service academies. The list is an excellent testimony to the success of the Marine Military Academy, its traditions, and its graduates.

Today, more than ever before, America needs young leaders. The Marine Military Academy is a virtual laboratory that cultivates cadet leadership in a perpetual, dynamic and nurturing process. Leadership at MMA includes the Marine Corps JROTC course of instruction, leadership seminars, guest speakers, and constant ethical decision-making projects.

Dave Christain, father of Matt Christain, Class of 2001, stated: "There are many college preparatory schools but there is only one Marine Military Academy. MMA prepares young men for more than college. It prepares them for life by showing the consequences that arise from each decision. MMA instills the values of honesty, integrity and discipline. My son first enrolled at MMA for his freshman year. My only regret is that we did not start earlier. Year after year we have seen a noticeable improvement in his confidence and personal skills."

During Plebe training, an intense four-week introductory training period designed to teach and promote honor, courage and commitment, new cadets learn discipline, self-control, respect, courtesy, neatness, punctuality, teamwork and the history and tradition of the Marine Corps. It's here that a solid foundation is built – discipline leads to discipline, good follower-ship leads to great leadership. Under the direction of a former Marine drill instructor (a retired Marine Staff Noncommissioned Officer) plebes learn to treat others with dignity and respect, to band together as a team and to rely upon their peers to accomplish their tasks. The drill instructor and his family live with their cadets in their barracks. Drill instructors teach leadership through formal and informal classes and by serving as superb role models. Then they give the cadets responsibility and stand back and mentor.

At the Marine Military Academy, it is important that cadets participate in a physical activity after a full day of academic, classroom studies. The training and competition in athletics offer cadets the opportunity to learn teamwork, discipline and sportsmanship, while maintaining a healthy body.

In an effort to promote the "whole cadet" concept along with teamwork and sportsmanship, MMA's cadets are required to participate in extracurricular programs and community service projects. These are specifically designed to enhance their character, their will to win, their individual talents, and their concerns for others. Each year, cadets host blood drives, clean up the beaches, tutor elementary school children, usher at the community playhouse and volunteer at the hospital. Cadets also participate in annual events like the American Cancer Society's Relay for life and Christmas in April where homes for underprivileged families are refurbished. Add to this over 2,000 man-hours in Eagle Scout projects and cadets stay busy all year.

The Marine Military Academy's foundation was framed from the desire to emulate those Marine traditions and values that have earned the respect and gratitude of our great nation. In a world where many prefer to take shortcuts and offer less than their personal best effort, the Marine Military Academy challenges each cadet to strive for excellence and to reach his greatest potential. These goals for personal excellence extend through academics, athletic/physical activities, moral and other personal development endeavors. When a cadet graduates, he will have the academic foundation, morality, self-confidence, self-discipline and leadership traits that will guide him successfully throughout the remainder of his life.

To inquire about the Marine Military Academy or to give a donation to help those young men who do not have the means to attend MMA, please contact Lieutenant Colonel Robert R. Grider, USMC (Ret), Director, Institutional Advancement.

Marine Military Academy
320 Iwo Jima Boulevard
Harlingen, Texas 78550
(956) 423-6006 ext.230, (956) 412-3848 fax
www.mma-tx.org
E-mail: grider@mma-tx.org

The Women Marines Association

The Women Marines Association (WMA) is the only nonprofit, veterans' organization for women who have served honorably or who are currently serving in the United States Marine Corps and Marine Corps Reserve. The Association was established in Denver, Colorado, in July 1960 and has nearly 4,000 members. Most of these women comprise approximately 80 chapters in 10 geographic areas across the United States, but many are members-at-large in the U.S. and abroad. They range in age from 18 to 90+ years, but all share the common bond of being Marines.

Purpose

The WMA has seven purposes which are to:

- Preserve and promote the history and traditions of women in the Marine Corps from World War I to the present;
- Foster, encourage, and perpetuate the spirit of comradeship of women who have served or who now serve in the United States Marine Corps, regular or reserve components, through social and recreational activities for Association members;
- Counsel, assist, and mutually promote the welfare and well-being of elderly, disabled, and needy women Marine veterans, as well as women serving in the Marine Corps;
- Provide entertainment, care, and assistance to hospitalized veterans and members of the armed forces of the United States;
- Promote the civic and social welfare of the community;
- Sponsor or participate in activities of a patriotic nature, particularly those that perpetuate the tradition and esprit de corps of the United States Marine Corps;
- Conduct programs for charitable and educational purposes.

For many years after its establishment, the WMA only gave its National President a fifty-dollar operating budget for each two-year period.

Then in 1978, an unusual event took place that would ultimately establish a treasury. Nita Bob Warner became National President in 1976 and had to carry through with a decision that had been made two years prior: the biennial convention in 1978 was to be a cruise convention. When Nita Bob went to Miami to check out the various cruise ships and was debating on how many spaces to reserve, 200 or 400, the cruise director asked, "Why not take the whole ship?" Nita Bob agreed to buy out the 1000-passenger ship for 850 passengers and signed her name. When asked what collateral she had, she put up the five family farms she owned in Arkansas! For the remaining months until the actual cruise convention, Nita Bob lay awake wondering if she would lose everything. When she did manage to fall asleep, she had nightmares. Thanks to the high interest rates at that time and a very diligent Convention Treasurer who deposited every check the day it was received starting two years in advance of the cruise, the WMA actually made money, Nita Bob kept her farms, and a WMA treasury was born.

Leadership

The WMA National Board consists of seven elected National Officers, ten Area Directors elected to represent ten geographical areas, and the Immediate Past National President for a total of eighteen. They meet during the biennial convention and once in the intervening year. Five or more active members of WMA residing in the same geographic area may apply for a chapter charter. Although still with a limited budget, the National President tries to visit most of the chapters during her two-year tenure. Ever the leader, Nita Bob Warner did so prior to the famous cruise convention using her own funds. In fact, when she visited Chicago, the Illinois-2 Chapter hosted her for lunch at a local racetrack. The owner of the racetrack named one of the races in honor of the WMA that day, and a horse named Pass Muster just happened to be running in that race. All of the luncheon attendees bet on him, unfortunately reducing the payoff substantially. Pass Muster came in first, of course, and all of the women Marines had their photo taken with him in the winner's circle.

Membership

There are two classes of WMA membership: active and honorary. Only active members have voting rights and are eligible to hold elected or appointed office. However, an honorary member may hold dual membership, active and honorary, at her option. Renewable dues for active members are for a one-year or two-year period. Anyone who is eligible for active membership may elect to become a life member. The life membership fee is pro-rated according to age. Current membership fees can be found on the website or by calling the toll-free number listed at the end of this section.

Honorary membership has been extended to all past Directors of the United States Marine Corps Women's Reserve; all past Directors of Women Marines; all past Sergeants Major of Women Marines; and the WMA National Chaplain from 1960 – 1979, Capt. Charles J. Covert (ChC), USN (Deceased). From time to time, complimentary one-year memberships are given to reward specific accomplishments. The most recent example of this occurred on August 1, 2003, when Patty Berg became the first woman Marine to be inducted into the Marine Corps Sports Hall of Fame. She was given a complimentary WMA membership at a special luncheon on the day of her induction. Patty holds the LPGA record of 15 major championship titles and has 60 career golf victories overall. She was also one of the six inaugural inductees into the LPGA Tour Hall of Fame. Patty served in the Marine Corps as a lieutenant during World War II.

Scholarship Program

The WMA is proud to award scholarships of $1500 annually to qualified applicants. In 2002, 25 scholarships were awarded, and in 2003, 23 were given. To be eligible to apply for a WMA scholarship, an applicant must satisfy one of the following requirements:

- Have served, or be serving, in the United States Marine Corps or Marine Corps Reserve;
- Be a direct descendant by blood, legal adoption, or stepchild of a Marine on active duty, or who has served honorably in the United States Marine Corps, regular or reserve components;
- Be a sibling or a descendant of a sibling by blood, legal adoption, or step-child of a Marine on active duty, or who has served honorably in the United States Marine Corps, regular or reserve components; OR
- Have completed two years in a Marine Corps JROTC program.

The applicant must also be sponsored by a WMA member and meet high academic and other standards. For detailed application information, go to the website. The application period extends from January 1 to March 31 annually.

Marine Corps Junior Reserve Officer Training Course (MCJROTC)

Believing that our youth is our future in this great country, WMA supports youth in various ways. WMA presents awards annually to outstanding MCJROTC cadets in participating schools across the nation. Members of WMA and chapters also provide significant support to the Young Marines Program and Toys for Tots.

Auxiliary

Loyal Escorts of the Green Garter is the auxiliary society of close relatives of WMA members. The sole purpose of Loyal Escorts, according to its charter, is to assist the WMA, and it does so in many ways. It contributes an annual scholarship to further the educational goal. It also sponsors and presents awards at each convention to chapters for noteworthy accomplishments, thereby promoting the seven purposes of WMA. Loyal Escorts members are pledged to "aid, assist, and escort WMA members in the performance of their duties as delegates to the convention and other official functions." The Loyal Escorts Board meets biennially in conjunction with the WMA national convention.

Emergency Fund Grants

WMA has established an Emergency Fund for veterans who have short-term emergency financial needs, such as skills training, loss of support, severe illness, and catastrophic accidents. It is a one-time, per-person grant limited to $1,000. The applicant only needs to write a short letter to the Chairman of the Bequest Advisory Committee explaining the financial need and request a specific dollar amount. Two letters from (1) reliable source (pastor, social worker, banker, doctor, etc.) and (2) a Veterans Service Officer or a Women Veterans Coordinator must accompany the applicant's letter.

WMA Logo

The logo of WMA is the Marine Corps Emblem with the head of a woman Marine super-imposed on the globe. Much to the surprise and delight of WMA members, they discovered in 2003 that that woman is the "spitting image" of Norrie Deem Zabriskie who served in the Corps from 1944 to 1947. Norrie was selected by General Vandegrift, the 18th Commandant of the Marine Corps, to be the Marine Corps "Poster Girl" during World War II. Her image, first in black and white and later in color, graced posters and billboards across the country. Twenty-five years later, her face was on the Silver Anniversary Edition of the sheet music of the March of the Women Marines and on the program for the first day of issue ceremony of the Five-Cent Women Marines' Commemorative Postal Card. To celebrate the 60th Anniversary of Women in the Marine Corps in February 2003, the WMA was instrumental in arranging for Norrie to travel to Arlington, Virginia, where she presented one of her original World War II posters to Colonel John Ripley, USMC (Ret.), Director of the History and Museums Division, Headquarters, U.S. Marine Corps. The presentation occurred at the Women in Military Service for America Memorial during a ceremony hosted by the Commandant of the Marine Corps in honor of women Marines.

Resource Manual and Membership Directory (RM&MD)/Finding Lost Friends

Every member of WMA receives a copy of the RM&MD which lists every WMA member by service name and also by married name. When a woman Marine joins WMA, she often discovers the names and addresses of women with whom she went through boot camp or Officer Candidates School many years ago. Many planned and unplanned reunions occur during the biennial conventions and other special events. Bettie Pruden Lerdall tells one such story. Following boot camp, Bettie became a platoon leader and was known as "Prudie" to her fellow platoon leaders in the company. They become close friends, but after being discharged and going their separate ways, it was hard to stay in touch. Prudie never forgot their names. In February 2003, she attended a luncheon at Camp Pendleton, California, to celebrate the 60th Anniversary of Women in the Marine Corps and took special note of the names of attendees. To her delight, she spotted the name of Geri Fiorello, who was one of the platoon leaders in her company. She and Geri had not seen each other since they were discharged in 1946. They discovered they share a love of the game of golf, are active in WMA, and live in adjacent states, California and Arizona.

Publications

The WMA publishes a quarterly newsletter which reports on current USMC events, veterans information, national and chapter activities, as well as other items of interest. It also contains a section for sales of merchandise such as books, cards, stationery, decals, clothing, jewelry and other items of interest to Marines. The newsletter is sent to each member as part of her membership benefits.

History

Because women have always comprised a very small percentage of the Marine Corps, special attention is required to ensure their history is captured. WMA has a committee that works with the Headquarters Marine Corps History Division, the Marine Corps Heritage Center, and others to collect oral histories, special papers, uniforms and memorabilia, and other items of interest. In this way, WMA ensures that a unique part of Marine Corps history and the significant contributions of women, from World War I to the present, are documented.

The Lady Marine Rose

The Lady Marine Rose was a ten-year dream of the Greater Oregon chapter of WMA in Portland, Oregon, known as the City of Roses. The idea originated from chapter member, Eva Rae Briscoe, and the dream was to have a rose developed that would represent women Marines everywhere and whose sale would benefit the WMA scholarship fund. It was not an easy task to create a rose of just the right color, but finally Montezuma Red was chosen, and the rose was grown especially for WMA by the Northwest Rose Growers Association in Woodland, Washington. The Oregon Chapter presented the rose to the National President at the

11th Biennial Convention in Seattle in 1980, and Mary Knapp announced its adoption as the official WMA flower. The Greater Oregon chapter subsequently changed its name to the Lady Marine Rose Chapter. By 1982, there were 2,000 Lady Marine Roses blooming all over the United States, in Japan, and in special gardens such as the Cypress Gardens in Florida, Rose Hill Memorial Garden Park in Whittier, California, the International Rose Test Garden in Portland, Oregon, and at the Home of the Commandants in Washington, D.C. All profits from the sale of the rose went to WMA's scholarship program. The Pacific Northwest winter of 1983 – 1984 was severe. Consequently, Roseway Nurseries, which had grown and distributed the Lady Marine Rose, lost the entire stock, and were forced out of business. The rose lives on in private gardens but is no longer a source of income for the WMA scholarship program.

Donations

The WMA gratefully accepts all donations, including Memorial Donations. Memorial donations are accepted in memory of deceased WMA members, their family, and friends. An acknowledgement note of the donation is sent to the next of kin, and the names of Memorial Donors are published in the WMA newsletter. For further information on donations, please contact Lieutenant General Carol Mutter (featured in this book), who has served as a National President of WMA. She can be reached through the website or toll-free number below.

Contact Information

The WMA has a great website, a toll-free number and an e-mail address. The WMA exists to serve all women who have earned the title Marine.

The Women Marines Association
PO Box 1907
Woodbridge, VA 22195
(888) 525-1943
www.womenmarines.org
E-mail: WMA@womenmarines.org

Corporate Index

H

I

N

O

P

V

W

X

Y